YOUTH SQUAD

YOUTH SQUAD

Policing Children in the Twentieth Century

TAMARA GENE MYERS

McGill-Queen's University Press
Montreal & Kingston • London • Chicago

© McGill-Queen's University Press 2019

ISBN 978-0-7735-5892-2 (cloth)
ISBN 978-0-7735-5893-9 (paper)
ISBN 978-0-2280-0031-0 (ePDF)
ISBN 978-0-2280-0032-7 (ePUB)

Legal deposit third quarter 2019
Bibliothèque nationale du Québec

Printed in Canada on acid-free paper that is 100% ancient forest free (100% post-consumer recycled), processed chlorine free

This book has been published with the help of a grant from the Canadian Federation for the Humanities and Social Sciences, through the Awards to Scholarly Publications Program, using funds provided by the Social Sciences and Humanities Research Council of Canada.

Funded by the Government of Canada   Financé par le gouvernement du Canada   Canada   Canada Council for the Arts   Conseil des arts du Canada

We acknowledge the support of the Canada Council for the Arts.

Nous remercions le Conseil des arts du Canada de son soutien.

Library and Archives Canada Cataloguing in Publication

Title: Youth squad : policing children in the twentieth century / Tamara Gene Myers.

Names: Myers, Tamara, 1964- author.

Description: Includes bibliographical references and index.

Identifiers: Canadiana (print) 20190131136 | Canadiana (ebook) 20190131187 |
ISBN 9780773558922 (hardcover) | ISBN 9780773558939 (softcover) |
ISBN 9780228000310 (PDF) | ISBN 9780228000327 (EPUB)

Subjects: LCSH: Police services for juveniles–History–20th century. | LCSH: Police-community relations–History–20th century.

Classification: LCC HV8079.25 .M94 2019 | DDC 363.20830904–dc23

This book was designed and typeset by Peggy & Co. Design Inc. in 10.5/14 Sabon.

For John

Contents

Figures and Table   ix

Acknowledgments   xi

Introduction   3

1   The Idea of a Youth Squad: Crime Prevention
    for "Children on the Verge" in the First Half
    of the Twentieth Century   18

2   The Montreal Miracle: Juvenile Justice, Gender,
    and the Making of a Youth Squad   42

3   Condemned by the Curfew   79

4   The Sports Solution: Surveillance and Athletic
    Citizenship in the Recreation Revolution   105

5   Traffic Tragedies: Police, Children, and Safety
    in the Age of Automobility   134

    Epilogue: Police and Schools   166

Notes   181

Bibliography   225

Index   241

Figures and Table

Figures

2.1 Juvenile arrests from the annual reports of the Montreal Police Department, 1922–1959   58

2.2 "Criminalité," *Revue des Agents de Police*, 1946   60

2.3 "Guerre à la délinquance: des policières montréalaises," *Coup d'Oeil*, 1952   68

2.4 Ovila Pelletier, CKAC radio program, *On the Spot*, 1954   71

4.1 Parc Ovila Pelletier   131

5.1 "First Day of School," *Police Chiefs News*, 1950   153

5.2 *Stay Alert, Stay Unhurt*, 1955   154

5.3 *One Little Indian*, 1955   155

5.4 *One Little Indian*, 1955   156

5.5 Elmer the Elephant   157

5.6 School patrol boy Kenny Cobbs   162

6.1 Parc Ovila Pelletier, Montreal   167

Table

5.1 Reported car crashes, injuries, and deaths, Vancouver, 1940–70   143

Acknowledgments

The making of this book was facilitated by many institutions, colleagues, and friends. I received crucial financial support from the Social Sciences and Humanities Research Council of Canada, the University of British Columbia, and Lehigh University. Most importantly, these funds ensured that I could travel to archives, hire a series of brilliant research assistants, and present findings to multiple audiences. The people I have met in preparing this book have deeply influenced its final form and it has been a privilege to have their company on this intellectual journey.

Helping to make this a rich and pleasurable research program long before I started to assemble chapters were archivists and librarians. I want to especially thank the staff at the municipal archives of Montreal, Calgary, Toronto, and Vancouver, the Musée de la Police de Montréal, Centre de Documentation/Service de Police de la Ville de Montréal, Harvard University Law Library, New York Public Library, the McGill University Archives, Université de Montréal library, Library and Archives Canada, Archives Nationales du Québec à Québec, and the Bibliothèque et Archives Nationales du Québec à Montréal. Without the dedication of so many archivists and librarians, books would not get made, including this one.

I had the great fortune to have a wonderful group of research assistants. I thank Meghan Longstaffe, Geoffrey Korfman, Sarah Thornton, Simon Vickers, Ben Stevenson, Claire Chevreau, Mab Coates-Davies, and Sarah Gibson. The indefatigable Hubert Villeneuve did exceptional work for me in Montreal; his enthusiasm and professionalism profoundly shaped the making of this book. Katie Hurlock and Kristin Tremper helped out in the late stages of manuscript preparation.

Colleagues near and far contributed generously of their time and expertise. The members of the Montreal History Group, especially Mary Anne Poutanen, Andrée Lévesque, and Magda Fahrni, provided insights into archival sources and materials for which I am deeply appreciative. In Vancouver, Michel Ducharme, Laura Ishiguro, Paige Raibmon, Tina Loo, Brad Miller, and the late Danny Vickers read grant applications and drafts of papers, and most importantly, listened to the project as it came into being. I am grateful for the time, friendship, and the extraordinary example set by my sometime collaborator, Mona Gleason. Mona, Megan Davies, Colin Coates, Mary Anne Poutanen, Andrée Lévesque, Bettina Bradbury, and Kristine Alexander offered their insights on my work and provided superb company. These are the very best colleagues and friends one could ask for.

My second academic home in Bethlehem, PA, has been an ongoing source of sustenance. For welcoming me into their wickedly smart and supportive circle of women in the academy, I thank Stephanie Watts, Vera Fennell, Julia Maserjian, Kristin Handler, and Holona Ochs. Seth Moglen and Kristin Handler have been a constant presence in my American life, lovingly helping to translate and advise. Kathy Hutnik, John Savage, Marisa Cerveris, Amy Munson, Ziad Munson, Sandy Clancy, Monica Najar, and Jen Kalembar provided outstanding companionship. My book club – Amy Munson, Claire Kowalchik, Julie Kibelbek, Karen Gennaro, and Jenny Landis – reminded me that reading and writing books are some of life's greatest pleasures. John Pettegrew introduced me to Sheyda Jahabani and Jonathan Hagel, and I'm grateful for their generosity and for what we shared – a deep appreciation of food, adventure, meaningful work, a rich sense of humour, and love. Thanks to all.

At McGill-Queen's University Press, Jacqueline Mason demonstrated an early interest in the project and remained dedicated to it over many years. Her enthusiastic reception to my ideas kept me going in dark moments.

The making of this book overlapped with the best and worst that life can offer. John Pettegrew and I worked out a bi-coastal loving relationship that distracted us from, and enriched, our scholarship. Over the years, ritually meeting over martinis and sumptuous food – in Vancouver, Vermont, Bethlehem, New York, Whistler – we discussed the details of research delights and difficulties. As I finished this book I became his colleague at Lehigh. He prioritized my finishing of it, reading and critiquing chapters, despite battling a terminal illness. He took great pleasure from my pressing "send." He died two months later. I have yet to find the words to express my profound sense of loss but know that he is on every page of this book.

And finally, I thank my family. John's children, Nick Pettegrew and Helen Keetley, are a constant source of love and amazement. In John's absence, their mother, Dawn Keetley, has been a great support and friend. My sister Friday Myers and her daughter Coco, my dad Peter Myers, and his partner, Fiona Lucas, reassure me daily about life, love, and loss.

An earlier version of chapter 5 appeared as "Didactic Sudden Death: Children, Police, and Teaching Citizenship in the Age of Automobility," *Journal of the History of Children and Youth* 8, no. 3 (Fall 2015): 451–75. I thank the editor and Johns Hopkins University Press for allowing me to reproduce it here.

YOUTH SQUAD

Introduction

In a place not far from where I live in Pennsylvania, teenage transgressions recently prompted extraordinary action from the local government and police force. Frustrated in the face of teen congeries that riddled the streets at night, the police chief complained bitterly about his inability to distinguish the vandals among them. Adolescents who linger and loiter by night have long provoked adults because in their teetering between childhood innocence and adult maturity they represent an incipient threat to the community, if not themselves. In this instance, the borough council of Coplay took the opportunity to criminalize all teens: the new youth curfew prohibits anyone under eighteen from being out in public from midnight to 5 a.m. on weekdays and 1 a.m. to 5 a.m. on weekends. Police Chief Vincent Genovese endorsed the curfew because, as a status offence, it allowed him to clear the streets of the teens without having to prove any crime had been committed. Like the age-old crime of vagrancy, curfew vastly expanded police discretion and reinforced "hierarchy and social order."[1] The chief might disagree with this assessment, preferring to see nighttime curfews as a beneficial act "for" the kids. "It would mean we can get to them early," he argued. "Every kid has a right to grow up. We're protecting them from themselves."[2] The chief's sympathetic words and actions are symptomatic of the paradox of protection wherein law and law enforcement are used to circumscribe and constrain youth for their own good. This safeguarding of childhood and policing of adolescence has undergirded arguments favouring curfews for more than a century. The trope relies on a seemingly recognizable category of worthy and redeemable young people called "the kids" while masking the particularism of regulation: the gendered, racial, and class identities of "kids" whose bodies and behaviours are spatially outlawed by curfew enforcement. This local story of troubled police–youth relations and the curfew solution is part of a long history of police implementing age-conscious mechanisms of social control.

Perhaps no relationship is more fraught with ambiguity than that of cops and kids. Today police officers collectively help children safely cross the street, sponsor literacy programs, and coach youth sports teams. But as agents of public authority with a mission to deter crime and enforce law, police officers also intimidate and repress youth. This tension between social service work and crime control, between protection (of property and citizens) and punishment, is hardly new: it has defined law enforcement since at least 1829, when Sir Robert Peel initiated the modern police force in London. From the inception of urban forces, children, and young people generally, lay within police purview both as objects of protection and targets of repression. By the interwar period, however, an identifiable bureaucratic reform had taken root in modern policing that promised to transform the relationship between law enforcement and the young: the explosion of youth squads. This book points to this watershed moment in the history of policing when, between the 1930s and the 1960s across northern North America, police agencies took what I call the "youth turn," implementing a set of policies and practices directed at children and adolescents.

Long before the youth turn and the emergence of police youth squads, Anglo-American law gave definition to the child, distinguishing young people, in capacity and responsibility, from adults.[3] British common law tradition set at seven the age below which a child could not be held responsible for criminal acts. The Canadian Criminal Code of 1892 further defined the category of young offender (to under fourteen) and provided for their separate trials.[4] Penal reform radically transformed the experience of criminal justice for the young by emphasizing classification, individual sentences, and treatment over punishment and retribution. Armed with the legal doctrine *parens patriae*, in the early nineteenth century local governments across North America expanded the state's role over children and child welfare, using age as a primary category of classification for new institutions like reform schools.[5] In response to rapid demographic and economic changes associated with urbanization and immigration in the late nineteenth century, social reformers deepened their response to child welfare, organizing to rid their cities of delinquency, child labour, juvenile prostitution, and generally protect the young. These reformers formed part of a religiously inspired middle class, a vocal minority who interpreted immigrant and working-class children's visibility on the urban industrial landscape as a problem: youths' vulnerability, poverty, unhygienic bodies, potential for abuse and neglect, and unruly demeanours demanded rescue and reform.[6] Under the rubric of child protection, reformers and their political allies diverted youth from the criminal justice system and instead processed them through juvenile courts with the ostensible aim not of punishing, but of treating dependent and delinquent youth. Cleaving young offenders from older criminals lay at the heart of this new conceptualization of juvenile treatment under the law; juvenile courts, beginning in 1899 in the American Midwest and spreading across Canada and the rest of the US in the early twentieth century, worked to generate youth-specific individualized rehabilitation schemes that would minimize exposure to negative influences that produced delinquency, including adult criminals and criminal justice processes. The youth turn in policing would follow on many decades of juvenile justice reform that highlighted the need for the state to protect needy and neglected children and to divert juvenile criminals from adult institutions. Child-saving rhetoric aside, historians of early juvenile justice regimes exposed them for focusing on "character deficiencies" instead of "economic inequality, power, and class," leading historian Eric C. Schneider to suggest for the case of Boston that they "ultimately did not aid or reform very many."[7] Juvenile justice was, however, productive of new spaces and forms of youth regulation.

This book emerges from a foundation in juvenile justice historical research. While researching my first book, *Caught: Montreal's Modern Girls and the Law, 1869–1945*, notations referring to the city's youth squad, called the "Moralité juvénile" or simply "MJ" in the juvenile court records, began to proliferate, especially after 1940. This earlier research focused on the daily practice of youth regulation through the courtroom, showing how local actors (judges, probation officers, reform school workers) shaped the "justice" that children and adolescents received, and underscored the processes that gave delinquency its gendered and cultural definition and meaning.[8] Like other scholars of the 1990s and 2000s who situated juvenile justice institutions into a framework of state "policing of families," I was interested in what case files revealed about adolescent lives and their social relations, not the role of law enforcement in juvenile justice.[9] My focus on girls' performance of modernity did point to an important development in policing, however: "bad" girls became the purpose of policewomen's work in the early decades of the twentieth century, although in Montreal their positions were marginal and temporary. Since late nineteenth-century child welfare reformers actively sought to divert children from police prerogative and power, it's not surprising that most of these studies lack consideration of the role played by police in the early juvenile justice systems.

Those responsible for the transformation in juvenile justice intentionally tried to minimize youth's exposure to police.[10] In the latter decades of the nineteenth century, as historians have stressed, police forces' main role was to keep public order and protect private property, not protect the general population. This legacy earned them a reputation for repression; scandals relating to bribery and patronage further undermined belief in their suitability for a role in child welfare.[11] Law enforcement functioned as a competing and regressive force adjacent to juvenile justice. Yet police institutions were not immune to progressive penal reform thinking; as sociologist David Garland has summarized for the United States and the United Kingdom, in liberal democracies, the reform agenda for modern policing at the turn of the twentieth century resulted "in theory at least," in police work "evolving from being a state instrument, protecting the propertied elite to being a more authentically public service ... providing security and protection to the whole population."[12] This process was of course unevenly delivered and often unfinished. David B. Wolcott's study on the policing of juvenile delinquents in three American cities from 1890 to 1940 helps to chart this evolution and adds police to the history of juvenile justice. In *Cops and Kids* he explicates the key role played by police in delinquency regulation, arguing that police constituted a front line of discretionary and often arbitrary juvenile justice, even while appearing to occupy a secondary role in it.[13]

This book substantiates Wolcott's findings and adds another chapter to the history of policing youth by illuminating how police agencies in multiple large and small North American cities embraced reform and became youth conscious from the 1930s through the 1960s.[14] My argument is that police sought to explicitly challenge their ancillary role in juvenile justice, pointing to its failure to deter crime and rehabilitate delinquents. In diverting youth from juvenile institutions, police agencies expanded the everyday forms of social control over children and youth, constructing themselves as a community authority governing delinquency, child welfare, and even childhood.[15] Not all law enforcement officers made the turn, of course. Tending to children and youth required a particular set of gendered attributes most associated with an avuncular officer or a policewoman. Certain officers became youth workers, who collectively formed youth squads, a catch-all term I use for the myriad anti-delinquency units that could be found in many North American urban forces at mid-twentieth century. These squads comprised a coterie of officers responsible for policing youth in conflict with criminal law and local regulations and for designing programs to reduce delinquency. In examining this youth turn in policing, this book charts the arguments and ideas, personnel, and programs that helped construct police as a vital force in the lives of children and youth. What follows is an excavation of the meanings and implications of youth consciousness among police, for both urban policing and young people.

In the early decades of the twentieth century, several factors coalesced to draw police into youth work. Most important among them, despite the efforts of the juvenile justice system, delinquency persisted, leaving the door open for police forces to assert new ideas and approaches in managing the "youth problem." Since the nineteenth century, civic authorities had defined delinquency largely as a working-class boy problem; their idleness and lack of proper upbringing led to petty theft, vandalism, and truancy.[16] The girl problem, in contrast, was linked to the relative independence and sexual autonomy expressed by adolescent working girls and young women. But following the First World War an apparent uptick in lawlessness, sensationalized by the American press, influenced a generation of police officers to focus on juveniles. Violent crime waves featuring racketeers, gangsters, and the unemployed (suspected Communists following the Bolshevik Revolution) grabbed the attention of law enforcement and the public on both sides of the border.[17] As the United States appeared to be overtaken by a crime wave, boys' attraction to, and imitation of, gangsterism and hoodlumism were particularly worrisome. Youth-oriented police officers embraced a spirit of progress for controlling crime and introduced a series of new measures to prevent the crime's undertow from claiming susceptible boys. Although Canada's crime problems paled next to its neighbour's, as historian Greg Marquis explains, Canadians consumed American films and pulp fiction that sensationalized crime, and the country's biggest crime fighter, FBI director J. Edgar Hoover, had the ear of Canadian law enforcement through the interwar period.[18] Crime waves and "new" youthful violent criminals gave "modern" forces the impetus to subvert the rise in criminality.[19]

At the same time that crime waves animated police organizations' discussions, popular notions of modern childhood and adolescence came to the police through contemporary criminology and sociology of delinquency. Youth squads imputed to the juvenile delinquent modern childhood and adolescence, claiming a new knowledge of, and expertise over, the young. This putatively resulted in a protective approach toward youthful lawbreakers and a focus on preventing delinquency. Crime prevention, a comprehensive strategy and practice predicated on the idea that criminals were made, not born, led police into childhood spaces. Environmentalism – the belief that certain social, economic, emotional, and educational surroundings produced latent criminality – had come to dominate criminological and police thinking by the 1920s. Infused with such ideas crime prevention programs proliferated in US and Canadian cities and towns. By targeting the environment that gave rise to delinquents and criminals, police officers aimed for access to children, youth, and their cultural spaces, landing youth squads squarely in the oversight and moulding of childhood. This paradigmatic shift in policing meant eschewing the model of the intimidating beat officer who scared the young, and stood as anathema to late nineteenth-century juvenile justice ideals.[20] It also stood in contrast to the era's crime control models championed by Hoover and FBI criminologists and municipal politicians, who nevertheless lauded prevention strategies that provided police with multiple access points to childhood as an investment in a better future and a way to make costly crime control less necessary.

Youth squad crime prevention programs shared several truisms. First came a determination that the provenance of criminality lay in a child's environment. This might include criminal influences and predatory adults, but also the idea that a childhood spent in idleness and dissipation could produce a life open to delinquency, then criminality. Second was the rejection of deterrence and correction in favour of rescue. The juvenile court appearance, according to crime prevention advocates, far from its original promise of shielding the child from the harshness of criminal justice, could be traumatic for youth, instilling in him or her a fear of, and hostility to, law and order. Avoiding court appearance and incarceration, even in juvenile reformatories, was central to steering children away from future crime. Third, crime prevention officers insisted that if children and youth interpreted police authority as friendly and positive, they would be less likely to become delinquent as they moved through adolescence. The goal was for youth to see the officer not as a harsh form of disciplinary authority but as a kind of public guardian who looked out for the best interests of the child and the community.

Changing the reputation of police authority – from enemy to *friend* of youth – was an oft-quoted ambition of mid-century youth squads. On the surface this aim was directed at the low regard with which communities held officers. As described in chapter 4, becoming a coach to young sports fans at the very least afforded police officers voluminous positive press coverage. But it also served a more instrumental function. By performing the role of friend to youth, officers sought out a new source of legitimacy for their authority over youth and their communities, one that could interrupt relations between other adults (like parents) and children, and insinuate officers within neighbourhoods under the guise of friendship.

A corollary to crime prevention was the construction of a new youthful subjectivity: the *incipient* or pre-delinquent. This new category applied to any and all children in a state of potential deviancy. Pre-delinquency could be determined by children's attitudes and demeanours, or suspect influences in their midst – friends, parents, neighbourhood. If the definition of juvenile delinquency was left intentionally broad and imprecise to allow for parents and officials to define when and how youth constituted a "problem," pre-delinquency was similarly a catch-all category left to youth workers to operationalize. Rhetorically at least, working with, and correcting, pre-delinquents steered young people away from delinquency's path while establishing positive relations between police and youth.

Transforming the police officer into a persuasive presence in young lives would not be easy, for several reasons. First, youth squads joined an already crowded field of youth organizations – from Boy Scouts and YM/WCAS to social service agencies and schools – that held prerogative over managing and moulding the young. Police youth squads did join in, though, using sports and social activities to draw youth close to them. Second, while neighbourhood policing had long involved work with women and children, police officers often found that their dubious reputation preceded them. Youth learned early to avoid the policeman.[21] The discretionary or "curbstone" justice wielded by police officers produced a weariness on the part of minority and working-class communities that were targeted by law enforcement; this is most evident in the policing of racialized communities where police discrimination and cops' "dirty work" found long-term resentment.[22] Unfavourable publicity around police corruption and a sense that police were strangers to those subject to surveillance and regulation aggravated this disposition toward individual officers. Massive public relations campaigns would help turn this around for youth squads. Still, in 1958 when Canadian journalist Sidney Katz tried to explain "Why do we hate the police?," he showed how tensions with the public remained strong throughout the period under study. Yet Katz admitted youth seemed ambivalent about the youth squad officer who self-identified as "a fun-loving, elderly Rover Boy – a combination of athletic coach, psychiatrist and dispenser of hot dogs at picnics."[23]

An examination of the youth turn in policing in the middle decades of the twentieth century permits a window onto the changing meanings of childhood and adolescence. For centuries, common and civil law defined youth in terms of chronological age, assigning rights and responsibilities to children and their guardians. Historians argue that age "has always mattered," but age consciousness as a central marker of identity would only shape cultural definitions of young people beginning in the late nineteenth and early twentieth centuries, especially modern childhood and adolescence.[24] As definitions of child, adolescent, and adult became increasingly distinct in these decades, new understandings of youth helped shape the purpose of police work. Youth police echoed the modern and idealized conception of childhood that emphasized a definition comprising education, play, and dependence. Their discourse emphasized children's natural state of innocence and a right to childhood in making an argument for how best to protect youth and quash delinquency.[25] When they articulated childhood as an ideal it was in the context of understanding that certain children – poor, racialized, single-parented – grew up in circumstances that made them prone to breaking bad. Crime prevention programs' well-timed police intervention with these young pre-delinquents signalled a belief in the possibility of restoring childhood to children.

Ideas about adolescence as a unique time of "storm and stress" spread following G. Stanley Hall's publication of *Adolescence: Its Psychology and Its Relations to Physiology, Anthropology, Sociology, Sex, Crime and Religion* in 1904. According to psychologists of the early twentieth century, adolescents occupied a liminal developmental stage between childhood and maturity, making them highly susceptible to poor judgment and reckless behaviour. Armed with laws that banned youth under sixteen from pool halls, bowling alleys, and dance halls, youth squad officers claimed to be setting teenagers straight by returning them to a safe place – home. As high school became the locus for shaping adolescent behaviour, police helped define the teenager – a term coined in the 1940s. Police-supervised leisure that took place outside of home and school was directed at those who were children and young teens – innocent and pre-delinquent. In the mid 1940s when Canada's federal police force, the Royal Canadian Mounted Police, embarked on youth programing, one constable explained, "most juvenile delinquents are not stupid or backward. They merely have an abundance of energy which took the wrong outlet to express itself simply because there was too little else for them to do. Today more than ever before, Canada's cities are awakening to the need for teen-age centres of recreation – places more conducive to the young person's well-being and more enticing than juke joints and cheap cafes and dance halls."[26] Police officers embraced youth offending as a natural part of growing up, a feature that was theirs to manage.

Police forces engaged in a type of age grading when they imbued great importance to pre-delinquency. Pre-delinquency was a status – beyond the innocence of childhood and on the verge of adolescence and delinquency. The delinquent had been initiated into bad or immoral behaviour and had developed a consciousness or knowledge of transgressing order. The pre-delinquent stood on the precipice of developing that consciousness – likely the consciousness of the potential to offend had been roused or his/her environment was likely to require intervention. In this design both children and pre-delinquents could be convinced to trust law enforcement and taught to avoid delinquent acts, sites, and people. Their impressionability and malleability were essential for crime prevention to work. Pre-delinquency was a state or stage that could be mapped onto chronological age usually in conjunction with other identity markers. Girls could be pre-delinquents for their entire adolescence, to age eighteen; pre-delinquent boys who were the major targets of crime prevention schemes were mostly under sixteen years of age.

Conceptualized and articulated by officers themselves as an effort to protect the young, youth-conscious policing is an example of what sociologist Stanley Cohen describes as an "inclusionary" mode of social control for regulating deviance. Where exclusionary modes of controlling deviants comprise "stigma and segregation" – in this case, punishment and incarceration – inclusionary modes promote "integration and absorption" and "assum[e] internal obedience."[27] Inclusive approaches to delinquency control held the promise of greatly influencing youth behaviour and gaining compliance with established rules, law, and order. For at least some youth, inclusion could be powerful. The formation of junior police and youth patrols during the Second World War exemplifies this thinking. In the face of youth gangs and rising delinquency in Washington, DC's 13th Precinct, Patrolman Oliver A. Cowan organized the Junior Police and Citizens' Corps. Where parents and custodial institutions had failed these would-be hoodlums and the poor black neighbourhood where they were being raised, Cowan had found a way to satisfy their desire for power and belonging. He empowered the boys to police themselves by reorganizing them into police ranks and putting them in charge of patrolling their neighbourhood.[28] When children and youth absorbed messages about curfew, joined police-sponsored sports teams, followed officers' advice about safety, or mimicked officers as street and school patrols, they participated in a process that bestowed incipient citizenship on those who fell in line. This may explain the popularity of certain programs like school patrols and police-led team sports – the internal obedience to that police presence in childhood registered as adherence to community and the greater collectivity. Yet the very process of categorizing children and youth into pre-delinquents, delinquents, and non-delinquents would be mapped onto contemporary understandings about who was likely to offend and who was redeemable. The exclusionary or punitive measures used to deal with deviant youth behaviour, like court appearances and incarceration, did not disappear; rather, they would remain for those who resisted or rebelled against normative youth behaviour.[29]

The rise of youth squads occurred at a particular moment in the twentieth century I refer to as the middle decades or mid-century.

More precisely, in terms of periodization, this development can be seen between the decades after the juvenile court revolution, roughly the 1930s, and the punitive turn of the 1970s.[30] Most youth squads were officially formed beginning in the 1930s. This era is one of dramatic social and economic change, from worldwide depression to war to postwar affluence. The effect of these developments on youth was a public concern throughout the time period: as symbols of the future their well-being and of course misbehaviour garnered much attention. Public anxieties over adult crime waves of the 1920s and 1930s were followed by successive delinquency panics. During the Second World War the seemingly parentless generation acted out: gangs of boys threatened communities while girls dropped their inhibitions and morals when they went "khaki-mad" for young men in uniform. The 1940s ignited what British historian Louise A. Jackson calls an "almost perpetual wave of public anxiety" about youth crime.[31] In North America, alienated youth seemed to be endemic to postwar society, rooted in a childhood spent during wartime. This psychological assessment of the roots of delinquency gave it a kind of universalism or generational thrust in the 1950s, though by the end of the decade, as youth gangs and violence captured headlines, delinquency would become associated with crises over masculinity, class, and race. In the United States, Michael Flamm shows, it was in the late 1950s that delinquency went from being everyone's problem to one infused with "racial overtones" and located in distressed urban environments.[32] The optimism of penal welfarism faded through the 1960s with the arrival of law and order politics. In Canada, youth gangs also drew the attention of media and law enforcement in the 1950s. Ovila Pelletier, head of Montreal's youth squad, hung on to the promise of crime prevention in the face of local leather-jacket gangbangers, advising the public to see this as a manageable problem rooted in the Americanization of youth culture.[33]

The middle decades of the twentieth century were infused with the promise of progress in police reform – what police historians identify as the era of professionalization and disruption.[34] Policing became more bureaucratized, specialized, and technologically informed with the use of radioed patrol cars, photography, and surveillance devices. Officers and forces organized into unions and affiliated with professional associations, giving them greater presence and power in this period. Marquis argues that professionalization was indeed linked to enhancing police power, and to convincing the public that the force was composed of "neutral, incorruptible and capable crime fighters."[35] Although efficient crime control dominated the self-definition of police organizations, this era also produced experiments in crime reduction that focused on youth and community. American historian Janis Appier's study of the emergence of coordinating councils in the 1930s is a case in point. These anti-delinquency organizations that brought together police, social workers, and civic organizations to discourage youth from offending theoretically offered a different strategy beyond repressive measures for winning the war on crime.[36] During the 1930s almost six hundred coordinating councils sprung up in twenty-four states. Fritz Umbach suggests that although they are often located as emerging in the late twentieth century, along with rising crime rates, community police squads have antecedents dating to the 1950s.[37] These programs that discursively attempted to overturn outdated modes of dealing with delinquency and criminals failed to live up to their promise of crime reduction and community safety, opening the door to the punitive turn.[38]

American historians of juvenile justice William Bush and Geoff Ward have argued that modern childhood and diversionary police programs that were meant to conjure a sense of belonging eluded specific children and youth.[39] Indeed, youth squads' crime prevention programs were aimed at bringing certain working-class children into mainstream society but not eradicating racial and class barriers to equality. As historian Elizabeth Hinton carefully outlines, by the 1960s federal law and order directives and monies for delinquency control turned preventive programs into an "expanding punitive apparatus ... increasing the chances that [young black urban Americans] would be arrested, accrue criminal records, go to juvenile detention centers, and eventually serve long prison sentences."[40]

Since youth squads and delinquency prevention programs operated both locally and transnationally, this book uses national and international newspapers, magazines, and police periodicals to follow discussions, ideas, and personnel across borders. The youth turn in policing occurred in many cities across Canada and the United States at roughly the same time. New York City and Montreal, for example, both established substantial youth squads in the 1930s; other cities and smaller centres followed suit. Canadian and US sources often lauded the innovative aspects of youth squad work and helped identify the discursive power of police reform work with youth. To illuminate the local details of crime prevention schemes, I use municipal archives, police annual reports, and police publications. For Montreal, which I use as an example of youth squad genesis and growth, I took advantage of juvenile court records and police and school board archives. The richness of local archives of police efforts around safety – from Vancouver to Calgary to Toronto and Montreal – suggests trends in messages to youth and also the momentum of youth consciousness.

Each chapter illuminates a different aspect of the youth turn in urban policing. Chapter 1 explores the idea of the youth squad. It identifies the historical and epistemological contexts that gave rise to crime prevention as a viable alternative to crime control after the First World War. Police agencies articulated with urgency the apparent rise of juvenile delinquency in the interwar period and the juvenile justice system's limited success in crime prevention. They also sought to reform their public reputation through good works with youth. Focusing on important early efforts in New York City, Berkeley, and Chicago, this chapter examines the pilot projects and efforts at delinquency prevention that would be replaced by the mid-1930s with extensive and enduring programs, expanded personnel, and new bureaucracies. Chapter 2 charts the birth and evolution of a youth squad, using Montreal's Juvenile Morality Squad (JMS) as a case study. The story of the JMS is instructive for showing how the rhetoric and goals of crime prevention were grafted onto an established police bureaucracy and practice. Originating in the mid-1930s, the youth squad under Ovila Pelletier's leadership embraced several structural changes by the 1940s, including expansion of personnel, the extension of membership to women, and a centralized and physically separate bureau. In an era reputed to have uncontrollable delinquency worldwide, Pelletier boasted to have successfully implemented a prevention-oriented police response that dramatically reduced the numbers of arrested youth and, according to Pelletier and the youth squad, fundamentally altered the relationship of police to children and youth.

The next chapters examine how crime prevention produced a range of youth squad initiatives. Chapter 3 uses the juvenile nocturnal curfew to show how age-specific laws gained popularity as a tool for crime reduction. Curfews did what parents had failed to do: protect children from themselves and others at night. Charting its use from the late nineteenth century, this chapter shows how police across northern North America agreed that juvenile curfews were a critical tool for policing modern young people. Beyond sending them home at a certain hour, police officers also sought to occupy youth leisure and invoked the "sports solution" to ward off bad behaviour. Chapter 4 charts this development, exploring the advent of police athletic clubs and the meanings of membership. Adopting the role of modern sports "men," officers playing coach were to be exemplars of moral and masculine citizenship. Montreal and New York City hosted highly organized and popular police athletic clubs especially, but not exclusively, for boys. These initiatives exemplify how the most profound changes in the relationship between young people and police forces occurred in recreational venues of North America. Hundreds of thousands of young people joined police athletic leagues, social and cultural clubs, and took advantage of membership opportunities to attend local sporting events, circuses, and the like. Through recreation programs police gained access to boys across class and cultural lines, helping to instill notions of hegemonic masculinity, class, and racially specific sportsmanship. Finally, in chapter 5 we see how youth squads also made their way into elementary and high schools, with the officers transitioning into educators through lessons focused on how children could navigate their own safety and avoid delinquency. In exchange for safety, wisdom, and protection from injury and possibly death, police expected children to incorporate the rules and regulations governing public space, accept that roads were for cars, and develop a new respect for the law. Becoming part of the solution to the traffic problem gave certain children access to a mid-century citizenship involving preparedness, obedience to authority, and conformity to automobility. These three chapters delve into youth conscious programming at the hands of youth squads, all of which in one form or another are still with us today. In the Epilogue I conclude with the normalization of police presence in schools and what it meant for the changing nature of authority and the governance of childhood.

In 1969, Montreal Police Chief Jean-Paul Gilbert pleaded with his colleagues at a meeting of the Association of Chiefs of Police to recognize "[o]ur collective failure" in the area of crime suppression. It, he argued, "should convince us to put the accent on crime prevention and education."[41] Calling for what he presented as a new role for the police*man* that eschewed the stereotypical characteristics of intimidation and repression, he and other speakers at the Police-Jeunesse (Police-Youth)–themed meeting promoted an invigorated campaign to address "pre-delinquency." Like many youth-conscious leaders in twentieth-century law enforcement before him, Gilbert embraced crime prevention as the solution to the seemingly never-ending problems of juvenile delinquency and criminality. Crime prevention was hardly a new idea when Gilbert headed Montreal's police force, yet new demographics – the bulge of baby boom adolescents – and behaviours made it appear urgent, even original.

This youth consciousness exhibited by most local and national police forces since the 1930s fundamentally altered the place of law enforcement in childhood and adolescence, especially by mid-twentieth century, yet it would not resolve the twin problems of delinquency and youth vulnerability, nor would it change the reputation of officers. Its appeal has been tenacious, however, as Police Chief Gilbert's words in 1969 suggest. Twenty years later, when the Quebec Human Rights Commission issued a report on the relations between the Montreal Urban Community police and visible minorities, it raised the idea that police programming for youth could help ease tensions. The press reminded Montrealers of the city's successful Police Athletic League–style program that had ended in the 1960s and noted that in no less than five hundred US municipalities, police officers coached and sponsored recreational activities in underprivileged neighbourhoods. Black community associations had advocated for such programs through the commission's inquiry. "Span[ning] the gap between youth and police" promised "social harmony" and would reform the cop-kid relationship, perhaps inspiring "more interest from minority youth in police careers."[42] This is the story of the emergence and potency of the idea that by including those considered likely to offend authorities could help render delinquency a thing of the past.

The Idea of a Youth Squad: Crime Prevention for "Children on the Verge" in the First Half of the Twentieth Century

In the early twentieth century, children and youth posed two evidently insurmountable challenges to urban North American police departments. Most obviously, the rising generation's predilection for trouble meant each decade of the new century witnessed a juvenile delinquency problem seemingly worse than the last. In 1938, the International Association of Chiefs of Police (IACP) went so far as to declare juvenile delinquency "the most serious police problem in North America."[1] Attendees to the IACP annual congress, held that year in Toronto, heard multiple speakers on the subject. Various factors, including public anxiety about escalating violence, the proliferation of gangsters and bandits, organized crime, and an apparent loss of political and social order, urged police officers to enervate delinquency and disrupt youth's path to future criminality. The second issue, related to solving the first, concerned public relations: how could the police transform their reputation with young people from untrustworthy and arbitrary authority to "public friend No. 1"?[2] These twin problems became the subject of public and professional discourse, giving rise to a "youth turn" in police practice.

This chapter examines the origins of youth-conscious policing and its expression as mid-twentieth-century youth squads. Historically situated in an era of penal reform that saw the professionalization of policing and a consolidation of the principle that law enforcement operated on behalf of the state to deliver a public service to its citizens,[3] youth squads reflected growing specialization within urban forces. Police departments, joined by civic leaders, advanced the youth turn in policing by embracing the crime prevention paradigm. Crime prevention, as crime-fighting

strategy and praxis, reflected the triumph of environmentalism in criminology. In this understanding of the etiology of crime, adult criminality
was causally related to an ill-spent youth: the social, economic, and
emotional surroundings of childhood. In the words of New York City
Deputy Police Commissioner James B. Nolan, the commanding officer
of that city's youth squad called the Juvenile Aid Bureau: "The most
recent trend in police work is to look in to the life of the offender and to
discover those factors which prompt his [sic] antisocial behaviour. When
we view criminal careers in retrospect we invariably find that the problem is one that first presented itself in childhood and through neglect
had developed into serious criminal behaviour."[4] This shift would mean
identifying and getting to know children "at risk" before they became
a problem: to teach them to respect authority, reject delinquency, and
exercise their idle minds and bodies.

Conviction that criminal wrongdoing could be snuffed out by positively affecting the worlds of children and youth held great appeal for
crime prevention advocates. The old police ways of brutalizing juveniles,
which increasingly threatened police legitimacy and hampered relations with youth, could be relegated to the past.[5] Yet this paradigmatic
shift overlapped with the rise of crime "control" strategies, advocated
by Federal Bureau of Investigation (FBI) Director J. Edgar Hoover. He
promoted repressive control mechanisms such as mass arrests and
mandatory punishment of offenders of all ages.[6] His get-tough-on-crime
approach, especially when applied to the youth problem, was controversial among experts who embraced the reduction of juvenile delinquency
and the production of would-be adult criminals through crime prevention. Crime prevention programs became the weapon of the new youth
squads that emerged in the interwar era. This institutional innovation in
crime prevention schemes recalled turn-of-the-century juvenile justice
discourse, which rejected correction in favour of rescuing children and
youth in conflict with the law, not Hoover's crime control mantra.

The idea of a youth squad emerged in the context of the changing
status of children and youth. Rising interest in prison and social reform,
which saw children as vulnerable and dependent on the state, challenged
the nineteenth-century liberal state, which provided minimal recognition and protection for children. Across the nineteenth century the idea
of a protected childhood, one that featured education, play, and moral
guidance, increasingly came to dominate the language of the "child

savers," middle-class reformers who advocated new approaches to raising their own children and also intervention into working-class and poor families. Although parents were relied upon to raise their children to be citizens, this social evolutionary process was too important to be left to happenstance and the spectre of inadequate parenting. Protection of childhood in the guise of orphanages, compulsory schooling, industrial and reform schools, which would produce juvenile courts at the turn of the century, reveals a shifting social contract between the state, private charities, and young people.[7] The state in its many guises set about promoting what it labelled as the "best interests of the child," shaping the rough material of childhood into liberal, moral, and disciplined citizens by rehabilitating juveniles in institutions and under the guidance of child experts.[8]

Nineteenth-century child welfare policies and practices constituted and upheld contemporary racial ideologies. Those with "child" status were malleable and had potential for citizenship, but this notion did not apply to all; colonialism in Canada conferred "ward of the state" status upon Indigenous peoples, resulting in the incarceration of Indigenous children in residential schools, while in the United States African American children "were rendered unsalvageable and undeserving of citizen-building ambition."[9] The parental state that oversaw child welfare institution building, as sociologist Geoff K. Ward argues, reinforced white supremacy and produced Jim Crow juvenile justice in the United States.[10] In urban centres in both the US and Canada, juvenile justice processed poor, working-class, and often ethnic minority youth deemed reformable. Crime prevention programs shared with juvenile justice systems these racial politics and a commitment to rehabilitative idealism making both exclusionary and largely directed at socio-economically marginal white youths and immigrants considered to have the capacity for full citizenship.

Juvenile justice systems that emerged to rescue and rehabilitate minors in the latter part of the nineteenth century worked at odds with many local police forces, whose purpose was to preserve order.[11] Beginning at the turn of the twentieth century, the juvenile court movement produced separate court facilities for young people that promoted a professional approach to youth and delinquency that featured rehabilitation over punishment. The socialized justice model explicitly invoked contemporary social science that promoted a search for environmental causes of bad behaviour (in the home, school, and community) and early, consistent intervention into childhood.[12] Seemingly sympathetic, avuncular judges and a host of probation officers trained in adolescent behaviour promised to spare children from the brutality of the adult criminal justice system and law enforcement and divert bad behaviour.

Beat officers perceived the youthful criminal underclass as a direct threat to the existing order and stood opposed to the empathetic approach that was characteristic of juvenile justice workers. Tensions between minors, police, and juvenile justice workers lasted well into the twentieth century. The juvenile court movement of the turn of the century effectively "marginalized" the police in the regulation of juveniles, as historian David Wolcott argues in his study of policing youth in Los Angeles, Chicago, and Detroit between 1890 and 1940s. However, the adoption of crime prevention measures created the possibility of a new role for police in the campaign against delinquency.[13] By the 1920s, as many as ninety large urban American police departments had begun to undertake crime prevention pursuits, largely directed at youth.[14] Crime prevention officers embraced a new identity vis-à-vis youth, reconstructing themselves as public parents or friends to youth and fomenting a revolution in public relations.

Crime prevention strategies led police into children's lives in unprecedented ways. This reconfiguration of police activity to incorporate prevention programs with young people was an expression of changing ideas about children's nature and the possibility of policing and citizen building for those considered malleable. This development was inspired by federal and local politics and included a vast array of new programs, institutions, and personnel situated within urban police forces; it furthered several trends within policing, including the hiring of policewomen and the importance of male officers as athletic and paternal role models, and as educators. Hatched during a paradoxical moment when both child saving and crime control were popular, anti-delinquency work required a massive educational campaign and a categorical change in the police's reputation with youth.

The Problem and the Impulse: Juvenile Delinquency and the Police

Misbehaving children are endemic to most historical periods, yet it was the nineteenth-century problem child that first provoked a revolution in sentiment, social action, politics, and law. Over the course of the long nineteenth century, juvenile justice and child welfare schemes responded to the rising visibility of white working-class male delinquency, especially the "waifs and strays" of urban life.[15] The main, often desperate, features of industrial modernity – urban poverty, ill-health, high mobility, cyclical unemployment – contributed to the growing presence of boys in public spaces of the emergent industrial cities. A lively nineteenth-century youthful, largely male, street culture emerged and expanded, evidence of a paradox inherent in modern society's progress. Modern city youth took to the streets as vendors, newsboys, rag pickers, delivery boys, vagrants, thieves, and sex workers. In large centres, like New York City, Chicago, and Montreal, a peer-based youth culture based around a casual and criminal economy provided a community for otherwise dislocated young people.[16] Girls, too, could be found among the street children of urban North America, selling and stealing what they could.[17] Given the dynamic sex trade of the nineteenth century, older girls and young women living rough in urban centres either engaged in prostitution or were presumed to be on its threshold.[18] Not surprisingly, the necessity of daily survival on city streets produced in street children what Timothy Gilfoyle has called "a confrontational and oppositional subculture relative to adult authority."[19]

This swelling public presence of minors elicited action on several fronts broadly directed at the regulation, if not amelioration, of children's lives and the elimination of a growing delinquent class of juveniles. Most notably, a concerned established citizenry founded a variety of institutions, from orphanages to public schools, expressing a new ethic of child saving based on an assumption that urban, industrial society had rendered children at once more vulnerable and more vicious.[20] The material manifestation of nineteenth-century child saving policies came in the form of industrial homes and juvenile reformatories that promised correction of youth morals and manners and the production of upright citizens.

Institutional settings – created as the antithesis of street culture – promised to instill bourgeois values in "lost" children, republican in America and imperialist in Canada, by mimicking middle-class domesticity and insisting on respect for law, order, and social hierarchy. Inflected with the racial politics of the day, these institutions targeted the salvageable and discarded the rest, leaving Aboriginal children to the residential school and African American youth to the prison.[21]

Nineteenth-century urban culture also brought police officers onto the streets in an attempt to preserve the social and economic order and eliminate its visible and insidious threats. In the middle decades of the nineteenth century, many major North American cities established police forces, following Boston's lead in 1838; initially, at least, urban forces served to address mounting crime and quell episodic riots. Police historians describe the early function of city police officers as fluid, if not amorphous, which undoubtedly led them into direct contact with youthful street cultures and to an ambivalent attitude toward the young. David Wolcott writes that nineteenth-century policemen conducted broad social service work, "inspecting streetlights and sewers, clearing roadways of obstructions, finding lost children, lodging vagrants, [and] controlling animals."[22] On the urban beat, uniformed policemen became a visual reminder of authority and a regular neighbourhood presence, finding, disciplining, and returning children to their parents. It was while maintaining order that new municipal police forces targeted older youth perceived as vagrants, petty criminals, and others opposed to the liberal order (especially anarchists and workers); police officers, then, came to know young people and to contribute to the construction and regulation of modern juvenile delinquency.

Unlike the new generation of late nineteenth-century child welfare reformers who were determined to preserve and when necessary restore the innocence of childhood and rescue youth from a street-centred life, the beat cops approached wayward youth in more practical terms. Although reformers and police forces concurred that street culture brought young people perilously close to the nefarious worlds of adults, police officers responded by exercising their paternalistic authority. Deterrence – meeting boys' shenanigans with stern reproach – was thought to best keep youngsters from developing into full-fledged criminals. Boys' "badness" was ordinary, the police claimed, and needed to be met with a firm hand. This would be effected through surveillance and the constant threat of real and potential punishment.[23] While some officers were undoubtedly sympathetic to delinquent children, collectively, Wolcott argues, they "embraced a goal of personal intervention and immediate individual correction."[24] This pragmatism was based on the belief that such discretionary justice was a powerful deterrent. Initially, it was also expedient given that police officers were scarce and responsible for a multiplicity of tasks; in nineteenth-century New York

City, for example, there was one cop per four hundred residents, half what it would become a century later.[25]

The early interactions of urban police with young people helped to produce enduring cultural stereotypes of police officers. From the neighbourhood, the beat cop acquired a reputation for being youth's everyday adversary: heavy on punitive measures and light on sympathy. As the juvenile justice system emerged, child advocates considered police treatment of youth to be part of the problem. North American juvenile justice turned young criminals into juvenile delinquents, a distinction that permitted the law to treat adolescents with a view to rehabilitation while expanding the definition of offences.[26] Juvenile justice administrators privileged probation officers and social workers over police officers when the new courts were founded, starting with Denver's in 1899 and Chicago's a year later; urban police forces were marginal to their mission of rehabilitation, though they continued to arrest and refer minors to the new courts.[27] Despite the emergence of progressive-era juvenile justice, some city police, like those in Chicago, remained antagonistic to youth and meted out arbitrary and sometimes brutal justice.[28] The reputation of early twentieth-century Chicago cops was predicated on the intimidation and violence common in their dealings with youth on the streets and in custody; the police defended these actions on the basis that dissolute kids needed to learn a lesson. Stories of cops threatening youth with weapons, exacting bribes, and committing physical and emotional abuse go some distance to explaining why youth mistrusted police authority, which was embodied in the bullies and corrupt officers of urban forces.[29]

Not all police forces deserved a reputation like Chicago's, yet ambivalence toward juvenile delinquents was common and persistent, as the spectre of a rising delinquent class of juveniles refused to fade. Spurred by a social construction of juvenile delinquency rooted in class and ethnic prejudice, fear for public safety and for the future of respective nations, police harassed young people whose presence on city streets implied they were up to no good, and enforced the law through informal discipline and rough justice.

In Canada, the complexity of the cop–child relationship and the growing uneasiness toward the rough justice meted out to youth became a frequent topic of discussion by police institutions in the 1930s. This turn is suggestive of a change in official police perspective – not practice

– on youth. The *Canadian Police Gazette* (a monthly compendium of articles about policing) discussed questionable incidents of rough justice in a mid-1930s article, "Spanked the Kids." In this story, the police chief of a small town in Ontario apparently "resorted to the good, old method of chastising several youths" who were "caught in the act of tampering with parked cars." He caught and cuffed them then delivered them home. The humiliated boys rejected the notion that what happened was run-of-the-mill chastisement, calling it, rather, "assault and occasioning bodily harm."[30] While making light of the boys' claims and, importantly, the officer's actions, the article's unnamed author admitted that corporal punishment at the hands of police officers was "troublesome" and suggested that "most" cops follow police procedures carefully to avoid "unpleasant repercussions" like being charged with physical violence. By the mid-twentieth century, in part because of the perception that growing up in depression and wartime had had a deleterious effect on youth, Canadian law enforcement organizations admitted that "a policeman [could] do ... irreparable harm" by browbeating children.[31] Slowly assumptions changed whereby scare tactics and bullying at the hands of the police were seen as ineffective and, in fact, had produced the child's justifiable psychological reaction to such treatment: "get[ting] even" with the police, resulting in a deepened schism between law and youth.

In the first decades of the twentieth century some police departments began to take a different tack with youth. The Detroit Metropolitan Police, for example, under Commissioner James R. Couzens (1916–18), sought to rescue the reputation of municipal police forces by reforming the duties and responsibilities of officers. A business leader, he convinced Detroit to implement a corporate model for a police department that emphasized efficiency, specialization, and scientific tools for policing. With respect to juvenile delinquency, Couzens embraced the idea that the police should emphasize social welfare services, and in the decade following the establishment of that city's juvenile court he instructed his officers to offer protection rather than punishment for kids.[32] Couzens's reforms included invigorating the juvenile division and, eventually following a trend across the continent, hiring women officers in the 1920s to oversee cases involving women and children. Perhaps ironically, this turn to protection resulted in more arrests and institutional placements of children and youth. For these reasons, young people in Detroit likely shared with their counterparts in Chicago a healthy fear of and antagonism toward the police. A long, slow campaign to change the reputation of cops began with police leaders like Couzens and others who wrote and spoke so as to construct the future of police work as child friendly.

The impulse to treat children in conflict with the law differently than adults emerged prior to a well-articulated sense of child-friendly policing. In the nineteenth century, typologies of children's care and regulation produced myriad institutions – from asylums to orphanages to industrial and reform schools – that carefully differentiated youngsters from their elders and each other, according to disposition and the nature of the perceived trouble. The new juvenile court system that dominated juvenile justice in the first decades of the twentieth century similarly produced a unique experience for offending minors, with its emphasis on individualized treatment and rehabilitation, and protection over punishment.[33] Though initially on the margins of the juvenile justice system, law enforcement agencies began to move in the direction of a child-specific approach.

Community service police work could also emphasize protection of children. In Toronto, for example, the first decades of the twentieth century saw the force busy with several types of community service work involving working-class neighbourhoods: locating deserting spouses, providing shelter for the homeless, and managing lost and errant children. This social service police work was assisted by the introduction of women officers in the early twentieth century; these women, it was assumed, rejected the notion that police were limited to exercising the "strong arm of the law." As historian Greg Marquis has argued, this social welfare role (including that played by female police) faded by the Second World War, as this municipal force turned toward crime control.[34] During the war, a shortage of male officers and growing street disorderliness prompted a call for a small group of uniformed policewomen, drawn from the Canadian Women's Voluntary Services, to help quell rowdiness on downtown streets.[35] This voluntary work did little to prevent the marginalization of women officers' roles in that city. In Toronto, this trend would reverse, but not until the late 1950s, when the Metropolitan Toronto Police Youth Bureau and a Women's Bureau were formed.[36]

At the same time that urban police forces turned away from social welfare services and toward crime control, many centres saw the creation of youth squads and bureaus that provided a place for women officers.

The formation of such specialty officers helped in some cases to retain, while in others, reintroduce women officers, as well as continue the protective work that stemmed from the social welfare role of urban police forces, at least as it pertained to children and youth.

Crime Prevention: Discovering "Children on the Verge"

Urban policing in the late nineteenth and early twentieth centuries emphasized protection and often institutionalization of children, but police youth squads originated with crime prevention programs that gained prominence among anti-delinquency solutions in the 1920s and 1930s. News stories of gangsters and exploding street violence, loudly amplified by J. Edgar Hoover of the FBI, captured the imagination of the public and policy makers in the interwar period.[37] The moral panics about a major surge in the crime rate tended to settle attention on the rising generation, who were engaged in transforming the morals and manners of their parents. The 1920s youth rebellion – made visible by middle-class young people eschewing their parents' sense of hard work and restraint in favour of personal pleasure – heralded a disorderly world as their wanton behaviour spiralled out of control.[38] This preoccupation with youth rebellion changed during the Depression to concerns about throngs of wandering and vagabond youth.[39] Criminal justice workers, like Walter Greis, a former prison warden from Wisconsin and an authority on delinquency, declared in 1937: "We are faced with the greatest delinquency problem of all time."[40] Hoover, who had declared war on crime, also helped to identify youth as a significant part of the crime problem; in the mid-1930s, he drew attention to the major crimes, such as robbery and auto theft, committed by young men. In an era in which the gangster was both vilified and romanticized, juvenile mimics horrified adults.[41] They were not the majority, but their numbers were worrisome, as was the fact that one-sixth of arrests belonged to repeat offenders who had first broken the law as minors.[42]

Hoover's get-tough-on-crime approach gained support as juvenile crime numbers soared. Yet the panic over youthful delinquency also elicited a more compassionate response. Greis, for example, determined that youth offences occurred as the result of adult action or inaction: broken homes, the inadequacy of institutions like schools and churches, and the dearth of recreational facilities. Growing up in underprivileged circumstances was "delinquency's best breeding ground."[43] Rather than round up juvenile offenders, he advocated keeping young people out of courts "at all costs." The community, he argued, meaning municipalities, should offer programs that significantly modified the child's environment, helping to avert the production of criminals.[44] Greis and his rejection of crime correction for young people joined a chorus of voices determined to control crime by turning to youth work.

"Our greatest problem today is the youth problem," opined Mrs E.T. Sampson of Montreal in the summer of 1939.[45] At that auspicious moment when war erupted in Europe and the fate of liberal democracy hung in the balance, acute anxiety over youth behaviour grew. This generation of Canadian boys and girls had suffered Depression-related depredation and dislocation implicating them in the soaring crime rates that not only pointed to the erosion of civil society, like the Axis powers, but also seemed to threaten the very pillars upon which society was built. "It meets our eyes in all the papers," Sampson wrote, regretting stories of the exploding youthful prison population and a nineteen-year-old sentenced to death.[46] Childhoods spent in adverse conditions, according to commentators like Sampson, may have turned youth vicious but it also victimized them. That autumn, C.A. Wylie, director of the Montreal Boys' Association, empathized with youth for being caught in a system that had both deprived them and transformed them into culprits of "serious misdemeanors."[47] Civic youth workers like Wylie took pity on mainstream working-class youth. Their calls to resolve the youth problem pointed to the need for jobs for young people to keep them occupied, housed, and fed, but they did not stop there. Rather, solutions became comprehensive, spirit-changing programs that addressed the moral, material, and physical deficits in modern childhood. Indeed, this was one moment of many when the shame of a society that spawned "degenerate" youth in a century that was hailed as belonging to young people repeatedly laid bare how that modern society had failed the rising generation.

As a would-be alternative to crime control and repression, the crime prevention strategy focused on examining the provenance of criminals, creating the opportunity for scrutinizing the childhood of gangsters and other criminals. "When we view criminal careers in retrospect, we invariably find that the problem is one that first presented itself in childhood and through neglect has developed into serious criminal behaviour," wrote one New York City policeman of his experience in crime prevention.[48] In pursuing the causes of criminality police looked to the social, economic, and cultural environments in which criminals were raised to identify the sources of bad behaviour. As noted in the Annual Report of the New York City Police Department in 1931, gangsters were once delinquents who were once just boys and, "[a] Police Department cannot be content with shooting down gangsters." The report concluded "It must at the same time put into operation programs to eliminate them."[49] In implementing crime prevention programs and units, police departments took a dramatic step toward embracing youth work that was being driven by academic criminology, sociology, and social work and practised by multiple community organizations focusing on child welfare. This trend hugely expanded and elevated anti-delinquency work in police departments beginning in the interwar period and had the unintended consequence of overlapping with, then usurping, juvenile court jurisdiction.

By the interwar period, prominent sociologists and delinquency experts like Frederic M. Thrasher, William Healy, Clifford R. Shaw, and Sheldon and Eleanor Glueck had produced volumes of evidence determining that "criminal careers begin in childhood and adolescence."[50] "Most criminals," Sheldon and Eleanor Glueck wrote in summarizing contemporary crime prevention thought and practice in 1936, "show definite antisocial tendencies of attitude and behaviour early in childhood."[51] This theory of crime causation had profound implications for the understanding of childhood and the treatment of young people. So important was the child's environment to predicting future criminal behaviour that crime prevention advocates, especially those who studied neighbourhood "ecology," insisted that certain children from high crime districts be understood as "incipient delinquents." Not surprisingly these areas overlapped with those known for high immigrant populations, poverty, and dislocation.[52] Such labelling was not restricted to racialized youth from high crime areas, though; in fact, the discourse on incipient delinquency did not suggest that practitioners of crime prevention should focus narrowly on those who showed potential for trouble but on a broad swath of children who were "on the verge."[53] Crime prevention programs were designed to be a line of defence against the troubled worlds that children inhabited or might inhabit. Would-be delinquents and criminals, according to crime prevention advocates, also needed saving from the formal criminal justice and police institutions, an "exposure that hardens" youth.[54] Thirty years of juvenile courts had not quelled the upward swing of delinquency, and as a peer of the Gluecks argued, crime prevention promised to examine "the problems of children rather than problem children."[55]

Crime prevention programs included a "skeptical eclecticism and an experimental attitude," according to the Gluecks, that would pull community organizations, schools, boys' and girls' clubs, and police forces into youth work.[56] Crime prevention squads within local forces developed as officers joined the ranks of that era's many child workers, embraced contemporary theories of crime causation, and became authorities on youth spaces and the sites of childhood, such as the family and school. The moment was right in the interwar years for police to move into resolving the delinquency problem, as the juvenile court system that had marginalized police forces now fell under scrutiny for not having lived up to its promise.

Civic leaders responded to the public panic over soaring delinquency rates by embarking on crime prevention work in the interwar period. As a crime wave apparently reached national proportions in the United States by the early 1930s, federal and local police turned toward crime control strategies, but civic organizations, educators, and youth and social workers headed down a different path, to "block youth's path to crime."[57] As historian Janis Appier demonstrates, the emergence of municipal committees for crime prevention did not see their cities as being besieged by lawlessness as the FBI's J. Edgar Hoover's war on crime would suggest, but rather, as constituting "a network of social agencies that could foster a safe and satisfying civic life." Coordinating councils, as they were called, developed a community approach to delinquency prevention by focusing on youth recreation programs and supervised leisure in impoverished areas, as well as casework with troubled adolescents. These councils coordinated the literal efforts for civic improvement directed at young people with the local police, juvenile courts, schools, and youth organizations. The councils' insistence upon managing the environment in which youth were growing up reflected their support for social science expertise and a rejection of Hoover's idea that criminals were born bad seeds. By the end of the decade, almost six hundred cities and towns across the US had coordinating councils.

As delinquency rates continued to climb during the Second World War, criminal justice experts expounded on the need for crime prevention measures to, in their words, "protect" youth from criminal law.[58] John Kidman, of the Canadian Penal Association, advocated a community watch system that could intervene in youths' lives before a crime was committed. Social workers' duty in this respect was to be in the community of youth or to seek them out along the "highways and hedges to find them before the trouble begins."[59]

Unlike child welfare reformers and those already involved in youth work through clubs and organizations, police had some distance to cover in fashioning themselves agents of young people. Rising delinquency and crime rates, along with the popularizing of child psychology, motivated the turn toward crime prevention. Turning away from crime control and repression toward crime prevention would require convincing the public that saving the children would bring the crime rate down. This was facilitated by the development of separate programs and squads that involved child specialists. The police insisted on the appropriateness of officers becoming youth workers: one New York City officer argued he had a "unique opportunity for close contact with youngsters," positioning himself as best qualified to know how and why kids got into trouble.[60] Work with children also allowed some gender flexibility, and, unsurprisingly, social workers and women could be found initiating and developing crime prevention programs in police forces. Overall the "crime prevention turn" in policing and the impulse toward remaking urban policing into a force for "child-friendliness" in large North American cities coalesced into a movement for separate squads aimed at childhood.

The example of crime prevention development in the Berkeley, California, Police Department is a case in point. Led by the trailblazing Police Chief August Vollmer, the Berkeley PD was one of the first to formally embrace crime prevention and create a separate unit or youth squad.[61] Vollmer's reform initiatives of the 1910s and '20s consisted of applying new methods to police training and work, effectively raising the standards of police work. With decades of experience with "runaway boys, truant, dependent, and incorrigible children," the PD followed a pragmatic approach, differentiating between the more serious acts of criminality for which youth were sent into the court system and minor misdeeds. For the latter, the PD engaged the Cleveland Common Sense

Policy, a system that ensured minor delinquencies were treated by invoking parental control and avoiding jail.[62] Yet this system's ineffectiveness frustrated Vollmer and resulted in rising numbers of youth in conflict and a commensurate increase in adult criminality. Under Vollmer, starting in the 1910s, the Berkeley PD experimented with a variety of crime prevention strategies, beginning with an effort to render the child knowable. He upheld the belief that police should work in concert with experts to root out the causes of delinquency. He brought in psychiatrists and psychologists to lecture to the police on juveniles and advocated for his officers to be social workers in fact if not in name.[63] In 1916, the University of California, Berkeley, offered criminology courses in crime prevention for police who worked with juvenile delinquency.[64] Vollmer also added a course to police training called "Treatment of Juvenile Offenders."

These training measures were insufficient, however, and in the 1920s, Vollmer, facing rising crime rates, championed the notion that police officers could interrupt the production of delinquents and criminals by intervening in the lives of young people to halt such "waste."[65] He sought out schools, community members, and child welfare workers, including the Director of Research and Guidance in the Berkeley Public Schools to identify the sources of the rising delinquency rates. He then established a Crime Prevention Division in 1925 because, in the words of the woman who ran it, Elizabeth Lossing, the PD "had neither the machinery nor the personnel" for combatting delinquency.[66] This early youth squad found the support of various local organizations including the Berkeley Coordinating Council and College Women's Club and, echoing the early juvenile courts, was expected to have a thoroughly "modern" Child Guidance Clinic.

The appointment of Lossing as head of the Berkeley PD's Crime Prevention Division is telling. A woman with significant training in social work and child psychology, she exemplified the new direction of crime prevention work in the Berkeley PD.[67] Lossing had taken psychiatric social work courses at the University of Michigan and the New School for Social Research and had experience in the Associated Charities (San Francisco), the Berkeley Health Center, and the Institute of Child Guidance in New York City. The benefit of having a woman officer in charge was not lost on Vollmer, who closely identified the kind of anti-delinquency work that would be accomplished, focusing "largely ... [on] ... pre-delinquency problems."[68] Lossing built on the work of the first policewomen, such as Alice Stebbins Wells (appointed to the Los Angeles Police Department [LAPD] in 1910) and Georgia Ann Robinson (the first African American appointed policewoman in 1916, also LAPD), who had initiated crime prevention work with young women and girls.[69] In reflecting on her first decade in charge, Lossing described crime prevention work as "dealing with defective conditions of home and neighborhood." Her approach was reminiscent of casework performed by the era's juvenile court probation officers.[70] Pre-delinquency work entailed pulling together a network of community agencies interested in children and youth and "promot[ing] interest in the health, happiness and welfare of children."[71] Vollmer advocated having a presence in the realm of childhood whereby early signs of delinquent behaviour could be met with the relevant social agents.[72]

In addition to pre-delinquency work, this early youth squad concentrated on female juvenile delinquents up to twenty-one years of age and boys under twelve. This gendered typology of targeted youth reflects the era's view that women police officers' role in the criminal justice arena was best suited to grappling with the sex delinquency of girls and pre-delinquent boys. The Crime Prevention Division took it upon itself to decide the disposition of these cases and ran an "unofficial probation" system. Its members also explicitly set about changing public attitudes toward the police department and such work with children and youth. Public relations campaigns involving the trope of saved young people became central to tasks of the division. After a decade of crime prevention work, Lossing was cautious about claiming its effectiveness in reducing delinquency and crime, yet she was buoyed by the national embrace of such police initiatives. Thus, she did not hesitate to promote Vollmer's focus on children and youth as thoroughly modern and essential to the future of delinquency control.[73]

Crime prevention programs in California were touted as successes to local and national audiences. Young people were diverted from lives of crime and childhood was vastly improved. Yet, as historians have shown, in an era when the public and police forces viewed crime control essential to reducing the threat to ordinary Americans, certain sectors of the youth population were particularly targeted. As Latinos moved to California in the early twentieth century, as African Americans did to the urban north, police "disportionately" blamed youth of colour for the delinquency rates.[74]

Thus, the early crime prevention initiatives helped to conjure a new target for police work: the incipient or would-be delinquent, or pre-delinquent. Since this kind of vague status had broad applicability, it potentially made any and all children the business of law enforcement, but in practice, it created exclusions, like the Mexican American youth of Los Angeles or those considered already delinquent. This orientation alone ensured that women's maternal qualities would be considered appropriate for crime prevention programs. But these would be credentialed, professional women, as the case of the Berkeley crime prevention unit demonstrates, who purportedly held the most up-to-date insights about children and youth; this meant officers found they needed post-secondary courses, if not degrees, in social sciences directed at building an academic expertise in youth work. Other requirements included dispositions suited to youth work, including empathy for youth, and providing good role models for youth. This particular casting of the youth squad officer influenced which male officers would best fit this work as well. Men would be youthful, athletic, and natural leaders of boys.

Getting closer to children and youth inspired some officers to volunteer to coordinate leisure-time activities. The histories of the crime prevention implementation are replete with officers who took boys on hikes, for swims, and who broke up gangs by offering club activities and sports (as will be discussed in chapter 4). One such story, from the Berkeley Police Department, is a tale of winning gang members' trust through sports: Officer A.E. Riedel apparently diffused a rivalry between Japanese and African American gangs by getting them to meet on the football field.[75]

Started by Ronald G. Everleigh, a member of the Vancouver police force, in 1937 to disrupt idleness of young people, the Junior G-Men of Canada gathered working-class boys, and eventually girls, into clubs to promote citizenship training. Aimed at teens who wouldn't typically join organizations, the Junior G-Men appealed to boys looking for leisure activities, which were what Everleigh considered "ordinary privileges" of young people. The G-Men name was a colourful reference to gangster films of the 1930s, one that the boys chose themselves; in exchange for club space and activities, hundreds of young people took a pledge of obedience to law, order, their parents, and the flag.[76]

The New York City Police Department (NYPD) embarked on similar youth work in the early decades of the twentieth century. Its Junior Police program of the 1910s was one of the first experiments that took a "special approach" to potential delinquents. The Junior Police, established as a temporary measure in 1914, allowed the NYPD to reinterpret its role with youth, essentially expanding the parameters of what cops might do regarding children with the added benefit of creating an opportunity to improve the relationship between children and police. Gaining control of the city's gang problem provided the impetus for the Junior Police program, which was directed at the city's socio-economically marginalized young people, who were thought to be vulnerable to gang recruitment. Junior Police functioned as a parallel police force for juveniles, with a hierarchy for aspirational youth, whereby junior "patrolmen" could work their way up to junior "chief inspector."[77] Through the auspices of this program, officers organized teams, games, and provided military drill, all the while forging a presence in parks and other areas of the city where children and youth were likely to congregate.[78] Establishing a presence in youth hangouts – eventually labelled by delinquency experts as "plague spots" – functioned as a way for police to engage and befriend the boys and girls found there.[79] Officers would no longer simply be assigned to arrest delinquents and criminals; rather, this new system emphasized correction through "admonition and warning" and encouraged officers to get to know youth to deter them from developing an appetite for petty criminality.[80] The basic principle of the Junior Police was deterrence; by occupying youth spaces and gathering knowledge about neighbourhood youth, police officers aimed to protect children from the pernicious influence of gangs, identify the vulnerable – such as "mental defectives" – among wayward youth, and make "friends" with groups who were characteristically enemies of the police.[81] The desire to cultivate positive relations between police officers and children led the former to create opportunities for education on such subjects as street safety and games for both boys and girls while surveilling the city's "plague spots."[82] In this capacity, officers sought to instill in the rising generation notions about good citizenship.[83]

New York City's Junior Police program did not outlast the decade, and much of the anti-delinquency work of the 1920s happened under the rubric of the force's Welfare Department.[84] Headed by a woman, this bureau comprised many retirement-age policemen and female officers who surveyed the "breeding places of vice and crime to which the youth of the city was exposed."[85] Concerns over rampant criminal activity in

the 1920s and the seemingly young age of offenders inspired serious
study of crime prevention toward the close of that decade.

Major developments in crime prevention took root when, in 1929,
the New York City Police Commissioner, Edward Pierce Mulrooney,
established an Advisory Committee on Crime Prevention, which led
to the creation of a Crime Prevention Bureau (CPB) the following year.
By December 1930, the CPB, headed by Henrietta Additon and an NYPD
Deputy Police Commissioner, comprised a main office and six district
units strategically placed in high-delinquency areas.[86] Highly experienced in social service work, Additon held multiple degrees from the
University of Pennsylvania and many positions of note. She was part of
the epoch's professional class of women workers whose specialty was
protection of women and girls, demonstrated by her positions heading
up the Big Sisters of Philadelphia, the US Interdepartmental Social
Hygiene Board's committee on women and work, and the Women and
Girls' Section of the [First World] War Department Commission on
Training Camp Activities. After the war, she worked as the director
of the Juvenile Probation Department of the Philadelphia Municipal
Court, taught at Bryn Mawr College, and lectured on probation at the
Pennsylvania School of Social and Health Work.[87] When tapped to
become the head of the CPB, she was working for the American Social
Hygiene Association.[88] Remarkably, she was not a cop.[89] The crime
prevention turn paved the way for women with a social service back-
ground to be meaningfully integrated into the force. Not that there were
no policewomen available: she allegedly won the position over Mary
Hamilton, a long-term city policewoman. Additon promoted the police
role in improving community conditions for New York City's boys
and girls and chastised social workers for long overlooking the critical
role police officers could play in triumphing over the destructive and
undesirable influences that led children astray.[90] Likely her experience
with delinquent children and troubled families made her candidacy
appealing. Parroting contemporary ideas about crime provenance,
Additon claimed that hardened criminals had a history of being "sickly
boys" and that the endemic unemployment of the 1930s portended a
dramatic rise in delinquency.[91] She held the position until May 1934.

This substantial bureau, comprising over one hundred male officers,
over forty policewomen, and twenty-five female social workers, was
created with the purpose of implementing the recommendations of

the Advisory Committee. As such, the CPB took a broad interpretation of the definition of prevention work: "determent, adjustment, treatment of the vulnerable and the delinquent." This definition included monitoring the spaces of youth culture, addressing pre-delinquency, and fostering among the city's youth a respect and appreciation for authority.[92] Additon's first directive to her officers was to find and ferret out the "crime-breeding places" of the city. Like protection officers before her, she focused on exposing commercial amusement venues such as dance halls, moving picture houses, and pool halls, for their pernicious influence on young people.[93] Like many of her peers, she argued that the perils of growing up poor, in broken homes, and with ill health produced a heightened risk for juvenile delinquency and criminal behaviour.[94] Consistent with this environmental argument, she fought against financial cuts to city playgrounds and other child-friendly spaces, claiming their curative effect for kids prone to delinquency. In 1933, the CPB surveyed the city's public play facilities, recommending the addition of 166 "play sites" as an "effective means of safeguarding [children] from street accidents and from conditions that lead toward juvenile delinquency."[95] One and a quarter million children would be reached by the proposed 51 play streets and 115 play plots. These play sites were to be spread throughout Manhattan and the boroughs in an effort to meet the "non-material" needs of children growing up in "poor, congested neighborhoods."[96]

By 1931, 130 patrolmen, 44 female officers, and 25 social workers staffed the Bureau. (Female social workers not from police ranks would be removed in the 1940s and eventually replaced by police caseworkers.) Although youth police existed in many precincts, the Bureau marked a shift toward the centralization of youth cases. The formalization of crime prevention into a bureau produced some concern about police work moving into what had been welfare service work at the hands of volunteers, who were on the verge of retirement. The press picked up on the fact that the children who came into contact with the CPB would effectively have police records and suggested a preference for the CPB removal from the police infrastructure, but to no avail.[97]

Change came in early 1935, when the CPB became the Juvenile Aid Bureau (JAB).[98] The JAB had a broad mandate, being responsible for developing delinquency prevention schemes for the city and "[h]elping secure adequate social treatment for juvenile delinquents and wayward minors."[99] The JAB continued in the same vein as the CPB and brokered relationships with the Board of Education, especially its Bureau of Child Guidance. The maturation of this prevention orientation resulted in a qualitative change in the approach to policing young people.

Under the auspices of the JAB, for example, crime prevention youth policing in New York City changed juvenile justice processes. A bureaucratic system empowered police to generate records on the city's youth, targeting those who lived in high-delinquency areas. Every NYPD officer carried JAB-2 cards on which they recorded interactions with delinquent or potentially delinquent youth. Officers wrote up youths under twenty-one who were engaged in "delinquent" conduct, even that not warranting arrest, recording the details of the act and important aspects of the youth's identity. These details included the young person's address, school, age, and race (denoted as "color").[100] Officers then sent this record to the local unit of the JAB. Receipt of a JAB-2 card precipitated a call to the Social Services Exchange to ascertain whether the youth and his/her family were known to any of the city's social agencies.[101] If no record was found, the JAB either followed up with a home or office visit or filed the card for future reference. The latter disposition of the youth in question applied to trivial offences and first-timers, although the JAB boasted about the efficacy of home visits, which provided officers with a better picture of negative influences on the child. In cases where the youth was arrested, another form, the WF4, was sent to the main office of the JAB, which then sent a record of it to the local JAB.[102] In the 1940s the Police Department issued a directive to officers that no child under sixteen be arrested unless a serious offence had been committed. Instead, the JAB treated these cases without court action.[103] The decision concerning the seriousness of the offence lay with the individual officers, their biases and prejudices, and ideas concerning the rehabilitative potential of the youth, a quality that favoured white boys over boys of colour.[104]

In addition to this expanding record-keeping on youth, the JAB generated a "trouble list" of potential delinquents from schools, parents, social organizations, and the like.[105] Within months of its creation, the Bureau of Attendance for the school system provided names of five thousand "truants" to the police who promised to use only the names to "draw the children into healthful, recreational activities."[106] This list would preoccupy the JAB, as the numbers of youths dealt with on an annual basis swelled; by 1940, for example, the caseload was over 66,000 youths, as many as 90 per cent of whom were labelled "potentials" for delinquency commission.[107] JAB field workers also conducted tours of inspections at youth hangouts, including dance halls, cellar clubs, movies, bowling alleys, poolrooms, Times Square, and parks and beaches in summertime, to root out underage children and identify wayward behaviour.[108] Other points of interest included bus and ferry terminals, the Navy Yard, and Harlem.[109] When necessary, JAB officers arrested adults for contributing to the delinquency of a minor. In these ways, the JAB fashioned a distinct form of casework with New York City's youth. This side-stepping of the juvenile justice system would raise another series of concerns about crime prevention work with youth, a fact that was most acute in the case of Montreal, as we will see in the next chapter.

Youth-conscious policing in New York City in the 1930s and '40s involved several bureaucratic changes in the practice of policing and the creation of programs to reduce the opportunities for youth to get into trouble. These would include taking a community-based approach to casework that linked the child with schools and various social agencies, pinpointing the communities and individuals that led children astray, and offering many recreational activities. The close contact with neighbourhood children was expected to help reform their attitudes towards law enforcement. It was the "constructive" leisure programs that made the NYPD most visible. For its part, the NYPD claimed to be addressing the needs of disadvantaged children by providing structured play. Through "child-friendly policing" a basic pattern emerged in which young people would find themselves more engaged and more monitored by local authorities. Police filled gaps in urban recreation, setting up and coaching athletic teams. Boys' and girls' clubs were established that would teach skills, and police gave children an opportunity to appreciate authority by playing at policing and by acting as juvenile police or safety patrols.

Conclusion

It would become an axiom of the twentieth century that due to unrelenting poverty, endemic social injustice, wars, crime waves, and escalating delinquency, each generation decried the condition of young people and its threat to liberal democracies. Youth problems in this period were seen as the result of children growing up in bleak economic times in substandard home situations, exposed to fast-paced cultural change, and dealt with by a harsh criminal justice system. Social scientists joined civic authorities and urban police departments in embracing crime prevention as a solution to youth problems. With this paradigmatic shift, communities acknowledged responsibility for producing delinquents and, by extension, criminals.

Over the course of the 1930s and '40s, crime prevention programs and youth squads transformed police relations with youth in countless cities and towns across North America. Experiments in youth policing like New York City's Junior Police joined other crime prevention programs, such as the Chicago Area Project (which targeted youth in low-income, immigrant communities), to reshape the approach to delinquency and youth in the early twentieth century.[110] Pilot projects and diffuse efforts at delinquency prevention would be replaced by the mid-1930s with extensive and enduring programs, increased personnel, and new bureaucracies.

Rather than seeing this development as an opportunity to become part of the juvenile justice movement, police forces sought to correct what was increasingly clear: the juvenile justice system's limited success in the realm of protecting children and preventing crime.[111] What stands out among these early prevention programs is the determination to steer youth away from the juvenile court system and corrections; as Elisabeth Lossing of the Berkeley Crime Prevention Division argued, "we … try to save our predelinquents and juvenile delinquents the necessity of Juvenile Court action."[112] The adoption of crime prevention measures created the possibility of creating a new role or identity for police in the campaign against delinquency.[113] A fundamental transformation in police work occurred. In an effort to contribute to the "constructive development" of young people, police-led clubs displayed a preference for protection and guidance over repression and retribution.[114]

Arguably, youth-conscious policing under the aegis of crime prevention programs and youth squads helped divert many young people from the juvenile justice system. Yet this was an imperfect and enduring experiment that garnered criticism at the time, embedded police authority in childhood in a way that was comprehensive and unprecedented, and ultimately did not succeed in putting an end to delinquency or children's vulnerability, although the continued presence of this goal to this day speaks to its implausible premise. Paradoxically, the persistence of juvenile delinquency as a major social problem in the 1940s and '50s was an argument for the expansion not only of the crime prevention activities, but also of further surveillance and correction of young people.

If crime prevention did not resolve the delinquency problem, police forces could – and did – claim that they had won the public relations battle to change their reputation with youth. In many cities, if we are to believe the press, young people came to see the police as benevolent neighbourhood figures who offered recreation and guidance and were worthy of respect. In the 1930s, the Toronto police boasted to the newspaper the *Mail and Empire* that their club activities had changed children's attitudes toward the police. Youth had "learned to regard the burly man in uniform as their friend and protector rather than their stern admonisher and perhaps the engine of their destruction."[115] Rhetorically, as police officers became youth squad agents, they fashioned themselves as child friendly, yet a deep ambivalence toward children and youth, especially racialized others, runs through this critical development in twentieth-century policing. Over the course of the twentieth century, municipal police forces would engage schools, welfare agencies, and youth organizations as they further embedded themselves in childhood.

CHAPTER TWO

The Montreal Miracle:
Juvenile Justice, Gender,
and the Making of a Youth Squad

Montreal's first youth squad emerged from the Police Department's Morality Squad. Starting in 1909, the Morality Squad (what would be called today a vice squad) policed offences against public morality, mostly gambling and prostitution, and is perhaps best remembered for its entanglements with Montreal's criminal underworld in the 1940s and '50s.[1] Its origins in the Morality Squad set this youth squad apart from those south of the border and in other parts of Canada. Along with the somewhat awkward moniker, the Juvenile Morality Squad (JMS) did not have an explicit crime prevention orientation; rather, like its progenitor, it addressed morals offences, vice, and delinquent acts of a sexual nature.

In terms of human resources, the Juvenile Morality Squad represented a tiny portion of the Montreal force and would garner far more public attention than its numbers would suggest. From its Depression-era beginnings, the youth squad grew from two officers to thirteen by the end of the Second World War, bolstered by the war's delinquency panic. But it was in the postwar era that the squad grew most rapidly, comprising more than eighty officers by the early 1950s. During the 1930s and early '40s, the Montreal force was 1,500 strong.[2] By the mid-1950s the police department's portion of the municipal budget grew as the number of officers increased to more 2,400.[3] The city itself reached a population in excess of one million in 1951 and that number would double in the following decade with the baby boom and high immigration rates. Bureaucratic changes and professionalization accompanied the growth of the police in Montreal. For the youth squad this meant, first, in 1944, that an effort to centralize the squad's work resulted in a physically independent office located in east end Montreal near the Jacques Cartier bridge.[4] Second, name changes – first to the Juvenile Morality Bureau, then, in 1946, to the Delinquency Prevention Bureau, followed by the Youth Aid Section in 1952 – signalled a shift in orientation toward crime prevention.[5] In the early 1950s, the squad boasted an international reputation based on its success in creatively reducing juvenile delinquency through crime prevention strategies.

Leading the youth squad was career officer Ovila Pelletier. In 1922, at age twenty-one, he applied to join the Montreal Police Force. Like most of the force, he was French Canadian and Catholic, from a family of modest means. He became a sworn constable in 1929 and would rise through the ranks to the position of detective inspector just prior to his death in 1958.[6] In the 1930s he would increasingly turn to juvenile cases and would spend most of his career working with youth, making a name for himself as head of the youth squad. In addition to delinquency control he won a major public relations victory at home for the police. This was no mean feat in an era known for police corruption; in these decades, the city had developed a reputation for being widely tolerant of vice and its police department (especially the "adult" morality squad) was weighted down by allegations of ties to organized crime and tolerance for gambling and prostitution.[7] The force, about 2,500 strong, had the reputation as "no place for an honest man."[8] In fact, in the early postwar period the deterioration of the police force's image in the press became a major preoccupation for successive chiefs.[9] Like many other Canadian police services, it did not reflect the diversity of its population, but was largely representative of the working-class French Canadian, Roman Catholic majority. Bringing esteem to a police force known for ignominious relations with commercial vice operations in the city helped endear Pelletier to the city.

In the 1940s and '50s, Pelletier and his colleagues reinvented the police officer as the youth worker, embracing renowned crime prevention schemes originating in Berkeley, California, and New York City. Reimagining police officer duty and identity in Montreal brought the reintroduction of female officers to the Police Department in 1947 and changed what it meant for men to police children. At the same time, the expansion of police youth work made police more integral to the city's juvenile justice system. Many observers applauded this development, but its usurpation of juvenile court authority led to major resistance from authorities at the Montreal Juvenile Delinquents" Court. In targeting pre-delinquents under its crime prevention programs, the squad also ran afoul of the city's well-established social service workers, who similarly complained of the squad's overreach into youth work, as we will see in chapter 4.

For young people, the youth squad had a paradoxical effect: it was at once a disciplinary apparatus of surveillance and regulation and a new source of protection, status, and inclusion in the community for those who conformed to its demands and ideals for youth. In the case of adolescent boys caught in same-sex sexual relations, this equation may have spared them harsh treatment by youth squad officers who determined that strangers – mostly adult men – had enticed unwitting and malleable youths into homosexual acts. Youth squad empathy for the teenager did not override mid-century homophobia; rather, when the squad engaged in a crackdown on the sexual corruption of youths, it found and punished adults, using such tactics as a bulwark against sexual transgression to teach boys conformity to the era's heteronormative imperative. Sexual regulation had long been directed at teenage girls, such that the juvenile justice system workers had considered all sex delinquents to be female; in the postwar era, embodied delinquency drew attention to all youths.[10]

The making of a youth squad in Montreal, as in other large urban centres, pointed to a consensus that juvenile delinquency had become, by the 1940s, one of society's monumental problems. During wartime and in its tragic wake, young people came to represent the promise of a better tomorrow. As a powerful symbol of the future, children and youth often evoked innocence. Experts and the media alike insisted that their delinquency was a product of contemporary society's ills and the individual's environment. Youth-conscious policing therefore produced and reflected an empathic vision of children, including delinquents, as victims of the adult world. Pelletier argued that a lack of "[m]oral and material happiness among children is the true problem [underlying delinquency]," and sought its root causes: ultimately, the world adults had created.[11] The mid-century discursive child who prompted youth squad action was a victim of hard economic times (a lack of employment opportunities and/or impoverished parents), circumstances beyond their control (depression and wartime, dislocation in the postwar period), adult predators, and above all bad parenting.[12] Even with the rise of the more threatening "hoodlum" in the 1950s, young criminals in the post-war period could blame their alienation on the "world made chaotic by their elders."[13] When the Montreal police youth squad joined the movement to tackle delinquency through prevention strategies, it confirmed a rhetorical commitment to at least protect children and redeem youth.

Origins

Prior to the establishment of a youth squad in Montreal, law enforcement officers encountered children and adolescents as part of their broad duties of keeping the peace. In Montreal, the municipal police service served as the front line in criminal justice enforcement and as agents of a rudimentary welfare system.[14] A perennial function of the Montreal force involved dealing with "lost" children; in fact, the police "found" more than two thousand such cases per annum in the early 1930s.[15] The police also arrested young people for public order offences (e.g., loitering, indecency, drunkenness, and theft), for behaviour specified in the Juvenile Delinquents Act (e.g., desertion, incorrigibility), and for breaches of municipal regulations (regarding soliciting/selling, traffic violations). Police officers brought young people to the Detention House and the Montreal Juvenile Delinquents' Court (MJDC), which handled complaints against juvenile thieves, vagrants, and those who had deserted their homes.

When the Canadian juvenile justice system emerged in the latter decades of the nineteenth century, it put into practice the impulse to reform and rehabilitate wayward children and youth through reform schools and separate youth courts by the early twentieth century. Most municipal police forces did not embrace this reform; social and judicial reformers, not to mention youths themselves, thought they lacked compassion, exercising brutish power over children in their midst. The practice of policing, then, appeared antithetical to the era's spirit of child welfare reform.[16] Montreal was no exception. The MJDC used probation officers and social workers to handle cases and minimized the role of local officers. Yet juvenile justice systems (and parents) required the input of police officers, who were best equipped to find lost children and runaways. Pelletier and his youth squad would be responsible for transforming the role of police in the juvenile justice system from the margins to a vital centre of youth work.

In the mid-1930s, Montreal Police Chief Fernand Dufresne made a relatively small gesture toward laying the foundation for a new youth squad. Dufresne seconded two members of the department's morality squad to deal specifically with minors.[17] Dufresne's aim reflected a growing youth consciousness among urban forces. His crime control strategy was to separate the policing of adults from that of youth. This directive was the first to explicitly assign specific officers to youth and delinquency. Pelletier and Louis-Philippe Durivage worked full-time on juvenile delinquency, with a view toward "eliminating it."[18] The advent of an identifiable youth squad helped the police to prevail in the city's delinquency regulation system, which had been dominated by the juvenile court since its inception in 1912. The early aims of the JMS emphasized youth protection work and co-operation with the juvenile court. As a sign of this shift the JMS placed a liaison officer at the MJDC in 1939 to be an essential intermediary between the police and the juvenile court judges.

The meagre size of the squad, its lack of special youth training and resources, and the omission of crime prevention techniques suggest youth policing was not yet a priority: this phase was only a transitional one toward youth-conscious policing. However, the small squad would have a lasting impact: it helped centralize police work on youth problems, so when public wartime anxieties arose over the vulnerability of youth, latchkey children, and "youth gone wild," there was a mechanism in place to channel the response. The greater the threat to and by youth, the more necessary the youth squad became.

The push to transform police officers into youth workers received a boost from community groups in the late 1930s. As stories about imperiled youth gripped the city, the police force was called upon to manage the growing problem. The Ligues du Sacré Coeur, a Roman Catholic men's association known for promoting Christian life and protesting what it claimed was unmitigated spread of vice in the city, launched a campaign directed at police and adult corruption of juvenile morality. Like other conservative organizations, the spectre of high unemployment, mixed with a radical political climate, gave the Ligues much consternation. Expressing concern over youth vulnerability was about more than protection of innocent bodies; it acknowledged a desperate need to win the contest over youth and by extension the direction of the social body. This public panic was not the first over youth trouble; in the interwar period, the arrival of a rebellious youth culture with a secular devotion to commercialism, hedonism, and recklessness had already "ravaged" youth morality.[19] Yet at the close of that decade, blame for the city's corrupted moral landscape was directed not at the gyrating bodies of "flaming" youth. Allegedly, a far more sinister scourge threatened young people: predatory adults. In this era adults under suspicion included those labelled "sex perverts," homosexuals, labour organizers, and Communists.[20] An "increasing number of corrupters of youth are at present carrying on their nefarious work" against both boys and girls in the city, reported the Ligues du Sacré Coeur in 1939.[21] In the face of this "dangerous" and "reprehensible" situation, the group petitioned the mayor to challenge apparent police inaction.[22] The source of the problem was manifold: the paucity of police officers dedicated to youth problems, parents' lack of moral guidance of children, the rise in vice among young people, and a growing number of "corruptors of youth."[23]

In 1939, Police Chief Fernand Dufresne appeased the citizens of Montreal with a promise to bolster his fledgling Juvenile Morality Squad and restore the moral health of youth. Just three years later, Juvenile Court Judge Arthur Laramée would write to Chief Dufresne congratulating him on the work of the Juvenile Morality Squad. Thanks to Ovila Pelletier and his colleagues on the squad, Laramée wrote, "adults who pervert youth" were arrested and convicted, and "children on the road to perversion" were steered toward the "right path."[24]

Montreal participated in the mid-century moral panic over the sex-crime menace.[25] Medical and psychiatric spokespersons, criminal justice officials, and the media fixated on immanent youth danger that helped produce work for the JMS. The two-man squad therefore initially paralleled the work of the larger Morality Squad – mostly involving investigating and policing prostitution and vice – with specific attention to immorality as it affected young people. With a view to expunging immorality – the social problem that had spread at a dizzying rate in the 1930s and early '40s – the JMS made liberal use of the court, the Juvenile Delinquents Act, and its authority over minors.

Policing Juvenile Morality, Arresting Adults: Article 33 of the Juvenile Delinquents Act

In 1940, Juvenile Morality Squad officer Ovila Pelletier arrested eleven adult men and brought them to Montreal's juvenile court.[26] According to court records, the accused preyed upon boys hanging around movie theatres on St-Laurent Boulevard, near Ste-Catherine Street East. In exchange for small sums of money, the youths accompanied the men to alleys and nearby rented rooms for sex.[27] According to the witness statements of the fourteen- and fifteen-year-old boys, this activity had been taking place over the course of several weeks. News of this crime ring and its centrepiece – gross indecency – likely confirmed to many Montrealers that a "veritable campaign" of corruption against children plagued the city.[28]

Five years later, JMS–juvenile court liaison officer Paul-Émile Naud processed several men for indecent assault on minor girls. According to the young teenage girls, these men had given them between twenty-five cents and one dollar for a range of sexual acts, including masturbation, oral sex, and sexual intercourse. These sexual exchanges occurred in small groups in rooms that the men had rented.[29]

In the above two incidents, the arresting officers could have taken the men to criminal court for violations of the Criminal Code of Canada. Instead Pelletier and Naud charged the men, respectively, with contravening article 33 of the Juvenile Delinquents Act, a variation on the offence "contributing to the delinquency of a minor."[30] Although the city's juvenile court docket comprised mainly minors, article 33 granted juvenile courts jurisdiction over adults in cases where delinquency of a minor could be attributed to the malicious or negligent actions of an adult. In practice, a range of adult behaviours fell under article 33 and the corruption of a minor: incest, rape, sexually explicit behaviour in the presence of a child, purchasing sexual favours, statutory rape, mutually agreed-upon sexual relations, and/or inciting minors to steal, receive stolen goods, and/or gamble. Most article 33 cases suggest coercion, many involved the commodification of a young person's body, and some were explicitly violent; all undoubtedly took an emotional and physical toll on the involved youth, not always visible in the legal record. Due to the insidious nature of these cases, and what must have seemed to be their ubiquity, the youth squad pursued adults vigorously, making article 33 a cornerstone of morality work with juveniles in the 1930s and 1940s. In 1946, Pelletier bragged that he and his colleagues brought to justice many adults for acts considered corruptive of youth – more than one thousand in the first decade of the squad's existence.[31] By 1948, as Pelletier's media star soared, the magazine *Saturday Night* featured his innovative police work, involving his own five hundred case files involving "perverts."[32]

Arresting an adult under article 33 of the Juvenile Delinquents Act allowed considerable flexibility for the youth squad and juvenile court officials. Adults accused of incest, rape, gross indecency, and so forth, could be sent to criminal or juvenile court. As Chief Constable Walter H. Mulligan of Vancouver explained in the 1940s, child molestation cases, for example, could be placed in one of two categories: indecent assault (a Criminal Code violation) or contributing to juvenile delinquency (article 33 of the JDA).[33] Youth workers, like the JMS officers and the juvenile court judges, often pursued cases of indecent assault on minors under article 33 in this period likely because they saw "corrupted" youth as their purview. Statutory rape and criminal seduction could be difficult to prove in criminal court, while article 33 subsumed these crimes and needed only proof of a corrupted minor.[34] One juvenile court judge critiqued article 33 for its vague "contributing to juvenile delinquency" clause, which he called "a lazy prosecutor's refuge"; it was also a choice weapon of the Juvenile Morality Squad.[35]

Article 33 targeted a range of adults, including family members of the victims. For their part, parents and guardians had the responsibility to remove the conditions that produced delinquent actions and ensure that children did not become delinquent. Other adults could be found guilty of an offence if they knowingly, or willfully, aided, caused, or abetted a child to commit an offence or tolerated her or his committing an offence; or if they committed an act that would contribute to making a child a juvenile delinquent.[36] Violations of article 33 were met with a $500 fine and/or up to two years', less a day, imprisonment.

Those accused of violating article 33 were most frequently male, with women arrested for neglecting their own children or exposing them to immoral, mostly sexual, situations including the informal sex trade.[37] Despite the fact that most child sexual assault involved men within the victim's family, contemporary expertise pointed to the sexual menace of strangers. Lewd and dangerous neighbours and "pathetic old men" were common culprits, explained Dr Rosario Fontaine, MD, who wrote a column called "Dr Watson's Corner" in the Montreal *Revue des Agents de Police/Constables Review*. "Old men," who were unable to achieve an erection, he wrote, "often seek genetic excitement by handling children or by having children commit indecent acts on them."[38] This kind of offender stood at one end of the scale, explained Fontaine – a nuisance more than a threat because of his inability to rape and therefore impregnate an innocent girl or to sexually assault a boy. A more socially threatening figure was another male character: the familiar (by sight) but estranged neighbour. Children apparently fell victim to neighbours who lured them into private spaces, such as garages, basements, and the like, often in groups. Single and without deep roots in the community, these men preyed on girls and/or boys. In the 1940s, court psychiatrists labelled their motivations "psychopathic" and referred to the men as sex "deviates," as in the case of fifty-four-year-old Arthur L., who was brought to juvenile court by Pelletier in 1943. A group of neighbourhood girls, aged seven to twelve, admitted that Arthur had called them into his garage, where he had engaged them in "immoral acts." According to the girls, he pulled down their pants, performed oral sex on them in front of others, and exposed himself to them.[39] A year earlier, a fifty-year-old man was found guilty under article 33 for committing indecent acts against girls and boys, all minors, who had been to his stable in their neighbourhood, where he fondled them, manually and orally, in exchange for candy or a dime.[40]

Although "corruption" of children and youth happened in and around their homes, the spectre of the stranger who preyed upon youth (especially in the anonymous youth-oriented commercial areas of the city) animated the call for a youth squad. These men might be transients (sailors, soldiers, for example) or they might be locals who took advantage of the readily available sexual commerce in the city. Attributing these acts to a stranger signified children's vulnerability in the complex world beyond the home. The "stranger-danger" trope had become culturally embedded by the nineteenth century. It gave rise to the criminalization of seduction (age-of-consent laws) in the 1880s to protect young women who lived beyond familial cover. By the 1930s, it implicated those children who roamed beyond parental supervision, casting them as sexually vulnerable to enticements (such as money and candy) offered by older men. Such strangers, increasingly called "perverts," sex deviates, or sexual psychopaths, were those imagined Pied Pipers of sin and debauchery who came from far away and offered what children could not refuse. According to the police experts, some children were more endangered by these men because of their poverty, apparently defenceless in the face of a promise of money or a treat. Cases processed by youth squad officers fixated on what the young people gained in the exchange: for example, in the 1945 cases that Naud presented at juvenile court, adolescent girls converted their monetary gain into a night at Belmont (amusement) Park.

The danger posed by strangers fortified the JMS's mission to protect the city's children and to caution parents. In the late 1930s, Pelletier arrested scores of men who fit the stranger profile; these cases represent the broad range that article 33 could embrace, from a forty-year-old man raping and molesting four girls under the age of eighteen, to a stranger who gave ten cents to eleven-year-old girls to masturbate him.[41] During the war, the juvenile court ensured that a man "addicted" to sex with young children was deported to England.[42] Two rare and tragic cases from 1945 and 1954, respectively, featuring the vulnerability of boys in the face of depravity, similarly helped to emphasize to the public the positive and necessary place for police oversight of youth and the danger posed by "sex perverts." The gruesome discovery of a nine-year-old boy who had been sexually assaulted and murdered on his way to ski on the slopes of Mount Royal sent a chill through the community in February 1945.[43] The spot where searchers found him, half buried in the snow with hands bound, was known as "the jungle." A place heavily scrutinized by police as a gay male hangout, the jungle was associated with arrests for indecency.[44] The prospect of a "degenerate" boy slayer generated "hundreds" of stories of indecent assaults by boys, girls, and parents who, according to the police, had been reluctant to come forward.[45] In the summer of 1954, the discovery of the dismembered corpse of a six-year-old boy similarly induced a panic over the safety of children. In this case, when last seen alive, the boy had been speaking to a "strange man." Subsequently his body was found in the man's rented room.[46] Both men in these cases were caught and hanged within a year of their crimes. Such monstrous acts committed upon children helped to keep stranger-danger stories circulating. Montreal was not alone in identifying a new sexual threat to children, as moral panics over "perverts" and "sexual psychopaths" spread throughout English North America.[47] As Mona Gleason has argued, the "powerful postwar association [of homosexual men victimizing children]" overrode "the fact that the vast majority of sexual assaults on children were perpetuated by heterosexual-identified men within the nuclear family."[48]

The youth squad used article 33 to police gay men. A "Dr Watson's Corner" article counselled the police in the 1940s that homosexuality was "sexual inversion": a "perversion which brings about the seeking of

sexual satisfaction between man and man or woman and woman."[49] He
acknowledged the common existence of "pederasty" in Montreal, making
a connection for readers between homosexuality and pedophilia.[50] His
explications of same-sex relations suggest that, by the mid-1940s, homosexual acts were associated with a fixed identity (the homosexual), but
the police were advised by the medical establishment not to harass gay
men unless they were found to be "mentally disturbed" with a predilection for children. In 1947, physician Émile Legrand described Benoît B.,
who had been charged with giving money to two adolescent boys in
exchange for sexual acts, as a "classic homosexual … with an effeminate
air, flowery language, and little mannerisms." His actions were found
to be the result not of "mental problems," making him less dangerous; rather, Legrand described him as "a sexual invert" and prescribed
distractions from his sexual preoccupations.[51] At the same time, other
men similarly convicted under article 33 (indecent assault on minor
boys) were labelled as "perverts" or "criminal sexual psychopaths," their
conduct the "most dangerous to the welfare of children."

Pelletier and his squad remained focused on the adults in these cases.
In its declaration of adult wrongs against children and youth, article 33
was clearly intended to be an instrument of protection, predicated on
the sexual innocence of the concerned minor. In court reports children
superficially emerged as "poor victims" and "innocents."[52] Yet, in practice,
article 33 cases contained a kind of circular logic concerning evidence.
When child witnesses admitted to committing an immoral act – itself
a highly subjective offence – with an adult, they confirmed their own
delinquency, which, in turn, could be used as proof of "contributing to
the delinquency of a minor" against the adults in question. Though child
witnesses were thought to be unreliable, when they admitted immorality
and described the actions in court, the very act of articulating – putting
into words and narrative – sexual behaviour was evidence that their
minds, if not their bodies, had been corrupted. This damning fact demonstrated to the juvenile court that the adult had not only corrupted the
child, but had also "aided him or her to commit the juvenile delinquency
offence of immorality. Thus, on the one hand its focus on immorality led
the JMS to tackle what was termed "child molestation" and other adult
transgressions against children; on the other, it exponentially increased
the regulation of youthful sexuality, especially that of boys. This shift is
abundantly clear in the cases involving same-sex sexuality.

When eleven adult men were arrested for immoral acts with boys in 1940, the implicated adolescents remained blameless even though they were clearly exchanging sex for money. Indeed, Pelletier and the juvenile court seemed to deny or minimize the role and intentions of boys at times. Yet several historians have shown that, in cities including Chicago, New York, and Toronto, this kind of sex work was undoubtedly part of working-class boys' urban experience.[53] During the 1940s, an era of shifting power relations, violence, coercion, lust, and gratification due to the anxiety surrounding the nation's rebound from war, boys might face condemnation for, or enjoy tolerance of, their sexual expression. The JMS interrogated boys and girls in conjunction with article 33 actions or their own cases, which ignited a process whereby information about adolescent sexuality was collected, assessed, and used to justify the development of prevention programs and punishment.

The JMS and the juvenile court often suspected that adolescent boys were being tainted by the immoral actions of adults. The epistemological shift in the 1930s – in which psychologists defined adolescent male sexual expression as normal, but that individuals needed protection and constraint – caused the slippage away from a designation of innocent.[54] Experts advised that boys, especially, should not be free of sexual knowledge and, therefore, could not be entirely innocent. Boys' sexual curiosity and sex play, then, were expected. In turn, adults who coerced or manipulated them into sex acts were now predators of the worst kind. They preyed on the "normal" instincts of boys, infecting them with "perversion."

Girls who had been raped or sexually assaulted and who were found immoral (i.e., sexually active) experienced strict surveillance through probation or institutionalization. Boys could similarly become "lost," although the threatening scenario played out differently. Once "initiated" into same-sex activities by older boys or men, adolescent boys were believed to become morally unmoored, which would, in turn, lead to criminality and becoming a "menace to society." In one of his 1946 speeches, Pelletier recounted the case of "Paul," a fourteen-year-old boy from a poor but "morally good family." The problem for Paul was not his grades or Catholic mass attendance, but rather that he wished to join his friends on Sundays at the cinema. Too poor to afford admission to the movies, his friends set him up with "an individual who furnished the required money."[55] Within a few weeks, his grades suffered and he was keeping late hours. When his parents confronted him, Paul deserted his home. Six months later police arrested him "in the company of a homosexual" and took him to court for immoral behaviour. Despite admonitions from the court, he deserted his family again. He eventually ended up in prison, having established a life of "depravity" and crime.

This cautionary tale about the "wasted" life of Paul is revealing about mid-century thoughts on the impact of same-sex sexual commerce and the source of homosexuality. Using the rhetoric of child protection, Pelletier mounted a homophobic tale that condemned not only the "depraved" adult, but the potentially gay teen as well. Although the adult was singled out as the culpable one in this story, and Pelletier expressed a modicum of empathy for Paul, he ignored the boy's own agency and voice. Pelletier did not differentiate between the actions of an adult taking advantage of a boy who wanted to go to the movies and a boy who was apparently willing to be in the company of a gay man when arrested for immorality. Pelletier's (self-interested) point was that had the law intervened successfully after his first exposure to adult same-sex "depravity," he might have been saved from a life of crime and punishment.

As the JMS pursued its laudable goal of wiping out child sexual abuse, it increasingly emphasized its jurisdiction over the regulation of boys' sexuality. The JMS expanded in the 1940s, having defined itself as essential to quelling the rising tide of juvenile corruptibility. Ultimately, the JMS's policing of boys' same sex relations was used to steer them "right," a type of social-sexual engineering that did not always result in the full weight of the law crashing down upon them. In this period, especially in the 1950s, society viewed boys' sexuality as dynamic and in need of restraint and (hetero)sexual education. Psychiatric and psychological experts helped to interpret boys' actions and minds for the court, drawing crude lines between boys whose behaviour was rooted in mental disease and those who could be "reoriented" into proper young men.

An important element of the JMS's work with boys, then, included interrupting sexual relationships and educating boys on proper behaviour. For the juvenile justice worker, once friends initiated a boy into masturbation and other indecent acts with boys and men, danger ensued, because, the probation officer cautioned, the boy could become homosexual.[56] Boys in their liminal adolescent state, though, could be redeemed. The 1948 article 33 case of a twenty-five-year-old man who was arrested for sodomy and oral sex (with a seventeen-year-old boy) demonstrates this thinking. Following his arrest by a JMS officer, Jacques J. was interviewed by a probation officer, who found that his friends initiated him into masturbation at age thirteen. And although he had frequented a club for a "bal d'homosexuels," where he met the seventeen-year-old with whom he had ongoing relations, the JMS deemed him treatable and not "lost" to homosexuality. Court doctors assessed his sexual instinct as "not perverted." Rather, quite simply, he liked physical stimulation. The psychiatrist viewed his same-sex relations – which we might assume were enough to condemn him – as a regression toward a "normal" prepubescent state, and therefore he could be helped by simply removing him from the conditions that produced it. In this case, the psychiatrist encouraged the young man to get married soon. Finding the reports on this young man positive and encouraging, the judge let him go under promise to work toward establishing heterosexual marital relations.[57]

The records of the JMS show that the police and court workers became increasingly aware that normative sexuality for teens held a different definition than conventional heterosexuality of chastity before marriage and fidelity within it. Children and adolescents experimented and played with their bodies, and they coerced others into fondling and orally stimulating them. They were capable of sexually assaulting each other and being victimized by adults of any age. Youths also engaged in an emergent same-sex subculture for which Montreal would become well known in the coming decades. The JMS and the juvenile court believed that in addressing adolescent sexuality directly, boys could be "set straight" without the need for institutionalization.

Reading against the grain of the records, we see the JMS frequently intervening in an emergent gay subculture: gay dances, restaurants, rooms to let districts, and "homo-sexual hangouts."[58] As the police stepped up surveillance of adult men, the JMS tried to stop teenage boys from indulging their same-sex desires. In a 1946 case, we see this in practice. Three seventeen- and sixteen-year-old cross-dressing boys, picked up for "loitering" one February night, admitted – with varying degrees of boastfulness – to being well acquainted with gay hangouts as well as same-sex sexual experience. Apparently smart, talented, and given to "exuberance," these teenagers faced lenient treatment; the judge counselled one boy to return to his home province and others' parents to do a better job.[59]

In another 1946 case, article 33 was used alongside the juvenile offence of immorality. One late June evening, seventeen-year-old Jean R. took a walk on Parc Mont-Royal to a place the police called "le chemin des amoureux" [lovers' lane]. In his version told to the investigator forty-five-year-old René C. approached him. The older man opened the teen's pants and performed oral sex on him, described by Jean's probation officer euphemistically as "des rapports contre nature" [unnatural relations]. The police came upon them (likely in a habitual raid as the area had long attracted night-time revellers since it opened in the nineteenth century) and arrested the older man and referred the younger man to the Juvenile Morality Squad. Both were ultimately found guilty in juvenile court. René C. was charged with violating article 33 and fined $25 plus court costs, and Jean was charged with immorality and fined $5 plus court costs. That the boy intentionally sought out lovers' lane and was not obviously coerced resulted in a light (though not insignificant) fine for the adult and a commensurate fine for the teen. The judge instructed Jean's parents to do their "duty" and watch their son's behaviour more carefully.

The large number of men arrested under article 33 was a triumph for the police and also a shocking confirmation to the public of the extent of youth "corruption" in theatres, restaurants, and other commercialized youth spaces. The cases speak to boys' and girls' roles in the commodification of sex that existed adjacent (and often integral) to the commercialization of youth culture as well as the youth squad members' prescription about youth malleability and vulnerability in the face of their presumed poverty (or need for money) and adult predation. In the 1940s and '50s, Ovila Pelletier and the JMS continued to run a campaign against adults who befriended youngsters and committed indecent acts on them.[60] As the squad grew, JMS neighbourhood beat cops surveilled playgrounds, alleyways, and other areas where children congregated, watching for suspicious older men who struck up conversations with youth.[61] Recognized as an important feature of youth-conscious policing, this aspect of youth squad work persisted through the 1960s and 1970s – despite the reorganization and decentralization of the youth squad – in the form of a sexual crime section of the Youth Aid Section of the Montreal police department.[62] Despite the youth squad's fight against the sexual abuse of children, policing the boundaries of juvenile morality drove officers to investigate and regulate teenagers whose behaviours they found wanting, leading to charges, probation, or incarceration.[63]

The 1940s: Innovations in Youth-Conscious Policing

The escalation of delinquency rates during the Second World War and in the early postwar era helped increase the Juvenile Morality Squad from five members in 1941 to twenty-eight in 1946 and eighty by the early 1950s. For Allied nations, these were turbulent years, set against the backdrop of war, victory, and early postwar reconstruction and renewal. The scholarship on juvenile justice has long acknowledged how war produced delinquency, delinquents, and youth work.[64] As historian James Gilbert noted, Second World War home front conditions laid the groundwork for a rise in juvenile crime: "From the middle of World War II, a great many Americans, led by federal law-enforcement officials, concluded that broken families, mobility, and absent working mothers had caused a spurt in delinquent behavior."[65] Other Allied nations like Britain, Canada, and occupied France similarly experienced an exceptional growth in delinquency with concomitant expansion in policing of children and youth. After the war, the challenges of family reconstitution and the absence left by fallen fathers meant concern over youth and the delinquency problem did not fade.[66] Rather, as reported regularly in the Canadian police press, delinquency raged across North America and Europe.[67] As juvenile crime soared despite the peace, Canadian observers could be given to hyperbole, announcing lawless youth "more of a danger to our society today than any atomic bomb," but the cause for consternation was the ostensible fact that juvenile delinquency no longer respected the boundaries of class. It was not a working-class problem, but rather a function of generation and age.[68] As youth problems became a constitutive feature of postwar society, troubled teens alarmingly represented all sectors of society, rich and poor.[69] Wartime anti-social behaviour of youths could be seen as a temporary result of relatively accessible employment and good wages, freedom, and excitement on the one hand, or blackouts, absent parents, and ever-present death and destruction on the other. Either way, as the high delinquency rate threatened to continue beyond the war, the JMS took action.[70] In 1946, Pelletier announced a new campaign to "stamp out" delinquency.[71]

Canadian news media reported a "sense of unrest and unsettlement" among youth during the war.[72] It was not difficult to find proof that youth were out of control: nationwide, the number of juvenile delinquents rose from under 10,000 to almost 14,000 in 1942, according to

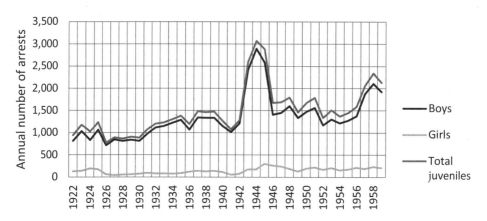

2.1   Juvenile arrests from the annual reports of the Montreal Police Department, 1922–1959
Source: Annual Reports of the Montreal Police Department, 1922–1959.

the Dominion Bureau of Statistics. By 1942, vulnerable and delinquent children were making headline news in Canada, and by 1944 Montreal experienced a full-blown juvenile crime wave.[73] The number of children who appeared before Montreal's juvenile court judge increased by 20 per cent in the early years of the war (from 2,979 in 1940 to 3,680 in 1942).[74] Many parents and guardians of these children and youth claimed an inability to control and contain their charges. For their part, Montreal police arrested over 3,000 minors in 1944, a 240 per cent increase over 1,284 arrests in 1942.

The great rise in numbers of arrested youth in Montreal in 1943–44 generated much anxiety about a trend that seemed out of control. (See figure 2.1.) Yet a closer look at the mechanisms and processes that helped to create this surge in delinquency requires some attention. Beyond the usual media-identified causes for delinquency, such as family breakdown and neglectful parenting, one can certainly attribute its wartime rise to an altered landscape. War's impact on the home front resulted in more opportunities for youth in terms of work and mobility, but there were also structural changes to policing that helped produce higher numbers. In Montreal, it is arguable that the spike in the delinquency rate was only tangentially related to wartime: in 1942, the provincial government raised the official age of the category juvenile delinquent from under sixteen to under eighteen and the city implemented juvenile nocturnal curfew.

Despite the multiplier effect these structural changes had on the number of youth categorized as juvenile delinquents, the wartime spike in juvenile crime made headline news as it tore into a sense of order on the home front.[75] Some blamed youth, while others, adhering to a crime prevention framework, represented delinquency as a disease or natural disaster. For example, in an illustration in the US journal *Survey Midmonthly* (reproduced in a Montreal police journal), two giant young people stand in a city about to be consumed by a wave of criminality. This flood threatened not only the girl and boy but also the fundamental structures of society.[76] (See figure 2.2.) Social commentators and journalists also used disease metaphors, describing juvenile problems as the contemporary plague.[77] News stories of errant children and wild youth were translated onto the silver screen by Hollywood, which produced an excess of cautionary youth tales through the 1940s and into the 1950s.[78] After the war, many recognized juvenile crime as one of the war's worst consequences.[79]

Pelletier and the youth squad responded directly to the rise in the delinquency rate by claiming that they were "saving the children" from these external forces and from themselves, which became the clarion call of youth work and the crime preventive measures that Pelletier and the Juvenile Morality Squad would introduce in the 1940s. This approach meant becoming visible to young people by augmenting patrols of youth spaces of the city (schoolyards, parks, streets, alleys) and surveillance of commercial hangouts (dance halls, bowling alleys, restaurants, etc.). Bureaucratic and legal innovations also helped extend the reach of the youth squad. In 1941, the Juvenile Morality Squad was officially recognized as a separate squad from the Morality Department; in 1942, the JMS gained expanded powers over young people in the form of the curfew that applied to children under fourteen years of age and with the expansion of the category "juvenile offender" from under sixteen to under eighteen years of age. In 1944, the squad was physically consolidated in its own separate office in central Montreal.[80] In 1946, it would be renamed the Juvenile Morality Bureau and eventually the Delinquency Prevention Bureau (DPB) or Bureau Préventif de la Délinquance Juvénile.[81]

This bureaucratic development centralized and streamlined the policing of children and youth. When a minor was detained for committing a criminal offence (e.g., theft, assault) or an infraction of municipal

2.2   "Criminalité," *Revue des Agents de Police* (March 1946), 2.

bylaws (e.g., curfew, disturbing the peace, public nuisance) police officers
would immediately alert the Juvenile Morality Bureau, which would
then take over the case. In principle, this system meant that all children
in conflict with the law would be dealt with by the youth squad. The
addition of radio police cars in the mid-1940s facilitated this process.
Only these officers would be responsible for the paperwork on the child

(which was now centralized) and for informing parents and deciding whether to take him or her to the juvenile court. If the juvenile court route was taken, a Bureau liaison officer handled the report at the juvenile court.[82] In the case of minor infractions, the youth was often taken home.[83] This design ensured that police could verify quickly and easily if a child had been previously apprehended.

This new system of processing children and youth was reinforced by the 1944 Delinquency Prevention Week conference, which was organized by Montreal's social and welfare service institutions in cooperation with corrections officials. The conference's main message, "Be a Good Citizen ... help build another," urged the home-front public to participate in delinquency prevention strategies. The first five of seven objectives of delinquency prevention underscored parental and civic duty to provide children with "good family" lives, leisure and recreational time/facilities, better housing and schooling, and protection of young people in the workplace. The last two objectives insisted on the "enforcement of laws affecting minors" and "improved correctional facilities for children," for the "punishment and regeneration of the young offender."[84]

It was in this context of high public support for centralizing youth work and expanding the squad that Pelletier confronted the wartime and early postwar delinquency problem and, at least initially, contributed to the wartime rise in delinquency rates. According to the JMS annual reports, the squad actively pursued children and young people in public spaces; places of "youth corruption" were under surveillance, and Montreal delinquents' hangouts and habits were well known by the squad.[85] The number of youths arrested by the JMS bears out this increase. For those fourteen to eighteen years of age, vagrancy and loitering charges went from 85 (70 boys and 15 girls) in 1942 to 899 (808 boys and 91 girls) in 1944. Other offences that account for the boom in delinquency arrests include public disorder and theft. The number of boys arrested for disturbing the peace more than doubled from 190 in 1942 to 391 in 1944, while those charged with theft rose just over 65 per cent in the same period, from 271 to 414.[86] While the high arrest numbers demonstrated that the youth squad was working, paradoxically, a good crime prevention squad would eventually reduce youth crime. In 1946, Pelletier began to speak publicly about his new plans for reducing youth crime rates. The principles of the prevention mission given to his expanding squad included: demonstrating respect for the child, making friends with children, getting to know and appreciate children's problems, showing encouragement, remembering that children of today are the citizens of tomorrow, and keeping a positive attitude.[87] He maintained that teaching children about the law was not so much about punishment as it was about their protection. To accomplish this prevention mission, he embarked on a new foundation of youth policing that included female squad members and a police boys' club in 1947.

Gender and the Youth Squad

During the 1940s, thousands of mainly working-class youth encountered the police during the course of a day or week. These officers were no longer the archetypical beat cops considered the "natural" enemy of children but, rather, male authority figures one might associate with avuncular benevolence.[88] In the 1930s, one Canadian newspaper observed that a policeman had to be "a male governess to all the children on his beat." In the postwar era, he became father on the beat.[89] Police forces planted the idea that young people now thought of these men as "Dad."[90] The tropes of familiarity and goodwill were strategic and central to changing the relationship of police to children. Postwar prescriptions of masculinity and fatherhood worked well alongside police paternalism to help reconfigure the cop as emotionally caring and responsible for children. Old gender systems didn't die quickly, however, and since youth policing called for attention to a younger category of youth and a softer, kinder approach – a female touch, to speak stereotypically – the availability of jobs for women in municipal police forces expanded based on their prescribed psychological and biological affinity for child care on a community scale. In fact, some reports suggested that "girl cops" were better than policemen because children trusted them more readily than men. In the end, a combination of male and female attributes personified by youth police turned them into new models for better handling of delinquency. Whether male or female, youth police fashioned a new gendered identity for cops in mid-century North America.

When the Juvenile Morality Squad took the prevention turn in the 1940s, its mandate broadened, as did the definition of who was best suited for work with children and youth. In 1947, the Montreal force deemed policewomen, who had been summarily fired at the close of the First World War and absent for decades, useful for police work.

While policemen guided fourteen- and fifteen-year-old boys to a less dissipated adolescence than might otherwise await them, policewomen tackled children at the other end of childhood. Highlighted in the 1952 *Maclean's* magazine article entitled "The Cops Who Change Diapers," policewomen were back on the force because of the kids, especially really young ones.[91] Although the practice of hiring women officers was not new, prejudice against it in Montreal only began to diminish with the establishment of the prevention orientation of the JMS, which gave female cops a home (or ghetto) on the force. By the 1950s, Montreal employed the largest contingent of female police in Canada with twenty women, and they fulfilled their purpose of "help[ing] children of poor neighbourhoods grow up into good citizens with a respect for the law."[92]

Canadian cities were well behind the US trend of employing substantial numbers of female officers. At the end of the Second World War, New York City boasted 195 "lady cops," and Chicago had as many as 60 policewomen.[93] Through the 1930s and '40s, the *Canadian Police Gazette* (CPG) – "A Magazine Devoted to the Explanation of Police Activities in Canada" – regularly ran positive articles about policewomen in other countries and covered the local campaigns to add them to the forces in Canada.[94] Although the CPG declared in 1946 that policewomen "have definitely become an accepted fact," progress was slow, with Vancouver and Toronto claiming four female constables each, Calgary only three, and, at the time the article appeared, the country's largest city, Montreal, had none.[95] Canadian cities seemed to operate under the assumption expressed by Montreal's Deputy Director of Police Charles Barnes that the hiring of women would not resolve manpower shortages. He claimed in a 1945 report that policewomen's work was "complementary" at best and would "not replace a single policeman as far as strict police duties are concerned."[96] He noted that policewomen were used to great, if limited, effect by the Metropolitan Police of England in watching over and escorting arrested women, female prisoners, and children. By this time, New York City policewomen served on the missing persons, pickpocket, shoplifting, and narcotic squads in addition to the Juvenile Aid Bureaus.[97] Still, it was the bureaucratic establishment within the police force of a separate bureau for delinquency prevention and the force's youth consciousness that provided women with a permanent foot in the door of the Montreal force.

In addition to the positive coverage of policewomen in police journals, campaigns were mounted by women's groups around the need to hire female officers. The policewoman movement had ebbed and flowed over the course of the early twentieth century, but the postwar marked a turning point, as Jean Short, executive director of the Girls' Counselling Centre of Montreal, noted. In 1946 she wrote, "it is also a woman's world" and thus time to accept women into "all professions."[98] Policewomen, she stated, would reinforce the police's role of safeguarding children, "who are the strength and future of this land of ours."[99] Short argued that policewomen were especially important as a friendly neighbourhood presence; their ability and talents contributed to the health and welfare of children, and inspired "respect for law and order" and "self respect."[100] Civic-minded women appealed to city politicians and the police administration. As it had in the 1910s, Montreal's Local Council of Women took the issue in hand in the 1940s.[101] In 1946, the Council's Social Behaviour Committee turned its efforts to this one goal. The committee's letter-writing and media campaign was fruitful a year later, as the first ten recruits began training in the winter of 1947.[102]

Over one hundred women had applied for new female police positions, but, according to Barnes, initially only nine qualified.[103] A memo approving the future hiring of policewomen stated that candidates needed to be at least twenty-five years of age and five feet three inches tall. They were required to have at least grade 9 education and have language facility in both English and French. The Montreal Police Department wanted women who showed "integrity, robust health ... and good judgment." They should be able to exercise authority over other women with "tact, sympathy, and discretion."[104] Since an understanding of the social problems and issues related to the public disorderliness of women and families lay at the heart of what the administration imagined policewomen would be responsible for, experience in what was broadly known as social work was an asset.

The 1947 hiring of policewomen marked a small window of opportunity. Not since the 1910s had the city seen a patrolwoman[105] and it would take another twenty-five years for another woman to be sworn in as a policewoman.[106] The reasons behind the dramatic change in policy are diverse, involving both internal issues related to personnel shortages and public pressure stemming from the perception that juvenile delinquency was spiralling out of control. The war had depleted the Montreal force, and in the immediate postwar period recruitment continued to be difficult because of the strict age and physical requirements. On the other hand, the now-available female war veterans – women who had served with the army, navy, and air force – appealed to the police administration because of their recent training and experience.[107] Proving themselves during the war was certainly part of the story. In 1946, City Councillor J.O. Asselin, chair of the executive committee, requested City Hall's generous financial support for an expanded force and noted that if not enough men could be found women could fill in, "supervising the parks, taking care of children near schools, driving cars and many other jobs of the kind that women did so efficiently during the war."[108] Not coincidentally, Inspector Albert Langlois, who had served with the Royal Canadian Air Force and trained the force's Women's Division (WDS), led the training of women police recruits.[109] The establishment and good reputation of the anti-delinquency squad, now the Delinquency Prevention Bureau, provided a gender-appropriate place for women on the force, making their hiring somewhat less contentious than it might otherwise have been.

In 1947, ten women began training under Inspector Langlois. From the beginning, it was assumed that their value lay in their ability to work with children and combat juvenile delinquency through supervising playgrounds and other "hangouts" of youth, and directing traffic in front of schools.[110] In keeping with Ovila Pelletier's crime prevention motto "to teach and not to punish," these female recruits would "teach youngsters that [the] tree of crime bears bitter fruit."[111] Although their contribution to police work was intended to be quite specific, this group's training more closely approximated what male recruits received and they were not "spared the tough parts of the syllabus," unlike the situation in the 1910s.[112] The training covered police and judicial procedure, criminal law, as well as lectures on troubled youth from experts including juvenile court judges, social workers, and psychologists. Physical training was also emphasized and included military exercises, swimming and lifesaving, and martial arts.[113]

The constant reassurances in the press that women did not take men's jobs nor sacrifice their womanliness speaks to the continued ambivalence about women with authority in civic positions. The media represented policewomen as entirely competent at their gendered jobs. At times, this conflict led to odd and untrue declarations. In 1952, Zoe Bieler wrote in

Maclean's that "[a]ll [Montreal] policewomen are more accustomed to diapers than guns" and "[n]one of them ha[ve] ever touched firearms."[114] Placing a domestic spin on policewomen's work, Bieler emphasized their "rescue" work with neglected children, including bathing and clothing them.[115] Montreal's police force forbade female officers from bearing arms until 1972 because of public resistance, although they were trained to use them.[116] Several Montreal policewomen, including Bieler's main interviewee, Constable Marguerite Cloutier, were photographed in 1948 with guns, their shooting scores recorded and compared with that of male officers.[117] In this instance, the *Constables Revue* emphasized their competency and their right to be part of the police force yet reinforced traditional gender roles; in the photos women were obviously wearing makeup, and most wore skirts. As late as 1968 the *Montreal Gazette* ran a story confirming that "talking is the only weapon these [police]women want to wield."[118] Yet we needn't lose sight of Bieler's main point: the first postwar generation of policewomen was meant to work on behalf of children and use skills of feminine intuition rather than the threat of firearms.

This new generation of female constables worked neighbourhood beats and kept an eye on areas of the city where youth congregated: schoolyards, parks, playgrounds, bowling alleys, dance halls, street corners, and restaurants. Cloutier patrolled what was known as the "Faubourg à m'lasse (Quartier Centre-sud)" in the city's east end, to deal with juvenile crime, prostitution, runaways, gangs, and inebriated youth. The small number of policewomen meant they could survey only certain areas of the city, mostly working class.[119] Cloutier, along with her sister Régina, walked a beat that was considered "tough," with "squalid tenements," "filthy" lanes, and "inadequate parks."[120] According to Bieler, in this 80,000-person neighbourhood in east-end Montreal, Cloutier was considered a welcome presence, a friend.

Policewomen worked in pairs and developed a reputation as an effective police force that emphasized prevention.[121] Their work reflected an assumption about children's vulnerability and endangerment especially in working-class neighbourhoods. In following Cloutier and her partner for a day, Bieler described the various ways that they pursued prevention, including enforcing traffic regulations so children did not get hurt, surveilling suspicious men who passed by and engaged children in playgrounds, and visiting the homes of families known for delinquency troubles. These methods involved gently scolding a couple of boys who "doubled up" on a bicycle, putting an end to an alleyway game of coin toss, and inspecting newsstands for sexually explicit materials. Cloutier confessed to reticence over making juvenile arrests and insisted that her priority was ferreting out adults who accepted or encouraged anti-social behaviour in children. Neglectful mothers, perverted strangers, and conniving entrepreneurs all got Cloutier's attention as she walked her beat and made house calls. In the case of the corrupt storekeeper who directed boys to steal for him, Cloutier saw him as the guilty party: the "kids were not bad, but they were poor and needed money."[122] Arresting kids, she claimed, indicated "failure"; this reflected the beliefs of her boss, Ovila Pelletier: "if we, the police, have to arrest a child – then we have failed him [*sic*]."[123]

Despite the emphasis on neighbourhood preventive work with children, women were sometimes needed beyond the kiddie patrol. For example, in the mid-1940s, the homicide squad pursued those responsible for a handful of abortion-related deaths. The squad seconded two women in the first graduating class of policewomen to carry out a sting operation. Carefully selecting two married officers to pose as women seeking pregnancy termination, the force arrested four doctors involved in underground abortion services. This work by female officers received some media coverage, probably because it occurred in the first months after women had joined the force; it is plausible that women were seconded to other squads when the force felt it was needed.[124]

No matter how many policewomen existed in comparably sized cities and despite the declarations that policewomen were now a fact, this administrative and personnel change found resistance. Initially, and not surprisingly, the addition of a handful of women to the police service caused a scandal in the local newspapers. Old arguments about women's sphere and the impropriety of conflating appropriate femininity with the masculine endeavour of policing seemed to rise and fall as the women officers remained. Women's work was circumscribed by two facts of their employment: their attachment to the Delinquency Prevention Bureau and their gender, which necessarily meant work with children and families. They were responsible for abandoned children, working with various establishments to place them,[125] and for young women in conflict with the law, "so there can be no complaints that women have been manhandled by the police."[126] The lack of police

2.3   National Film Board of Canada, "Guerre à la délinquance: des policières montréalaises," *Coup d'Oeil*, no. 37 (Eyewitness in English), 1952.

uniforms and their seeming gentle dispositions were helpful, according to Pelletier, in putting families at ease and getting police work done.[127] By 1948, the "service féminin" was pronounced "satisfactory." Four years later, a National Film Board of Canada Eyewitness short film celebrated Montreal's "feminine patrols" on the campaign to defeat delinquency. The film places the efficient force of two women officers at the right place and the right time to halt the getaway of a young shoplifter, to call for backup after a serious bicycle accident, and to clear a pool hall of kids under sixteen years of age.[128] (See figure 2.3.) One might even argue that this youth squad was increasingly feminized, with 20 women and 45 men in 1948; however, by 1952 the Prevention Bureau had expanded to 85 officers and the female count remained at 20.[129] Not until the 1970s would this gendered "policewoman" role gain more equal footing in police services in Canada: in 1979 the Montreal force hired its first regular female officer.[130]

     Male members of the JMS and the DPB also modified the job of cop to better suit the expectations of youth policing. Ovila Pelletier told the media in 1954 that his officers needed to be "interested in boys and understand family problems."[131] The squad and then the bureau appeared to attract men who might otherwise have been youth workers. Julien White, for example, joined the force in 1939 after five years as secretary general of the Jeunesse Ouvrière Catholique in Montreal, a Roman Catholic organization aimed at working-class youth and social action. As he mentioned in his application letter, this work with youth was "proof of my good will, honesty, [and] good spirit."[132] White joined the JMS, which comprised only Durivage and Pelletier in 1939, and became Pelletier's right-hand man during the expansion of the squad and establishment of the Bureau in the 1940s. He would occupy several jobs managing the squad and the bureau, creating forms, assembling statistics on delinquency, writing Pelletier's speeches, and training personnel. During the war, he acted as a special investigator in cases of sexual assault against young people and instructed other officers in how to conduct such inquiries with young victims.[133] Paul-Émile Naud joined the force in 1936 at age twenty-one and came to the JMS in 1944. He worked as the squad's liaison officer at the juvenile court and pursued an intellectual curiosity about delinquency through sociology classes at the Université de Montréal. In 1951, he took a three-month leave without pay to study juvenile justice in Europe. Upon his return, he lectured at the École de Police on youth and the law.[134] Despite being a career police officer (joining the force in his twenties and remaining there until his death), Ovila Pelletier was seen as the initiator of important youth programs, and by the mid-1940s was hailed as a national expert on youth problems, despite his lack of formal training. His wise and paternalistic demeanour and great energy for youth policing earned him high praise locally and beyond.

An illustration accompanying an article in the *Constables Revue* (Montreal), "Juvenile Crime, a Social Evil," summed up the prescriptive role for postwar youth squad officers. In the first diagram, a large fist is threatening a boy; in the latter box a policeman is shown demonstrably giving advice to a youth. The caption read, "Less violence, more head work." The message could not be clearer: the once-brutal orientation of police (where force ensured a disciplined public) should be replaced with understanding and goodwill toward young people. For Pelletier, "head work" meant several conclusions about youth crime and prevention: how a child spends his/her leisure time is critical to predicting delinquency; early detection of youth problems is essential for avoiding full-blown delinquency; youth police can and should instill in children a positive attitude toward authority; children must understand police to be friends who are there to help and protect them; police must treat children with respect and consideration in order to win their trust. "Mutual understanding" between cops and kids, according to Pelletier, would lead to a decline in delinquency and a better society.[135] This transformation involved a paternalistic policing that opened doors for female officers and gave rise to the fatherly officer.

The Montreal Miracle: Taking Stock of an Innovative Decade of Youth-Conscious Policing

As hoodlums and youth gangs captured the public's imagination shortly after the war's end, delinquency authorities watched in vain as the number of delinquents escalated.[136] It was in this very public context that the Montreal youth squad pulled off a "miracle." By 1948, Pelletier's plan to reduce delinquency was a media sensation. Compared to the "sharply rising trend of delinquency in most cities," *Saturday Night* magazine reported, Montreal's numbers plummeted; 1943's 4,000 juvenile arrests had shrunk to 1,800 by 1948.[137] Through the 1950s, many observers celebrated and revered Montreal's anti-delinquency program.[138]

Montreal officers would explain that the astonishing reduction in juvenile delinquency over the course of the 1940s was the result of a "master plan of operation" to combat the roots of delinquency and involved a reconceptualization of the role of the police officer in contemporary society.[139] This plan began by putting places of youth corruption under surveillance during the panic over youth morality during the war and operationalizing the new juvenile nocturnal curfew. This municipal bylaw enabled the squad members to interrogate any child on the street at 9 p.m., regardless of age, as we will see in chapter 3. These surveillance strategies were augmented with twenty female officers who, according to one journalist, really made the difference.[140]

The centrepiece of Pelletier's crime prevention scheme was the founding of the Police Juvenile Clubs for Boys (PJCB) in 1947, which addressed the paucity of working-class boys' recreation and the rise of street-corner sociality among youth. The sports solution to wayward kids was indeed a new avenue of policing Montreal's children, directly aimed

2.4 Ovila Pelletier, CKAC radio program, in National Film Board of Canada, *On the Spot* program, "Police Juvenile Clubs," 1954.

at pre-delinquents and "redeemable" delinquents. This network of boys' sports clubs was meant to foster "better understanding between youngsters and policemen." These clubs added a new dimension to the city's network of organized activities for young people, which were largely church-based and arranged along linguistic and religious lines (e.g., the Young Women's/Young Men's Christian Associations and Catholic or parish youth groups). The PJCs stand out for recruiting members regardless of religion or language.[141] These non-denominational clubs claimed to offer a new site for boys' socialization where they would wear not gang colours but police department colours and badges.[142] (See figure 2.4.)

The Montreal youth squad's focus on prevention techniques for boys relates to the massive gender imbalance in arrests. Across the 1940s, girls comprised only 5–10 per cent of arrests, their numbers hovering just under two hundred per year. In fact, the number of girls arrested remained steady and was not part of the major decline in delinquency rates upon which Pelletier capitalized. In 1944, for example, most girls were arrested for loitering by night during curfew. These "sunset violations" accounted for 91 out of 175 arrests; desertion (of the family home) and incorrigibility counted for 33; disturbing the peace arrests amounted to 13, and the rest were a smattering of sexual crimes (indecent or immoral behaviour), offences related to work (peddling or selling without a licence), and violations of public morality (drunkenness and being found in a gambling house). In 1948, girls' arrests totalled 190, with the categories of offences remaining steady. Notably, however, sunset offences dropped to 26 from 190 (13.7 per cent of girls' arrests) whereas desertion and incorrigibility climbed to 124 (65 per cent). Boys' numbers were far more mercurial. In 1944, the Annual Report of the Juvenile Morality Squad recorded 3,070 arrests – 2,895 of them boys. By 1948, this number had dropped to 1,791 juvenile arrests, of whom 1,601 were boys – meaning 1,294 fewer boys arrested. Most boys found themselves written up by the youth squad for sunset crimes, public nuisance offences, and variations on theft. In 1944, 808 (28 per cent) boys were arrested for sunset crimes; 764 (26 per cent) for public nuisance; 613 (21 per cent) for theft, robbery, and larceny; 327 (11 per cent) for property crimes, with the rest of the arrests involving offences against public morality (drunkenness, gaming), desertion, incorrigibility, or that were related to work (peddling or soliciting without a licence). What accounted for the big decline in the number of boys arrested by 1948 from the wartime high was a drop in sunset offences (808 to 286); public nuisance arrests (696 to 187); and theft (764 to 613). Only desertion and incorrigibility offences rose (58 to 286). This decline in arrests should not be read as a decline in the policing of teenagers; rather it should be noted that at the same time the youth squad admitted to fewer arrests it claimed to increase the number of informal interrogations of youth.[143]

In 1949, the international press lauded the work of the Montreal police force in stopping the "rising tide" of delinquency. That year, a European journalist, allegedly reporting from the streets of Montreal, told the story of a gang leader called Archie. This youth and his band of "little rascals" targeted a corner grocery store, smashing the front window. At the sight and sound of breaking glass, Archie fled the scene, only to be stopped by a police officer. In cautioning Archie, the officer resolved to set him on a different track and took him to a "welcoming place" where there were boys his own age. Rather than court, prison, or even home for a scolding, gang leader Archie was given a membership card to the Police Juvenile Club for Boys.[144] In the mind of the journalist, this "miracle" of Montreal – the decline of the juvenile crime problem, in fact the *reversal* of the trend – was causally related to the so-called "direct method" of policing delinquency: a rejection of corrections and a full-scale embrace of police prevention methodology.

Montreal's multi-pronged approach to juvenile crime was not unique to that city or to the 1940s – it simply seemed most effective there. Anti-delinquency programs predicated on a thorough understanding of the child and an emphasis on crime prevention over correction had emerged and spread throughout North America in the previous decades.[145] The delinquency panics of the 1940s and '50s provided the impetus to expand, coordinate, and fully fund earlier police efforts at preventing delinquency.

In various speeches and press interviews Pelletier trumpeted the merits of prevention: getting to children before they turned to delinquency. His understanding of young people was not innovative or new and undoubtedly sounded familiar even to 1940s ears. Delinquency's cause was simple, he stated in 1948: find a release for the "overabundance of excess energy" found in most children, otherwise they would express it through "destructive and malicious acts."[146] This basic tenet of child rearing – that "idleness leads to sin" – lay the foundation for an explosion of good works with youth, especially in the realm of physical culture. Organized sports, spectator sports, and various hobby clubs organized by police officers sprang up across the city. In fact, the JMS message was that if even one child landed in jail, they had failed.

In the latter 1940s, policemen and women were engaged in both casual and sporadic, highly organized activities with children and youth. The Social and Welfare Committee of the Canadian Brotherhood of Policemen (the Montreal Police union) organized good works with youth. The committee members visited incarcerated youth at Boscoville (a residential rehabilitation facility for youth, located in the town of the same name) in the summer of 1948, bringing them candy and cigarettes. Similarly, the committee visited the boys' reformatory, the Mont St Antoine, bearing gifts for Christmas time. The committee also organized to bring three hundred incarcerated youth to see the Montreal Royals play a baseball game. It transported girls and boys from orphanages to play in the city parks. The committee estimated that through its visits to public parks, it handed out treats (candy, peanuts, ice cream, and pop) to 1,500 children.[147]

The Montreal "miracle" may have resulted in a decline in the official Montreal juvenile delinquency rate, but it meant an intensification of policing certain sites of youth and childhood. As the numbers of men and women on the youth squad increased and the technologies of youth surveillance broadened, police had unprecedented opportunities to encounter youth. Although the squad had made itself an essential part of the juvenile justice system, its innovative crime prevention program usurped the juvenile court's long-term prerogative over deciding how to deal with young people.

As Pelletier and his prevention squad accumulated accolades in the press, a counter discourse also emerged. In early 1946, members of the juvenile court became alarmed, if not indignant, at the Juvenile Morality Squad's new system for managing arrested children. Rather than delivering children to the juvenile court as they had done in the past, police now took children to the JMS, where none other than Ovila Pelletier decided the outcome of the case. Previously minor offences had been handled by the police, avoiding the juvenile court altogether, but now the squad processed most cases. Listing the sections of the Juvenile Delinquents Act (1929) and provincial law concerning judicial tribunals, lawyer Marcel Trahan, working for the Montreal Juvenile Delinquents' Court, accused the police of usurping its jurisdiction over processing juvenile cases. Further, he argued, the police were breaching municipal regulations concerning police procedure by refusing to take all prisoners to the appropriate tribunal "without delay."[148] The complaint extended to the cases that ended up before the juvenile court judge. Even in these cases, the police officers allegedly interfered with the gathering of information on the child and family, thereby overriding the jurisdiction of the court's probation officers. With rhetorical bite, Trahan asked if Officer Pelletier was operating as a magistrate.

The response from the office of the Attorney General was a sign of the times. Not only did the government side with the Juvenile Morality Squad, it encouraged the court to make more room for the youth police in juvenile justice in Montreal. Many cases before the juvenile tribunal, the Assistant Attorney General Léopold Désilets pointed out, concerned the frivolous rather than the serious, tying up valuable court time with the mere "peccadilloes" of the young. Determination of which cases were benign, he wrote, should be the work of juvenile court probation officers, police officers, and members of interested social organizations. Calling for a spirit of collaboration, he asserted the JMS officers' right to protect childhood, instructed the juvenile court probation officers to consider the JMS members "volunteer probation officers" and to assist the JMS in any way necessary.[149]

Since it was the provincial government's prerogative to determine juvenile justice policy, and given its support of the youth squad's innovations, the Montreal police force had become a sanctioned and unquestioned pillar of the youth criminal justice system. The juvenile court authorities jealously guarded their right to bring their expertise on the functioning of juvenile justice to bear, but the police were now fully integrated. This integration had been developing for several years, and from police personnel files we learn that at least two juvenile court judges appreciated the assimilation of the JMS into the juvenile court. In 1945, Judge J.G. Nicholson wrote to then-director of the Montreal Police Department, Fernand Dufresne, that he was "very pleased with the services rendered to our court by the members of the Montreal Police Force." He made special note of Constable Paul-Émile Naud of the JMS, who often worked at the court.[150] Three years later, Arthur Laramée wrote to Director Albert Langlois, congratulating him for promoting both Ovila Pelletier and Naud, the latter who worked "with us" at the court.[151]

How did youth respond to the youth squad's innovations? Recent historians of children and youth have demonstrated that young people participated in the dynamic of the social construction of youth. Children's interactions with municipal authorities shaped those people as much as it affected youth behaviour. That said, it would be difficult to argue that there was only one response that captured youth's response to police interest in them. We do have partial, imperfect evidence that hints at how at least some young people responded.

One place to start examining children's reactions is to look at what the youth squad was trying to do. If there is an overarching message that the police strove to communicate to children at mid-century, it could be summed up by the 1946 National Film Board clip *The Policeman*. First, in a series of educational films called *Junior Community*, this short delivered to kids the message that the policeman is "your friend."[152] The story's narrative concerns little Freddie, who gets over his fear of policemen when he gets lost one day. Afraid that the policeman will "take him away," he first hides from the beat cop, but ultimately learns to trust him. The repeated images of the swift and easy physical intimacy between the lost boy and the policeman – mostly of them holding hands – shows the audience that a policeman is indeed not unlike one's own caring parent and should not be treated as a stranger to be feared. We have already seen that police used the media to advocate a new image vis-à-vis children. When Montreal Police Director Langlois spoke on the subject "The Policeman Is Your Friend" in 1946, his words repeated the message of the film: "Do not run away from [policemen]."[153] Evidently, children needed to be taught that cops were their friends, and so these tropes of friendly beat cops were repeated to children in various media. This discourse of friendly police aimed at children suggests that a transformation in attitude was necessary before kids could have confidence in the the police.

Conclusion

In the mid-1930s, Montreal's police department acted to create a vehicle for investigating youth troubles. The nascent and tiny youth squad engaged in morals policing and claimed to be motivated by a discourse of child protection. This is particularly apparent in the Juvenile Morality Squad's focus on the corruptibility of youth late in the decade and into the 1940s. The JMS liberally used article 33 of the Juvenile Delinquents' Act to target adults who were committing sexual abuse of children and sexual commerce involving young people. This focus on youth corruptibility continued through the various guises of youth squads in the city's history; from the 1950s through the mid-1970s the Youth Aid Section (la Section Aide à la Jeunesse) included a division called the "Sexual Crime Section" that investigated all sexual crimes against youth.[154] The youth squad's ambivalence about youth is evident in cases in which youth transitioned from being victims of adults to being delinquents acting out.

The youth squad took its crime prevention turn in the 1940s under Ovila Pelletier's leadership. This shift in the policing of young people involved several structural changes to the youth squad, including expansion of personnel, the inclusion of women, and the creation of a centralized and physically separate bureau. To take aim at pre-delinquents, the youth squad inaugurated the police youth club, as we will see in chapter 4. Prevention would earn the Delinquency Prevention Bureau considerable praise, except from the juvenile court whose work it infringed upon.

In an era that demonized the delinquent and raised delinquency to the level of international emergency came the "Miracle of Montreal."[155] An expansive, highly coordinated, prevention-oriented police response, this miracle dramatically reduced the numbers of arrested youth and, according to Pelletier and the youth squad, fundamentally altered the relationship of police to children and youth. As the story is told in the press, Ovila Pelletier delivered the city from the crisis of youth, effectively tackling *incipient* delinquency.

What occurred in Montreal had a counterpart in many large North American cities – crime prevention programs that emerged in the interwar period. Urban police forces were motivated by at least two related impulses: first, the desire to be part of the expanding juvenile justice system, and, second, to correct the juvenile justice system's limited success in the realm of protecting children. As David Wolcott demonstrates for Chicago, Detroit, and Los Angeles, the way in which these prevention programs played out depended on many factors, including police leadership, the perceived nature of delinquency, and the determination of who was allegedly at risk and committing crimes. Prevention programming by youth squads was meant to reverse the tough attitude historically taken by police toward youth. By the 1940s, delinquency prevention in cities like Montreal seemed to have resolved this ambivalence. Yet alongside the prevention discourse was the emerging practice of surveilling youth spaces, of assessing who was or was not a delinquent, and, ultimately, of determining which kids were redeemable, deserving of prevention and protection, and which ones were to be criminalized and excluded.

Montreal's youth squad continued as a discrete part of the police department until the 1970s, when it was decentralized. From the 1950s to the 1970s the Youth Aid Section, as the youth squad came to be called, developed an elaborate bureaucratic system of monitoring the city's pre-delinquent and delinquent youth. The youth officers acted as liaisons to the Social Welfare Court (which replaced the Montreal Juvenile Delinquents' Court), sought out runaways and missing adolescents, conducted night patrol for violations of municipal regulations, and kept "pace with juvenile movements (crazes) in order to formulate projects and programs" with the city's social service organizations and schools.[156]

CHAPTER THREE

Condemned by the Curfew

Ubiquitous today, teen curfews have been, since the late nineteenth century, one of the most persistent methods of youth-conscious policing. Curfew bells, sirens, and whistles announcing the day's end and the hour at which children should vacate the streets were a popular solution to delinquency and child vulnerability in Canadian and US towns and cities. Juvenile nocturnal curfew ordinances gained currency in three specific periods: the closing decades of the nineteenth century, during the Second World War and early postwar era, and at the turn of the twenty-first century. Each era gave rise to a historically specific rationale for deploying nocturnal control of young people, relating to the status of youth, the politics of policing, and anxieties over public order. In all three eras, the curfew solution criminalized the public presence of unaccompanied children (defined anywhere from everyone under eighteen to those under fourteen) between specified hours (between 8 p.m. to 10 p.m. and 5 a.m. to 6 a.m.). From their origins in the late nineteenth century, nightfall curfews for youth have been based on the argument that clearing the streets of young people is a powerful crime prevention strategy and in the interests of children's well-being. And yet, legal scholars in our day have convincingly argued that curfew laws are only superficially and sentimentally about the protection of children and the prevention of delinquency; rather, as illustrated by the torrent of curfew law enactments and lively debates of the 1990s and 2000s, curfew is simply an age-old instrument of crime control that "emphasizes accountability and more severe sanctioning of juvenile offenders ... [that] has largely supplanted the

rehabilitative justice model that dominated juvenile justice since the
early twentieth century."[1]

As a social control mechanism, curfew regulations date back a millen-
nium, but the first ones to target minors emerged in the modern era
under the guise of child protection. Child welfare activists – known as
child savers – embraced them as a way for the state to shore up parental
responsibility and to interrupt the spread of negative adult influences
on vulnerable children. As part of a broad child-saving enterprise in the
1890s to restrict the presence of "night children," curfews laws created
discourses about proper childhood and were a practical solution to the
problem. At mid-twentieth century, curfew laws experienced a crisis
brought on by the Second World War and the escalating delinquency
rates that followed the armistice.

Throughout the early 1940s commentators noted that teenage
decorum had become one of the Second World War's most serious
casualties. Governing bodies – especially municipalities – widely
marshalled curfew laws to regain control of youth during the turbulent
war years and the early postwar period. Although the reputation of teenagers animated the discussion and drove the passage of some curfew laws
at the time, the child-protection goals of the curfew and recent crime
prevention practices fit neatly within the curfew's mandate. In 1942, for
example, Montreal's municipal government passed bylaw 1715 to clear
the streets of children under fourteen years of age by 9 p.m., even though
it was an older cohort that was wreaking havoc on the city's sense of
order. The wartime emergency prompted many towns and cities to pass
black-out regulations as a matter of home-front preparedness, safety, and
civic discipline. Montreal's curfew looked like a quintessential crime
prevention mechanism because it targeted pre-delinquents. Directed at
reinforcing the family and intervening in childhood, the 9 p.m. curfew
interrupted the production of the next generation of delinquents and
criminals. This nocturnal curfew emerged in the wake of the formation
of the city's first youth squad; between September 1942 and the end of
1945, police logged over nine thousand Montreal youths for violating
bylaw 1715.[2] Not since the advent of the North American juvenile court
at the close of the nineteenth century had a legal solution brought such
hope for preventing children from becoming delinquent.

More recently, since the 1990s, municipalities across the United
States and Canada have vigorously embraced age-specific sunset laws

as a remedy for bored, potentially violent, and destructive teenagers.[3] Curfew's "triggers" have most often included vandalism or acts of shocking violence. Canadian examples include the curfew fury that shook a small town on the outskirts of Montreal in 2004 or the one that gripped Winnipeg in 2006 due to violence perpetrated by Aboriginal youth. Both curfews point to the enduring belief that curfew could be a critical solution to local teen "problems." They also bring to light the unconstitutionality of age-specific status offences and how their deployment overwhelmingly targeted minority youth.[4]

This chapter historicizes the curfew law in the context of the rise (and subsequent fall) of the rehabilitative model of juvenile justice and youth-conscious policing, exposing its endemic usage and contentiousness, and its role in drawing police further into the management of childhood. The regulation of "night children" and youth's access to public spaces developed alongside the child welfare reforms of the nineteenth century. These reforms brought elaborate categories of age-specific institutions from orphanages to reform schools to primary and secondary public schools. These institutions were central to state formation, as was the development of policing organizations. In the 1940s and '50s wartime-fuelled panics over errant children and youth spurred calls for the renewal of curfew laws. Toward the end of the century, deep ambivalence toward teenagers and the sensationalized views of the risk they posed to themselves and society again led to a mass embrace of curfew's potential for correction. In each era, the imposition of both spatial and temporal restrictions on young lives effectively brought them into closer contact with police authority.

Becoming Modern: Juvenile Curfews in the Nineteenth Century

The modern era of the teen curfew began in the 1880s when two small towns – Omaha, Nebraska, and Waterloo, Ontario – adopted their countries' first age-based curfew ordinances. These early curfews targeted children, rather than adolescents, and were lauded as a necessary step toward protecting them from the dangers of the night and of the street.[5] In the 1890s, pre-eminent child savers in both countries – J.J. Kelso of Ontario and Colonel Alexander Hogeland of Kentucky – took to stumping for curfew laws.[6] Hogeland made a career of trying to reform the lives of newsboys and was colloquially known as the "father of curfew" after he sent state legislators an extensive proposal for juvenile curfew laws in the 1890s.[7] For his part, Kelso led Canada's campaign for the juvenile curfew in conjunction with his reform work, which included founding the Ontario Children's Aid Society in 1891 and seeing through the passage of the Children's Protection Act in that province in 1893. These successful campaigns of the late nineteenth century drew upon curfew's rich past.

Proponents of youth curfew called for its "revival," pointing to the fact that such nocturnal population control was not new. Nineteenth-century child savers displayed knowledge of the importance, longevity, and centrality of this regulatory practice in Western culture. In advocating curfew law in late nineteenth-century Canada, child saver Beverley Jones emphasized the long and venerated tradition of curfew in seventeenth-century England and its arrival on North American soil at the insistence of the Pilgrim fathers.[8] In 1940s Montreal, curfew implementation debates provoked the *Gazette* to wax historical about its origins, stating that it began in the time of William the Conqueror.[9] Opponents were less generous, calling it "a relic of the dark ages."[10]

In medieval times, curfew referred generally to the practice of clearing the streets at nightfall or, more precisely, of extinguishing fires; thus the origins of the word *couvre-feu*: to cover the fire.[11] The most oft-cited enforcer of curfew was William the Conqueror, who was said to have set an 8 p.m. curfew for England in 1068.[12] Fortified European towns imposed curfew hours and shut down at nightfall. For centuries, night watchmen ensured the streets were vacated and fires were out. Generalized curfews continued with bells announcing the "advance of darkness" in pre-industrial Europe.[13] In the seventeenth century, the French white settler town Ville-Marie (now Montreal), implemented a general curfew as a public safety measure against possible raids by local and eventually displaced Indigenous peoples.[14] Curfews became less practical in larger European centres throughout the eighteenth century as a transformation in social and commercial behaviour opened up the urban night to "pleasure and profit," according to historian A. Roger Ekirch.[15] Aiding the decline in the general curfew was the changing characterization of the night – from sinister to compelling – and the impracticality of a general curfew in growing urban centres. By the nineteenth century, civic authorities invoked general curfews as emergency measures, as in the example of Chicago's Great Fire of 1871.[16]

Kelso, Hogeland, and others did not insist on the broadly directed curfews of centuries past but rather sought out implementation of the "targeted" curfew. In the nineteenth century, it was often specific cohorts of people, usually minority groups and youth, who fell under curfew's rule, revealing the highly arbitrary and discriminatory character of this social control mechanism. In the antebellum American South, for example, towns enacted curfews to keep enslaved African Americans out of the public realm at night.[17] As late as the twentieth century, racist policies in "Sundown Towns" beyond the South insisted that African Americans and other people of colour vacate town boundaries at the sound of a whistle each evening.[18] Children were another frequently targeted cohort subjected to night-time restrictions.

The emergence of the modern night helped to vitalize curfew as a mechanism for saving children. Nineteenth-century industrialism was built on time consciousness – where work organization became increasingly about time or hours – creating discussions about appropriate time schedules that divided a child's day.[19] Industrialization also transformed towns, cities, and night-time landscapes, providing new possibilities for sociability and work. Nightlife critics worried generally about night-time's "spectacle of moral diversity," rising crime rates, and nocturnal disorder. The night delighted and frightened commentators, who pointed to the unshrouding of sensuality and eroticism after dark, which led some to call for curfew's rule over certain groups of people, particularly vagrants, prostitutes, and beggars.[20] Concern over nefarious influences affecting children turned into campaigns to save them from the adult night-time world, requiring that they be home not just at nightfall, but, more precisely, at 9 p.m. The late nineteenth-century moral reform of child rescue and child protection produced separate justice systems for youth and favourable conditions for youth curfews. Protecting children from the night presented an opportunity to update a "relic of the dark ages" and transform curfew – with its attention to time, age categories, and standardization – into a tool of modernity.

At the close of the late nineteenth century the impetus behind the child welfare movement and the juvenile curfew was a growing consciousness of the centrality of the street in the lives of working-class, often immigrant, girls and boys.[21] Stories of children occupying the streets after dark abounded in North America. The author of the *Globe*'s column "Woman's World" claimed that Toronto streets in 1888 were "teeming with little children from the toddler of two years to the vile-tongued youth of almost any age, who defiles the air with his blasphemy and the street with his slimy spit."[22] She implored the city to put an end to the common appearance of dirty, bullying, and pathetic boys on streets at night. In arguing for the curfew, Kelso wrote about witnessing "unlimited street-roving after dark" that was "destructive of pure instincts [of children]." Under the shroud of darkness children were "inculcat[ed]" with "vicious, soul-destroying thoughts," exposed to "filthy communications and the plottings of street-corner loitering."[23] The ubiquity of "night children," as Peter C. Baldwin writes about the US experience, was caused by their involvement in both "nightlife and night work," pointing to the place of working-class children in modernizing cities.[24] Decrying truant and tramping children, curfew advocate Mrs John D. Townsend of Nebraska wrote of their "awful precocity."[25]

Night-time's negative reputation was well ensconced in nineteenth-century urban culture.[26] Publications like *Montreal by Gaslight* (1889) highlighted the problem of the ill-lit street, as the darkness allowed for nefarious activities to multiply and for the depraved and indifferent to go unobserved. Anti-night commentators in New York City pointed to the "promiscuous intermingling" across gender and class boundaries.[27] Even with the introduction of street lighting, night-time maintained its power to obscure and delight. Mark Caldwell writes that between 1870 and the 1890s, "[n]ight became a theater of sudden appearances and quick escapes, lonely crowds, wanderers, strollers, and predators – spinoffs of a burgeoning and diversifying population, the proliferation of new things to do after dark and the technologies that invented them, lit them up, and transported their patrons."[28] An otherwise respectable citizenry mixed with the so-called low-brow element known to most urban settings, producing an industry of vice and immorality under night's cover. Canadian social purity activists hoped that their cities would be spared the moral degeneration witnessed in New York City and London and actively sought out prevention controls on the supposedly most vulnerable urban souls, such as women and children.[29]

J.J. Kelso warned about the rampant spread of a desperate and delinquent child population in his pleas for child protection legislation in the 1890s that would champion the forced return home of children each night. Leading Canada's campaign for the juvenile curfew, Kelso embarked on several child welfare reforms in the 1880s and '90s, including founding the Children's Aid Society in 1891 and lobbying for a Children's Protection Act in Ontario, which found successful passage in 1893. Following the implementation of the act, the province appointed him Superintendent of Neglected and Dependent Children. For decades, he worked to create a network of Children's Aid Societies.[30] Juvenile curfews were integral to this dynamic era of child protection. The 1891 Report of the Prison and Reformatory System in Ontario recommended that a curfew be implemented to help prevent and "cure" juvenile delinquency.[31] Two years later, the province's Children's Protection Act included an enabling clause for municipalities that wished to adopt curfew bylaws.

As curfews gained in popularity following the 1893 act, Kelso lent his support in a widely distributed pamphlet containing his 1896 curfew speech to the National Conference of Charities and Corrections (in Grand Rapids, Michigan). Kelso's main argument for the juvenile nocturnal curfew was predicated on the ostensibly well-proven fact that children's exposure to night-time was destructive to themselves and therefore to society. Canadian Evangelical Protestant reformers such as the members of the Woman's Christian Temperance Union (WCTU) joined him in this position, pursuing the curfew to protect children's bodies and souls from exposure to the "devil's playground" that was the night.[32] Cities worked on the technological front to install better lighting systems, while bourgeois reformers like Kelso and the WCTU tackled the threat posed by moral and spiritual lapses produced in night-time pursuits.[33]

Kelso's US counterpart, Hogeland, similarly lectured across the country and appealed to state authorities to adopt curfew ordinances. His long-standing work among newsboys and the Boys and Girls Home and Employment Association gave him credibility and access to thousands: he reached as many as six hundred cities in his tours.[34] He and his supporters spoke of the need to support the police officer who worked against the rising crime rates caused by a combination of bad parenting and what they perceived as an inundation of the immigrant population.[35] Hogeland celebrated curfew as a mechanism to discipline working-class and immigrant adults who, in failing to restrain their children, endangered American social progress.

Discursively, with curfew laws on the rise, children became innocents unable to resist the temptations of nocturnal cultural life. These children were not bad themselves but were too weak in their tender years to avoid being swept into a path of moral descent, sin, vice, and crime. "Darkened young life-histories," Kelso warned, began with the "evil stories and suggestions heard while loitering in the streets after sundown."[36] Kelso's language is suggestive of the religious scaffolding of reformers' activities, but other curfew supporters focused on the "nature" of children. Children's night-time "wanderings" caused "moral injury," producing an "excitable and uncontrollable" temperament.[37] In this state, the child rejects the domestic world, "grows contemptuous of civil authority, and [is] initiated into criminal practices."[38] Reformers argued that the night introduced children to a vice-ridden, criminal, and sexualized adult world from which return was difficult, if not impossible. Unable or unwilling to return home, the child would turn to gangs (referred to at the turn of the century as clubs or coteries) for sociability and community. Thus, evenings spent on the streets foreshadowed a future life spent bound by the four walls of the reformatory, prison, or penitentiary.[39] In echoing support for a Toronto curfew, Kelso's child-saving colleague Beverley Jones asked rhetorically: "Why build and maintain gaols and refuges, workhouses and reformatories, and at the same time refuse to support a measure that will reduce the necessity for these institutions?"[40]

Both girls and boys were vulnerable, but the threat of the night and street-corner culture was expressed by social commentators and reformers in gendered terms. In the case of boys, petty crime and an awakened taste for lust and vice held no future alternative than adult criminality: "the evil impress made upon the soul remains indelible, and can seldom if ever be eradicated."[41] While boys were largely the subject of reformers' rants against night-time effects on childhood, Kelso also underscored the particular danger facing girls who had fallen for the "allurement of dimly lighted streets and street-made acquaintances."[42] Girls, he claimed, were not "wicked" but rather "foolish and giddy" and therefore not equipped to resist the situations arising from these encounters, leading them to their shame.[43] Kelso's musings on the fallen girl and street-corner loitering insist on a close relationship of children's access to the street after dark to the production of depraved and criminal adults. For girls, once shame had befallen them their only recourse to survival was prostitution. This image of children lost to crime and immorality inspired Kelso's campaign for the juvenile curfew. This argument, largely evocative of the child protection discourse of the 1890s, would persist through the early decades of the twentieth century.

Kelso's secondary argument promoting curfew related to his contention that the state must enter the private realm of familial relations where insufficient parenting was present. An idealized, bourgeois "haven in a heartless world" was the foil to pernicious street life. Kelso believed in the power of the home to inculcate children with values and lessons necessary for model citizenship: a good home provided a child with moral instruction, proper rest, and early sleep.[44] Parents were encouraged to improve the home environment – "make it attractive" – so that children would choose to be there and would "not regard compulsory detention there as a form of imprisonment."[45] When children were absent from home in the evenings, Kelso argued, they accumulated a series of deficiencies that would endanger any prospects for a healthy transition to adulthood.

The process of becoming an adult and a good citizen became much studied and discussed in the early decades of the twentieth century with the birth of the concept of adolescence. The popularizing of G. Stanley Hall's 1904 *Adolescence* and Freudian theories meant that discussions about children's health increasingly favoured curfew.[46] Imperative for ideal maturation was a good night's sleep and freedom from over-stimulation of the senses, especially at night (or by those elements associated with the night, such as sensuality). This line of reasoning gained ground through the twentieth century and predominated in the 1940s.

Kelso and Hogeland were child-saver leaders in an era when the state and legislation were deemed an intricate part of the solution to modern urban social ills. Canadian age-of-consent laws, for example, had been implemented in the 1880s, passed with the express purpose of protecting young womanhood and criminalizing carnal knowledge of girls under fourteen (later sixteen); this legislation implied that families and communities could not protect girls sufficiently and that the strong arm of the state was necessary to truly do the job.[47] In an 1888 "Woman's World" column in the *Globe* on the subject of the curfew entitled "Evils of Street Education," the author rhetorically asked: "Are not all laws moulded and framed with the direct object of making us better people ... and might we not use its [the law's] august arm to supplement the laxity or incapacity of parents?"[48] Similarly, Ontario's

Assistant Superintendent of Children wrote to the *Globe* responding
to the argument that parents should determine children's curfew hour
with the point that "government is but the cooperative act of parents
who need to act together in cities and villages ... [W]here the individual
parent does not do his duty it is not only the right but the duty of the
municipality as a means of self protection."[49]

The engine behind the child protection movement – and its cousin,
the juvenile justice movement – was the state and its critical role in
ensuring the welfare of children. The implicit assumptions in the state
acting *in loco parentis* were that parents were negligent, and the task
of raising the next generation was too important to leave to those
substandard parents. Therefore, the state had a vested interest in playing
public guardian. Evidence of deficient parenting was often anecdotal,
and reformers needed only to point to the emergent lamp-post youth
culture to prove it. Industrial and reform schools originated from this
thinking, and curfew law became popular in an era when the institutionalization of children fell into disrepute.

J.J. Kelso asserted that Canada was the first country to implement
curfews on youth, in the 1880s in Waterloo, Ontario. He explained
that the town council of Waterloo moved and adopted successive
resolutions requiring the ringing of a bell at 9 p.m. each night, signalling the hour at which children under fifteen must return home if
unaccompanied by a responsible adult.[50] Through the 1890s, city and
town councils debated following Waterloo's lead. The popularity of
this street-clearing measure spread during the 1890s mainly to other
small towns in Ontario and across the country, as part of a robust
child protection movement. Through that decade, women's Christian
organizations and child welfare reformers across Canada lobbied local
governments for the passage of curfew bylaws.[51] In Ontario, petitions demanded that municipalities act upon section 31 of the 1893
Children's Protection Act, which provided for a curfew ordinance (it
effectively enabled legislation for local governments to pass curfew
bylaws and local police to enforce them). In 1897, the Ontario WCTU
chapter proposed that the government make it compulsory for municipal corporations to pass curfew laws and enforcement mandatory
for those that already had such bylaws.[52] Women's efforts were not
successful in getting the province to act, although on the local level,
many towns and cities passed curfew bylaws.

The proliferation of the curfew to as many as fifty Canadian towns and villages in the 1890s sparked debate in municipal councils and in newspapers about child welfare, public order, and individual rights.[53] Most curfews specified that children would be home by 9 or 10 p.m. and set the age requirement at less than sixteen years, although it could be set as low as twelve years. In some cases, there was a gender differential, with older girls also required to respond to the curfew bell. In Newmarket, Ontario, for example, the mid-1890s curfew required boys under fourteen and girls under sixteen to be off the streets after 9 p.m. unless accompanied by a parent.[54] A *Globe* reader picked up this discrimination against girls and wrote to the editor to register her dismay: "a girl of sixteen is as mature both in judgment and morals, as a boy of nineteen or twenty, and not one-half as likely to be led into wrong-doing." She also advocated greater parental control of children.[55] Curfews could also target specific racialized youth, as in the example of the youth curfew implemented in 1934 to govern young people on the Kahnawake reserve outside Montreal.[56]

Skeptics persisted in the face of the widespread endorsement of curfew laws across small-town Canada. In the 1895 electoral race in Toronto, for example, one candidate for alderman rejected the idea of a youth curfew bell on the basis that no one should have the right to legislate for another's children.[57] Another joked that it made more sense to have a curfew for men over thirty-five years of age rather than one for minors.[58] Others argued that if there were, in fact, "street contamination after dark" the appropriate response would be to target it, rather than all children.[59] Individual freedom was at stake, curfew's detractors argued, and a repressive law served only to make the street more attractive to youth.[60]

Curfew laws were passed and intermittently used. They did not become the remedy to childhood derailed by modern industrial life. In 1906, J.J. Kelso publicly admitted that although the curfew campaign had been a success in calling attention to the nightly "Cry of the Children," he was disheartened by the impact of curfew law. Many towns and cities had enacted curfew bylaws, but he noted that the bells and sirens marking the time the children were to return home were "treated with indifference" by young people and adults alike.[61] Night historian Baldwin argues that curfew's association with small towns worked against its broader popularity in the United States.[62] A more practical goal, Kelso now thought, was to target the "worst cases of street wandering" and have the Children's Aid Societies deal with the culprits. This indifference to the curfew hour appears to have spread across towns and cities: by the 1920s and 1930s, women's groups and other concerned citizens were again asking city councils to either revive old 1890s curfew laws or to implement new ones.[63] It would take emergency conditions during the Second World War to revive the promise of youth curfew.

The Teen Problem and the Curfew Solution during the Second World War and the Early Postwar Era

The Second World War had a profound impact on the generation that came of age during the 1940s, as historians have illuminated.[64] Wartime childhood and youth were inflected with new levels of conformity around patriotism and sacrifice that produced examples of both brave and anxious teenagers. Children and teens devoted countless hours to the war effort, turned their imaginations to fighting the enemy while playing and reading, and learned to contend with an uncertain future.[65] The exigencies and opportunities on the home front reorganized families, as white men and some white women were recruited into the armed services. Other women and racial minorities sought out new employment venues that sometimes required moving great distances or implementing alternative child-care arrangements, including leaving young children alone. For youth, the war brought contradictory developments: adjustment to new cities and neighbourhoods, new responsibilities in the absence and or death of parents, and better opportunities for wages and freedom. Adults paying attention to how the war infused children's culture, behaviour, and attitudes noted their restlessness and anxiety; they saw teens drop out of school and engage in unprecedented violence, sexual promiscuity, and hoodlumism.[66] The war's aftershocks included the continued rise of juvenile delinquency rates, especially the spectre of the youth gang. The home-front emergency helped put youth curfew at the forefront of debates about what to do with latchkey children and youth who had "gone wild." This attitude to youth would result in the re-emergence of the curfew solution through the 1950s.

In the 1940s, juvenile curfew laws became a popular solution to latchkey loiterers and "roving bands of teen-age rowdies."[67] Whereas sociologists had linked overcrowdedness and poverty to delinquent subjects in the 1930s, during the war both Canada and the US experienced what experts labelled "prosperity delinquency" – behaviour linked to youth having more money and little regard for property and the safety of others. For example, midway through the war movie-going boys had become a "menace" across the US. Boys assaulted ushers, set fires in bathrooms, flung lit cigarettes and matches in the theatre, slashed seats and drapery, and picked the pockets of other patrons.[68] In the United States, wartime appeared to impair (sexual) impulse control in girls, increase rowdyism in boys, and heighten racial conflict among youth.[69] The rise of youthful zoot suiters across North America – named for their penchant for jazz-inspired, flamboyant dress – seemed emblematic to authorities of a generation and a cultural minority that had rejected the discipline, conformity, and sacrifice demanded by wartime. Clashes between police, servicemen, and other adults were often violent and resulted in the arrests of youth. During the most famous of the zoot suit riots, in 1943 Los Angeles, US service men attacked Mexican American youth, leading to the "largest round up [of young people] since Prohibition."[70]

In 1944 Montreal, zoot suiters – working-class French Canadian, Italian, and Anglo youth – brawled with soldiers, leading to scores of arrests.[71] In both countries, zoot suiters were held responsible for the violence, and those who could be were cited for curfew violation. As records from Montreal Juvenile Delinquents' Court reveal, youth under eighteen participated in and were shaped by a city geared for war. As a major recruitment depot and centre for munitions and other war-based factories, Montreal's economy absorbed young people as quickly as did its wide-open social scene, to the court's horror. In addition to zoot suit–sporting male youth, the court processed juvenile prostitutes, rape victims, and gay teens as the city struggled to maintain control of its youth. As complex delinquency problems confounded Montreal's local authorities in the 1940s, curfew ordinances became one line of defence.[72]

During the war, then, support for the introduction of curfew laws still emphasized the need for child protection, as it had in the late nineteenth century, but it was their older siblings' – the teenagers' – behaviour, along with deep shifts in familial roles, that compelled public discussion, policy development, and police action on restricting youth's night-time access to public space. Curfew debates, then, contained some of the elements of the late twentieth-century curfew arguments: out-of-control teen crime and a generation of parents unwilling or unable to assert authority. Curfew bylaws, though, continued to be contentious.

In Canada, the national emergency of the Second World War, coupled with the real and apparent rise in juvenile delinquency and latchkey children, helped the curfew's case in large centres. Montreal, Toronto, Ottawa, Edmonton, and Vancouver used curfew regulations to clear the streets of young people in the name of keeping the home front disciplined while fathers served overseas and mothers engaged in war work.[73] During the war as many as twenty-five cities with populations over 15,000 passed some form of youth curfew in which children under fourteen or sixteen years of age would be fined if caught on the streets after 9 p.m.[74]

The transition to a curfew-positive political environment could be dramatic. In 1941, the Toronto Police Department's Morality Bureau assured the Canadian Welfare Council that "[t]here is no Curfew Law [in the city]. The parents of the children of this city are responsible for the hour their children may be out."[75] City Hall had long had the power to pass a curfew ordinance under the provisions of the 1893 Children's Protection Act. With the unrelenting news about loitering children, youth crime, and mounting number of street gangs during the war, Toronto's City Council finally asked local police forces in 1944 to round up youngsters under sixteen.[76] With no youth bureau in place until the late 1950s, the Council instructed the police department, the juvenile court, the Children's Aid Society, and the St Vincent de Paul Children's Aid Society to enforce the curfew provisions of the act.[77] Any child caught "loitering" at night was issued a warning and a one-dollar fine for the first offence. A second offence led to a fine of two dollars; any further breaches of curfew would result in a five-dollar fine.[78]

Montreal's curfew law was embraced earlier than Toronto's, most likely because of its youth squad. The city's 1942 juvenile curfew bylaw was highly productive; from 1942 to 1945, the Montreal police logged nine thousand youngsters for being on the streets after 9 p.m. Just after the war, head of the youth squad, Oliva Pelletier, publicly declared war on delinquency and reminded readers of the critical role police played in "purifying the streets, alleys, and juvenile hangouts."[79] The city's 1942 juvenile curfew bylaw became a chief mechanism of clearing the streets of loitering youth. This city's curfew was notable because of the strong opposition to it prior to the war and its longevity; it far outlasted the wartime emergency that had given it birth. With an apparent delinquency crisis, curfew proponents gained the upper hand, leading to its successful passage in 1942. However, it too was not without controversy.

In the decade prior to the war, curfew law had attracted child welfare advocates in Montreal and sparked a debate that raged from the provincial legislature to the halls of Montreal schools.[80] A substantial campaign for the curfew was launched by the Comité des Oeuvres Catholiques de Montréal (representing the Société St-Vincent-de-Paul, the Association Catholique de la Jeunesse Canadienne, and L'Action Catholique), and a petition favouring the curfew was presented to city councillors in 1937. Smaller towns near Montreal such as Ste Anne de Bellevue already had curfew laws. Ste Anne's police force had used the curfew to resolve a youth loitering problem. The police chief aimed the curfew at twelve- to sixteen-year-olds who were not guilty of any criminal offence but who were "fraternizing, annoying people, and standing on the sidewalks in front of restaurants and theatres." Resistance to the curfew came from adults, who called it an infringement on their rights as parents to discipline their children. But, according to the police chief, eventually "everyone" got used to it.[81] Montreal city councillors and some police officers remained unimpressed by the evidence and support for the curfew prior to the war, resisting it on the basis that it intruded on the privacy of the family and required a substantial workforce.

The delinquency panic during the Second World War weakened Montrealers' resolve against the curfew. The curfew lobby not only focused on the law-breaking of young people but invoked a compelling argument on the need to shore up the imperilled wartime family. The threat of a full-scale delinquency problem appeared to be nationwide by the early 1940s. The Dominion Bureau of Statistics observed that the first three years of that decade were marked by a serious growth in the number of teens arrested. While delinquency rates in Canada increased by only around 45 per cent during the war, press accounts of delinquency, according Jeffrey Keshen, increased by 125 per cent.[82] *Maclean's* writer Mary Brechin wrote in 1942 of the youthful crime wave that covered Canada, pointing to the "danger ages" being those seven to sixteen years old.[83] Juvenile delinquency had "reached terrifying proportions," Doris Hedges wrote in 1944.[84] "High spirits, loneliness, or neglect by parents" were at the root of the juvenile problem, she claimed, and produced "disease, moral degeneration, and finally complete loss of a sense of citizenship."[85] Broader policing of youth during wartime helped to swell the numbers, but the population's willingness to believe that war-stressed families led to bad behaviour in children and adolescents generally caused the delinquency panic.[86] Blacked-out cities had apparently led to youth going bad. Boys loitered and looted, whereas girls lost their moral sense. With mothers at work and fathers absent from the home front, leaders sought a new tack to quell a mounting problem of neglected and delinquent youth. In wartime, the curfew law's reputation evolved dramatically.

By 1942, commentators writing in favour of the curfew represented a range of Catholic institutions, both English and French: the Archbishop of Montreal, teachers' federations, the Catholic school board, La Jeunesse Ouvrière, La Jeunesse Ouvrière Féminine, Le Comité des Oeuvres Catholiques de Montréal, La Société St Jean Baptiste, Catholic unions, the Fédération des Ligues du Sacré-Coeur, the Federation of Catholic Charities, girls' clubs, and women's leagues, among others.[87] Also in support were the Montreal municipal council, the Montreal Juvenile Delinquents' Court, the Salvation Army, the Montreal Boys' Association, the Local Council of Women, and the committee representing Presbyterian churches of Montreal and their social organizations.[88]

The groundswell of support for the curfew undoubtedly had to do with its being sold as nothing short of "a crime reducer, a child protector, and a home builder."[89] Perhaps the most compelling argument to many social and religiously based organizations was the latter: the curfew would shore up the family home that had been under attack since industrialization but acutely so during the current war. Curfew could be "a home builder," explained Catholic priest Archambault in his 1942 treatise on the righteousness of the youth regulation. Is it not in the evenings, he asked, when all members of the family come together and when concerned parents complete the education of their children?[90] John F. Dalton of the juvenile court committee elaborated: the "home was the natural habitat of the young child; without the curfew, he misses family life that offers the child a sense of belonging and security."[91] Evening family life had broken down because of the war. In the context of fathers leaving for armed service, curfew was a means to bestow authority upon mothers in their absence: "Mother is alone at home … she doesn't have the needed authority to make children obey. The children go out and run [in the streets] at night despite her." She is "powerless," "worried and sorry."[92] Montreal's mayor, Adhémar Raynault, who as a councillor in the 1930s tried but failed to see a curfew law passed, acknowledged in 1942 that "times are difficult ... mothers are working in war factories ... especially in working class areas, where children are without surveillance in the evenings."[93] The curfew, then, became a welcome support for parents, especially mothers, who faced new and difficult circumstances. This sentiment was echoed across the country.[94] From Prince Edward Island, Reverend Webster of the Children's Aid Society, in support of a more stringent curfew law in 1942, remarked that "the strong arm of the father is missed" and mothers are grateful for aid in this way.[95] Defining the problem as one of weakened paternal authority and the loss of a "good family life" helped ensure that curfew was passed in 1942 Montreal and kept its reputation strong throughout the delinquency crisis.[96]

As a "child protector" the curfew was supposed to restore the childhood missed by children who spent nights away from home. This line of argument focused on the child's health, spiritual well-being, and prospects for future citizenship and underscored how the curfew was targeted to pre-delinquents as much as to their older, rowdier siblings. The echoes of religious arguments about the effect of night on children's souls continued from the nineteenth century. Archambault referred to children's *sorties nocturnes* [night-time outings] as one of the "great evils" of the war. [97] Rumours swirled about children buying beer, carrying "loaded" weapons, and being lured into vice once they crossed the threshold of the city's "dens of iniquity."[98] Montreal juvenile court judge Robillard noticed that in the twenty years prior, parents appeared to take less seriously their responsibilities to keep children off the streets at night.[99]

Citizens and social commentators placed increasing stress on the physical and social costs of night time indulgence. In the late 1930s, a delegation representing the city's social organizations demanded that the municipal executive committee consider a curfew, arguing its goal was in the interest of "moral perfection, intellectual progress, and physical well-being."[100] During the war, Judge J.G. Nicholson of the juvenile court admitted that a high percentage of children who were brought to court were in the habit of being away from their homes until late at night. Every day he saw the price Montreal paid for sleep-deprived youth: impaired adolescent development. Without a curfew hour imposed on children under fourteen, sleep deprivation wreaked havoc with youth.

Sleep deprivation had long-term consequences for children's physical and mental well-being and especially for their morality. It resulted in poor "brain–muscle coordination," weak "powers of concentration and judgement," and irritability. Athletic and intellectual ability were compromised, Nicholson argued, leading to "feelings of inferiority" and poor morale. In turn, these problems exacerbated delinquent acts such as telling lies, bullying, and rudeness. Nicholson acknowledged that big-city nightlife offered a world of excitement for young people with "bright lights, gaiety, and movement of people," but by staying out late the child sacrificed development of such virtues as "calmness of thinking, sense of duty and responsibility, ability to concentrate, [and] the habit of industriousness." The curfew would save the child from such deterioration and missed opportunity, for if a child was a "building block for society," each one who "develops badly, contributes to the general store of misery and unhappiness." Each child lost to sleep deprivation and the street "lower[ed] the quality of our culture."[101] A curfew, Nicholson argued, was the panacea needed to ensure that the generation that came of age following the war would be ready to lead.

Curfew laws were received with ambivalence during the war, despite expressed great hope for strengthening the family, protecting children, and reducing crime. At the time of the Montreal law's passage, a fierce debate over curfew's effectiveness erupted, and within two years complaints were registered about its failure, no matter how many children were stopped by police.

The argument that the curfew helped protect childhood and build "better" children was an attempt to relieve the curfew of its disciplinary, repressive, and illiberal nature. Montreal Mayor Renault defensively argued, "[W]e don't want to put in place a harassment mechanism but rather we want to protect young children from the dangers of the street."[102] In Archambault's treatise on the subject he exposed the politics of sacrifice and submission underlying the youth curfew: night-time curfew taught children that when freedom was in danger, even they must "submit to a spirit of obedience and discipline ... They will only be better citizens, more devoted to their country, more disposed to serve and defend constituted authority."[103]

One of the strongest arguments made against proposed curfew laws in the 1930s and 1940s concerned parental responsibility, rights, and authority. Would not the curfew interfere with the job of parents? Juvenile court judge Nicholson argued that such a law did not "unduly interfere with personal liberty and with the exercise of parental authority."[104] For him, children's presence on the street at night was a sign of parental failure. Montreal city councillors were more reticent to intervene in the relationship between parents and children. In September 1942 this issue was front and centre as city councillors debated the curfew bylaw articles. Councillors Adams and Polson argued: "That while this council is in accord with the principle of juveniles being kept from loitering in the streets, parks and public places of the city after nightfall, it is very widely held that this should be a responsibility of the parents and that every effort should be made to avoid bringing the children under the stigma of police action."[105] While the juvenile court judges did not worry about the "criminalizing" of children under fourteen, councillors did. City Council accepted the idea that first offenders be taken home to their parents rather than to police stations or courthouses.

Other forceful arguments against curfew bells involved the expense of implementation. Police forces across the country had lost men to the armed forces and the curfew bylaw appeared to require a significant force of foot patrols. Montreal's police chief admitted to *La Presse* in September 1942 that he had only 150 men on the streets at night and therefore few of the 150,000 children in the city would be subject to policing. Suggestions were made that parish priests and night patrols consisting of responsible citizens could join together in eradicating "night children."[106] That is, the effectiveness of the curfew depended on the community's – including the children's – willingness to self-police. When curfew hour struck, anyone on the street could harass, cajole, and instruct young people to make their way home.

Thus, the wartime emergency muted opposition to curfew even in large urban centres. In September 1942, the municipal government of Montreal passed bylaw 1715.[107] The curfew stipulated that all children under fourteen years of age, unless attending night courses, were forbidden to "circulate in the streets, lanes and public places" between 9 p.m. and 5 a.m. Exceptions were made for children in the company of a parent or guardian. The bylaw required that with the first infraction the adult responsible for the child be brought before the juvenile court; a repeat juvenile offender would be brought directly to the court. Besides the ignominy of being brought to court, the child was also subject to a fine or detention in the case that he or she was unable to pay the fine.

Following passage of the bylaw, children were routinely rounded up after the curfew hour. From the records of the Montreal Juvenile Delinquents' Court, it is evident that children aged eleven to thirteen were brought to juvenile court for being on the streets at night. Most pleaded guilty and were fined between fifty cents and one dollar. Using a fine as punishment directly involved parents, who were called upon to pay. Failure to pay the fine within one week resulted in the child's incarceration in the detention home.[108] The court had used curfew law for decades to regulate specific youth who had been convicted of an offence under the Juvenile Delinquents Act (1908); these targeted curfews frequently required that the juvenile be at home after 6 p.m. While this might appear to be a harsh measure, the youth was spared reform school and permitted to return home. The immediate impact of the more generalized curfew was to create delinquent throngs of children whose only offence was not being at home in the evening.

But it was the juvenile morality squad officers on the streets who were charged with clearing the streets, parks, and laneways of loitering children and adolescents. The curfew law in conjunction with this newly constituted force resulted in the heavy regulation of children during the war, despite the police chief's complaint about too few officers on the beat. According to the Montreal Police Department's Annual Reports, the number of children arrested during the war skyrocketed – as many as nine thousand for curfew alone. The majority of these children did not end up in juvenile court but were recorded by the Juvenile Morality Squad as having been processed – likely sent on their way after a stern talking-to by the officer. The curfew effect can also be seen in the rise of sunset crimes for those fourteen and older. In 1939, prior to the curfew law's passage, 90 Montreal youth (76 boys and 14 girls) were arrested for loitering/loitering by night; in 1943, sunset crime arrests escalated to 489 boys and 55 girls.[109] Through the early postwar period, thousands of children were arrested by Montreal police, a legacy of the successful curfew campaign of 1942.[110]

Throughout the war and early postwar period the delinquency menace continued to make news. Theft, truancy, the pursuit of pleasure aided by growing salaries and less parental oversight meant teenagers, especially those over fourteen, were responsible for rising delinquency statistics during the war.[111] After the war, educators, legal experts, community workers, and politicians addressed the "alarming" increase in postwar delinquency spurred by the "chaos created by World War II."[112] Studies of, and solutions to, the youth problems abounded. The 1956 annual convention of the International Association of Chiefs of Police recommended that based on a survey of 153 police departments in the US, Canada, and Puerto Rico, municipalities consider the mandatory arrest of youth involved in serious crime, the potential to hold parents responsible, and a study of juvenile curfew effectiveness.[113] That year Philadelphia's mayor Richardson Dilworth approved a permanent curfew ordinance of 10:30 for those under seventeen and midnight Fridays and Saturdays.[114] By the mid-1950s, curfew laws were again spreading like wildfire, linked this time to the growing concern and media obsession with juvenile gangs and violence. This attention to an older cohort of youth whose behaviour shocked the public and law enforcement alike brought support for broadening curfew's application. Ordering teenagers off the streets at night to quell gang activity seemed urgent in Elizabeth, New Jersey, where a gang "street battle" involving one hundred youth led the city council to revive the Second World War curfew of 9:30 p.m. for boys and girls under sixteen.[115] In 1948, Chicago revived its 1910 curfew of 10 p.m. for teenagers under eighteen to deal with the postwar delinquency problem. By the end of the 1950s, police supported as an important element in the fight against youth crime the "street ban" of youth in six major US cities, including Philadelphia, Chicago, Detroit, San Francisco, Cleveland, and St Louis.[116] Although careful not to call it a "cure-all," Harry Fedele of Cleveland's Police Department Juvenile Bureau claimed it was an effective street-clearing mechanism that helped to reduce juvenile crime and gang fights.[117]

During the Second World War and postwar period the debates about children, teenagers, and curfew laws tended to minimize the voices of those most affected, the youths themselves. There are glimpses of acquiescence during the war, where teens claimed it wasn't such a hardship to the obey curfew bells.[118] Obeying curfew was one way for teens to distinguish themselves from "hoodlums." There are also examples of spectacular protests, like the Olive Hill, Kentucky, "mob" of one hundred that in the summer of 1943 vandalized the office of the judge who tried to impose a midnight curfew on minors.[119]

As race riots erupted in both the US north and south during the 1960s, general curfews became part of the arsenal used against minorities and the apparent lawlessness in embattled neighbourhoods.

Municipalities reinstated juvenile curfews, giving police an added weapon against mostly African American youth. In the summer of 1964, cities in New York, Pennsylvania, and New Jersey saw rioting in response to police violence against youth. Also in 1964, a youth curfew was called in the wake of protests against a police arrest in Centerville, Illinois.[120] In 1965, Los Angeles and Chicago used curfews in African American neighbourhoods to clear the streets as the riots' death toll rose.[121] In 1966, police enforced a state juvenile curfew law against African American youth in South Side Chicago because of gang violence.[122] As protests against poverty, discrimination, and racism spread across the US in the mid-1960s, youth curfews were invoked by the state to shut down the streets. Here, this old mechanism of nocturnal control, ironically once advocated as a tool to produce better children and childhood, was deployed against minority youth – those most often denied a chance at childhood. Curfew in the 1960s foreshadowed its more recent usage where policing is concentrated in minority areas and youth of colour are most burdened by its restrictive measures.

As the treatment of juvenile delinquents became punitive in the late twentieth and early twenty-first centuries, curfews again became popular and highly contested. Much of the scholarship on the explosion of curfew laws has focused on the United States, yet Canada has also witnessed a quiet growth in curfew regulations. In the summer of 2004, for example, nightly vandalism prompted the mayor of Huntingdon, Quebec, Stéphane Gendron, to take decisive action against young people, mandating their return home at the sound of a 10 p.m. siren. For this town that lies between Montreal and the New York state border, the loss of the manufacturing sector had directly affected youth culture. As one observer noted: "There are no commercial malls, video arcades or skateboard parks ... and no bus service ... to the nearest movie theatre."[123] Media coverage blamed inadequate provision of youth leisure sites for transforming the town's young into "restless youth," who became the first accused when widespread vandalism of public and abandoned properties hit the town.[124] Recent cuts to the police force servicing the Huntingdon area opened the door to embracing curfew as a broad solution to the nocturnal disorder of youth. Huntingdon's curfew proposal was immediately contentious. Not surprisingly, the notion of a curfew provoked Huntingdon's teenage population. Adolescent girls and boys raged against the unfairness of criminalizing their presence on the streets at night and the labelling of their generation "delinquent."[125] Less predictably, joining teens in protest were parents, members of the Quebec Legislative Assembly, and eventually the Quebec Human Rights Commission (QHRC).[126] The combined opposition to the teen curfew and the accompanying media frenzy caused the mayor to delay implementation; the law never materialized in the fashion the mayor had hoped.[127] In the meantime the QHRC argued that the proposed curfew violated the provincial Charter of Rights and Freedoms which guarantees freedom of movement and freedom of peaceable assembly regardless of age. Yet the mayor persisted, altering his tack by targeting parents. In August, his municipal council voted in favour of a bylaw that required that children under sixteen be accompanied by their parents after 10:30 p.m. A first offence was met with a $50 fine, and repeat parental offenders were to be fined $100. Gendron's argument was consistent, he claimed, with Quebec's Civil Code, which states that parents must always supervise their children and be responsible for them.[128]

Two years later, following the brutal slaying of a thirty-four-year-old woman in Winnipeg's west end, curfew again dominated public discussion about youth crime. Although the area held a reputation for regular incidents of extreme violence, the city woke to the especially disturbing news that Audrey Cooper had been the random victim of a prolonged beating by a group of teenagers, the youngest only twelve years of age. Such chilling behaviour prompted calls for a night-time youth curfew in the days following the murder, as politicians, local business owners, and others pointed to the urgent need to curb teen violence and gain control over an area associated with a growing Aboriginal population. The accused teens, assumed by the media to be Aboriginal, were described as "roaming" the streets at all hours of the night. These "Indigenous roamers," in turn, became the justification for supporting a broad juvenile curfew to keep the community safe. Resistance to such calls for curfew pointed to the unfairness of sending *all* children and youth home at a specified hour, not just those tainted by neighbourhood reputation.[129]

Exasperation over an inability to quell youth crime, and, in the case of Canada, the Youth Criminal Justice Act's apparent impotence in the face of violent young people, fuelled the decision to call for teen curfews in the case of Huntingdon, Winnipeg, and a host of cities across North America.[130] Yet, as Hemmens and Bennett conclude in their study of the legal response to recent juvenile curfews in the US, these city ordinances were less a "reasoned response" to delinquency than "a sign of public hysteria" that abrogated the rights of youth and often targeted racialized minorities.[131] Curfew laws resulted from episodic moral panics over youth behaviour and are an act of what geographer Gill Valentine calls an assertion of "adult spatial hegemony."[132] There are multiple problems with curfew regulations beyond their arbitrary enforcement, as this argument goes, including the assumption that youth have safe and welcoming homes and that violence and crime happen only after the curfew hour.[133] Notwithstanding these solid arguments against municipal curfews and the objections waged by teens and their advocates, they remain a popular regulatory tactic and the first choice of many city administrations and police forces.

In many ways, the rationale for curfews in recent decades resembles the earlier arguments from the late nineteenth and mid-twentieth centuries. For more than a century, the discourse supporting juvenile curfew has emphasized child protection and an acceptance of the police acting *in loco parentis* with varying levels of parental blame. Yet, in the nineteenth century a eugenic undertone to the curfew promise was evident. Many believed that a better child and citizen would develop from state-mandated sleep. Also in the nineteenth century and the 1940s, curfew supporters were committed to the idea that youth were malleable and could be rehabilitated. More recently, proponents of children's rights have invoked youth's constitutional rights in opposing curfew laws, although this position faces the counter-argument that young people are more dangerous and violent than ever before.[134] Thus, despite forceful arguments in favour of the rights of the child, the threat that youths pose to each other and to the community supersedes these objections to curfew.[135]

Conclusion

From the 1880s through the early decades of the twentieth century, curfew gained the support of a generation of child welfare reformers. The belief that evil lurked at sundown and made society's most vulnerable members powerless against its influence convinced reformers and townspeople to pass bylaws regulating children's use of the streets at night. Children were cast as victims or potential victims in need of the state's protective power; denial of the problem of "night children," reformers argued, came at society's peril, for the next generation would certainly consist of criminals and depraved individuals. Not everyone agreed with this legislative innovation; larger Canadian centres such as Toronto and Montreal resisted the calls for curfew, outlining the anti-modern orientation of the curfew and a reluctance to interfere with family prerogative in controlling children.

Curfew became popular again at mid-twentieth century with the Second World War and postwar increases in juvenile crime. The discourses that supported these curfews shared a similar characterization of children and childhood, yet they differed in important ways. In the 1940s, proponents of the youth curfew persuasively argued that it would encourage family stability and cohesion at a moment when these goals seemed unrealistic. Curfew not only cleared the streets of children at 9 or 10 p.m., but it supposedly stabilized families in a moment of intense familial disruption. In an era of weak parental control, it allowed the state to dictate youth behaviour. It also allegedly offered health benefits for youth. Eliminating the tired child would result in a better-formed adolescent and future citizen. It also had the effect of disciplining a generation of children about what was expected of them as part of wartime sacrifice.

The press and police highlighted the advantages of youth curfew in the postwar period, especially in the context of mid-century youth problems. Essentially, the curfew was a street-clearing tool that police could use without having to establish that an offence had taken place. As established by wartime reports about the effectiveness of curfew law, "without a curfew ordinance, police have little authority in regulating the nocturnal activities of the adolescent."[136] Curfew laws gave police the necessary power to question any young person on the street after dark, regardless of their activity. This discretionary weapon undoubtedly bolstered the policing of youthscapes and interrupted youth subcultures. It also provided the community with a directive regarding what time youth should no longer been seen. The audible marking of curfew's start each night produced both self-governance and vigilantism. Its role as crime control was clearly demonstrated during the 1960s, as police grasped for measures to shut down protests.

In 1943, authorities sought solutions to the "gangs of movie thieves," "mischievous youngsters," khaki-mad girls, and racialized rioting teens.[137] Curfew was a status offence (which permitted police to stop and question any youth who appeared unchaperoned after dark), so it had wide appeal for those seeking greater regulation of teenagers during and after the war. Of course, teens resented and resisted curfew's indiscriminate approach to their presence and they had their defenders. Curfews that "restrict … the normal youthful proclivity to go places and do things" made no sense to Catherine Mackenzie, who argued in the *New York Times* that the generation coming of age during the war was no worse than teenagers in the past. What they needed from adults, she claimed, was help in establishing teen clubs to orient them to "good clean fun."[138] Ovila Pelletier and his crime prevention colleagues could not have agreed more.

CHAPTER FOUR

The Sports Solution:
Surveillance and Athletic Citizenship
in the Recreation Revolution

In 1947, a group of gun-toting youths terrorized neighbourhoods and vandalized property, convincing Staff Sergeant Hilmer Nordstrom of the Saskatoon City Police Department to rethink his delinquency-control strategy.[1] The repressive model of policing boys seemed inadequate for the times, he thought; this generation, like their fathers' and grand-fathers', was raised in a gun-positive culture with its reverence for sport hunting, widely available mass-produced toy and real guns, seductive depictions of Hollywood gangsters and cowboys, and prevailing messa-ges that linked firearms and masculinity to British imperial superiority.[2] Whether through hunting or the "manly game of war," guns facilitated what historian R. Blake Brown asserts was a boy's induction into mascu-line citizenship.[3] It was in this context that Nordstrom endeavoured to transform the boys' promiscuous shooting and vandalism into an educational and disciplinary moment.

That year, Nordstrom established the Police Boys' Rifle Club to teach ten- to fifteen-year-old boys the middle-class values of sportsmanship and liberal citizenship through the responsible handling and shooting of firearms. In this updated twist on employing military drill to quell rampant juvenile delinquency, Nordstrom insisted club membership could buttress boys' obedience to authority and provide a meaningful path to manly virtue for working-class boys while giving them the martial skills they desired. Within five years, this Canadian prairie city's police force had enticed more than 350 boys to its club meetings held in the base-ment of the police station on Friday nights. Nordstrom's innovation in delinquency prevention was featured in the 1954 docu-drama, *A Sergeant*

Sees It Through, starring Nordstrom, civic leaders, financial supporters, and the alleged delinquents themselves. This thirty-minute informational film showed how police youth clubs turned delinquents and would-be delinquents into boy-citizens. The founding of the rifle club was at once an ad hoc response to a local crisis and part of a significant trend in preventive delinquency programs for youth prior to and after the Second World War, becoming a popular cornerstone of youth-conscious policing in northern North America in the mid-twentieth century.

The story of the Police Boy's Rifle Club exemplifies how the most profound changes in the relationship between young people, especially boys, and police forces occurred in recreational venues of North America. Hundreds of thousands of young people joined police athletic leagues, social and cultural clubs, and took advantage of membership opportunities to attend local sporting events, circuses, and the like. This popular development was propelled by the belief that such a movement could fix incipient delinquents who, without such intervention, would be tomorrow's criminals. Born in the era of crime prevention schemes, such police-led youth activities were effective in meeting the goals of mid-century policing; in large urban settings, like New York and Montreal, comprehensive sports and cultural programs became a major part of the solution to what observers called the "serious and tragic problem" of rising delinquency rates and youth gangs.[4]

Police-led clubs for youth represent a fusion of interwar crime prevention with prevailing progressive-era ideas about children and youth. In particular, police-led sports clubs adopted reformist beliefs about the need to develop the male body and youth's sense of morality, citizenship, and belonging at a time when manhood and, by extension, boyhood seemed imperilled by industrial modernity. The sports solution to this "boy problem" dovetailed neatly with the crime prevention turn embraced by North American police in the early decades of the twentieth century, which opened the door to influencing youth "before it was too late" and lives were lost to crime and dissipation. So acute was the concern over boys that the vast majority of police-initiated sports teams were exclusively available to them, and when girls were considered, a different kind of activity was encouraged, often involving reading, writing, and crafts.

Police-led leisure and sports programs not only reflected the era's prevailing gendered understandings of the roots and nature of delinquency and youth, but they also inscribed hierarchies of race and class despite the rhetoric of inclusion. In theory, local police youth clubs were open to all children and youth, though their provenance would suggest specific young people in certain geographic areas were particularly targeted. Directed at boys in what were considered marginalized, though redeemable, neighbourhoods, the police club movement focused on areas that lacked amusement venues to fix potential delinquents' "misdirected" play.[5] In the case of Saskatoon, for example, this meant working-class white youth gained an opportunity for citizenship, whereas racially marginalized Indigenous youth did not.

What did it mean that local police forces across North America became leaders in recreational clubs for youth? This development directly challenged youth street (sub)cultures that appeared threatening and inherently criminal and drew youth into a more quotidian relationship with individual officers. Not surprisingly, local and international media lauded these efforts that put hockey sticks, basketballs, and baseball tickets into the hands of otherwise idle and disadvantaged youth. Replacing the appeal of the street gang with club membership provided an opportunity for police to take on new forms of leadership as club masters and coaches. As such, they sought to teach young people fair play and healthy competition, and to follow rules, all the while observing and scrutinizing them. Youth too seemed to welcome these opportunities according to membership statistics and media interviews with happy joiners. For the police departments, this innovation permitted a way to not only control crime but also influence the public's attitude toward police work. Through involvement with youth, police sought to interrupt the deeply embedded negative impression of police authority that seemed to pass from parent to the rising generation in certain neighbourhoods.

Yet let's not forget that the police-led clubs and the insinuation of police into recreational and youth spaces and clubs amounted to an expansion of police supervision and surveillance. This development exemplifies what Michel Foucault and others have referred to as the shift from disciplinary societies to societies of control, where internment ceases to be the most common technology to handle deviance, giving way to incessant control, apparatus of security, and normalization.[6] This program of recreation helped the police gain access to boys across class and cultural lines, helping to instill notions of hegemonic masculinity, class, and racially specific sportsmanship, as is suggested by the example of rifle shooting on the Canadian prairie. By embracing sports as a disciplinary power, the police were in a position to insist on and define a "legitimate use of the body" and a code of liberal morality endorsed by the state.[7] Officers exercised a disciplinary power while assuming a pedagogical role over children and youth who were not found breaking the law or even the rules. As Pierre Bourdieu states about sports in general, it is "an extremely economical means of mobilizing, occupying, and controlling adolescents" from marginal neighbourhoods who likely had not bought in to the idea that modern liberal society included them. Club membership, in overt and subtle ways, was an act of recruitment to the mainstream consensus of obedient, male, middle-class, heteronormative citizenship.

This chapter explores how recreation as a strategy of crime prevention refocused police work. Its implication for young people was similarly profound, reordering youth's material use of urban space (and their lifestyles therein) and providing new possibilities for youthful subjectivities. That is, police recreational programs for youth should be seen as part of a contest over urban space that had specific implications for both young people and the police. These clubs and activities helped assert adult hegemony over young people's use of the "the street," defined broadly as all public spaces that youth occupy. They also contributed to what geographer Sarah Mills calls a positive counternarrative to the negative association of youth in public space during the postwar period.[8] These programs therefore helped dissolve the binary that often emerges when considering young people's occupation of public space – as either a "polluting presence" or as the very essence of vulnerability.[9] As the police programs interrupted boys' own hierarchies of authority and autonomy, youth could be seen to have benefited from the transformation of reputation with the broader community. Those who obeyed and joined found a new kind of belonging whose benefits went beyond a ball game. By becoming a member of a police club and wearing police colours rather than gang colours, youth gained at least temporary access to liberal citizenship. In creating insiders – those who belonged – these programs also produced outliers: those who did not fit in, who were denied membership.

Two cities developed extensive and comprehensive police clubs for boys and girls and were noted as successful examples of what could be done by local officers to thwart the making of young criminals. New York City's early experiments with police-led recreational activities formally organized into the Police Athletic League (PAL) in 1936. Montreal's Police Juvenile Clubs for Boys (PJCB) was established in 1947. Youth squads in those cities produced the PAL and PJCB, using radio shows to reach out to young people, membership cards to produce feelings of belonging, and incentives like free tickets to spectator sports.

The Origins of Police-Led Youth Clubs

Police-led youth clubs that became popular in the 1930s and '40s developed from a tradition of boys' clubs, which in turn resulted from a crisis of boyhood in the nineteenth century. Late nineteenth- and early twentieth-century American reformers and writers identified an emergent "boy problem" as an affliction of urban modernity. These commentators noted the ill effects, especially on newcomer and working-class families, of childhoods spent in the poverty and violence endemic to industrial cities: a surge in mischievous behaviour and homelessness among American boys. If the brutal context of modern urban culture made "gangsters and thieves"[10] out of immigrant and native-born working-class boys, their middle-class counterparts were not much better off, suffering from overly civilized, sedentary lifestyles.[11] These privileged American boys were considered ill equipped to inherit the leadership roles appropriate to their class; education, often at the hands of women, had left their bodies atrophying and their characters lacking strength and vitality.[12] Across class lines, then, boyhood had lost its hardy, resilient essence. The solution, known as boywork, would harness boys' nature and mould them into good citizens, workers, and patriots.

Expounding upon the "problem" of the modern boy as an intellectual and academic issue were religious leaders, writers, and the day's rising lay authorities: social scientists. Although expressed in different ways, the discourse surrounding the boy problem suggested an assumption about a universal boy nature and the need to nurture and manage it. Boys, according to nineteenth-century commentators, were most at home in nature, full of "animal spirits," and adventure. Nineteenth-century fiction, exemplified by *Huckleberry Finn* (1885), championed "untamed boyhood" and promoted the idea of a universal boy nature under attack by modern industrial society.[13] This anti-modernist critique made the causal link between the detrimental effects of city life on a boy's true nature and the rise of middle-class "sissies" and working-class delinquents.

The boy problem became the focus of "boyology" and "boywork" at the hands of social reformers, religious organizations, and civic leaders. In addition to the perceived need to harness youthful male energy was "muscular Christianity," a moral conviction about the importance of boys' health and physical fitness. It originated in England in the mid-nineteenth century and spread to North America at the close of that century. Muscular Christianity overturned evangelical Protestants' objections to the brutishness of sports and helped reconfigure physical exercise as an antidote to the sedentary and effeminate boy/man.[14] Organized sport also reinforced discipline and hierarchy to quell the rise of delinquency. Proponents of muscular Christianity and sport maintained that a new manliness cultivated by physical strength and moral character development could be achieved through the rules, regulations, and self-discipline required of athletic activities.

A major advocate of muscular Christianity was G. Stanley Hall, the developmental psychologist best known for *Adolescence* (1904). He based his ideas about the growing adolescent boy on the theory of recapitulation, whereby a boy evolves through developmental stages from primitive to modern.[15] His ideas applied to working-class boys not because of their overly cultivated demeanours, but their rowdy selves. The propensity for boys to play rough and perilously close to criminal influences provided an opportunity to modify their habits by masculine recreational pursuits, which essentially guided them through developmental stages toward becoming men. The promise was great: boys would be able to transcend class and ethnic difference toward a hegemonic masculinity and proper citizenship.[16] Turn-of-the-century experts in boyology believed that with proper socialization, recreation, and education, the boy problem could be resolved, boys rescued, and proper manhood ensured. Infused with muscular Christianity, boys' clubs became a central tenet and a major expression of boy work in the US and Canada at the turn of the twentieth century.[17]

On both sides of the border the locus for reforming young people was the youth club. Boys' clubs, such as the Boy Scouts and activities run by the Young Men's Christian Associations (YMCAS), proliferated toward the end of the nineteenth century and into the next, encouraging character building and physical fitness among boys as a response to the perception that physically weak men resulted from inactive boyhoods.[18] While middle-class boys turned to organized sports, child welfare reformers attempting to redirect wayward and aggressive behaviour targeted the "problem" of working-class boys' street play. As Grant notes, urban boys' clubs emerged as a fundamental part of mission work in poor urban areas in the closing decades of the nineteenth century.[19] In New York City, the club movement began as a way to remove juvenile gangs from the streets; the first club opened in 1876, and by 1901 a sizable network of clubs had been established.[20] These early clubs varied in what they offered boys – from food and games to drama and singing – but all intended to develop and channel boys' "natural" spirits and monitor their peer culture. These early clubs were based on a commitment to environmentalism and the centrality of play to childhood. By carefully manipulating youth's environment (including constructive play and competitive sports), reformers believed, boys could follow a productive path. The YMCAs emerged in North America in the 1850s and experienced dramatic growth in the closing decades of the nineteenth century. Begun as Protestant centres to provide lodging and homosociality for unmarried working men, the "Y" would become an important site for the promotion of masculine athleticism by the turn of the century.

In turn-of-the-century Canada, Protestant churches were especially active in developing and supporting boy work as an antidote to secularization and its foreshadowing of national decline. With dwindling numbers in Sunday schools, Anglican, Methodist, and Presbyterian churches supported the club movement for boys' spiritual enrichment and inoculation against the feminization of religious practice.[21] Programs emphasized outdoor life, recreation, and masculine development in increasingly non-denominational settings. By the interwar period formal Protestant churches in Canada supported the endeavours of the new clubs and programs for boys and girls, in the guise of Scouts, Girl Guides, and the Young Men's and Women's Christian Associations.

Most of these organizations promoted natural surroundings and/ or militarism as ideal contexts for character development. These clubs' purpose was to instill the middle-class virtues of self-reliance, patriotism, and manly duty, all the while focusing on proper development of the male body. Clubs like the Boys' Brigades (founded in 1890 in the United States and subsequently spreading to Canada),[22] and the Sons of Daniel Boone (founded 1905), exemplify the orientation toward military training and outdoorsmanship, respectively, and these emphases were brought together in the enduring British-originating Boy Scouts (brought to Canada in 1908 and the US in 1910).

The Boy Scouts of America organized eleven- to seventeen-year-old boys into patrols and set out to teach them lessons in moral living and patriotic masculinity. English Canadian boys were brought up in a culture saturated with moral and gendered imperatives around British imperial military "adventure" that were delivered in schools, literature, clubs, and through games.[23] The Boy Scout movement in both English and French Canada became an important socializing agent for respective nation-building and maturation projects that insisted on historically contingent notions of masculinity imbued with religious and racial imperatives. In French Canada, the Boy Scouts movement substituted British imperialism for a sense of pride in the French Canadian nation and Catholic subjectivity, as James Trepanier demonstrates.[24] With Canada signing on to fight alongside Britain in both world wars, Scouts emphasized military preparedness. Nordstrom, the police officer who opened this chapter, might have found models for his Police Boys' Rifle Club from early scouting in Canada, which followed its founder Robert Baden-Powell's edicts over the importance of shooting, "obeying orders," and preparing for war.[25] The development of the cadets movement at the end of nineteenth century and especially in the early twentieth wed the Canadian militia to schools, further emphasizing the monitoring and militarism of boys' leisure time.

The club movement provided an obvious model for urban police forces to follow in the mid-twentieth century. Another source of inspiration came from prominent contemporary sociologists like Chicago's Clifford Shaw, who developed programs in disadvantaged areas of the city explicitly to transform the context in which boys were growing up and getting into trouble. Shaw helped found the Chicago Area Project (CAP) in the interwar years, a community-based delinquency-prevention experiment that focused on recreation for youth, mediation for gangs, and grass-roots community renewal.[26] The first project was located in the Russell Square area, a European-immigrant area where delinquency and youth gangs attracted the attention of Shaw and his colleagues. Recreation for boys became central to CAP's mission. Street workers set up basketball, football, baseball, and other sports leagues, converted abandoned lots into playgrounds, and aimed to both acknowledge and temper boys' aggression through contact sports like boxing and wrestling.[27] Local boys responded favourably.[28] Although primarily focused on boys, CAP included gender-conformist activities for girls like sewing, handicrafts, and library clubs.[29] CAP was a broad assortment of efforts to improve communities from within. As such, it relied on a community council, local faith institutions, and schools, which helped foster neighbourhood spirit and redirect youth to programs rather than crime.

Early youth clubs and the Chicago Area Project shared an assumption about boy culture that embraced universal boyhood traits. The idea that boys' natural instincts led them to form gangs and perpetuate violence, and that these inclinations could be channelled by organized recreation and sports, attracted the attention of police officers. At the time, this kind of organizing was hailed as a major success, yet its insistence on what sociologists of the time referred to as the "natural groupings" of boys that emphasized cultural sameness had the effect, according to Julia Grant, of "reinforc[ing] pre-existing ethnic and racial boundaries and hostilities."[30] In the case of the YMCAS, most catered predominantly to white boys, but other clubs gathered locals regardless of cultural differences. Subsequently, they became sites of expression for racial, ethnic, and religious tension.[31] And yet this model became a major feature of youth clubs founded by urban police departments.

The Chicago Area Project's apparent success made it a model for anti-delinquency work within urban police forces. Detective-Sergeant Ovila Pelletier of Montreal's youth squad pointed to CAP as a "proven" recipe for quelling juvenile criminality, especially its focus on community involvement and adolescents' "intelligent use of ... spare time."[32] Among other urban police forces, CAP was known for identifying the importance of combatting delinquency before it developed, as well as the idea that youth's natural tendency was to form gangs. In post–Second World War Toronto, men working within their local YMCAS sought out juvenile "gangs" to turn them into clubs. Focusing on areas of the city that appeared to need the most attention due to the evident boy problem, such as Riverdale in the east end, these boy workers brought footballs, hockey sticks, and other recreational aids to distract boys into becoming "better teenagers."[33] Not as comprehensive a program as the CAP and with a shortage of adult workers, these small gestures toward averting delinquency crises employed the basic tenets of boy work by accepting their proclivities for belongingness (expressed in either gang or club membership) and their apparent need for physical activity. The inadequacy of recreational spaces and supervised play provided by social organizations such as the YMCA would lead police commentators to advocate for greater co-operation between those organizations and the police as well as a greater role for the police in such activities as a preventive measure against the rising rates of delinquency.[34]

The youth club movement provided a solid model and intellectual justification for urban police institutions to develop their own clubs, but the crime prevention turn swung that door wide open, as we saw in chapter 1. This new direction and responsibility of law enforcement led the police to participate in boy work. The slogan of the Victoria, British Columbia, Police Boxing Club – "It is better to build boys than to mend men" – captures the spirit and strategy of police work that would spread across northern North America in the 1930s and 1940s.[35]

Cops: Scout Masters and Coaches

Despite the close connection between the boy problem and delinquency, law enforcement came late to "boy work." Through the 1930s, and especially in the 1940s, youth-conscious policing had emerged across North America in the form of police-led recreational and sports clubs. The media, including police publications, regularly lauded this development and heralded individual officers who volunteered with organizations like the Boy Scouts. This movement began in ad hoc fashion at the hands of individual police officers who helped coordinate sports for young people who were perceived to have little access to recreational facilities. By the 1940s, participation in clubs became fundamental to modern policing.

Although individual policemen and women may have volunteered for youth clubs prior to the 1930s, such participation became widely publicized and more formally part of police work as youth bureaus and programs were established in this decade and the next. As crime prevention schemes emerged and became central to the era's approach to juvenile delinquency, individual police officers joined established youth clubs like the Boy Scouts. That organization's aim to help the "boy to become a better man and a good citizen" overlapped with crime prevention goals. Seen as a "supplement" to the home, school, and faith institutions, Boy Scouts focused on character building and offsetting negative environments by "engaging boys' leisure energies in outdoor games and activities."[36] Police organizations noted that the Boy Scouts, like the YMCA youth programs, often served the "non-delinquent" parts of urban areas, meaning they served boys who were "already moralized."[37] Police officers worked with the Boy Scout organization but aimed to extend its reach beyond the already "moralized" areas in order to get to know, and intervene in, delinquent communities and what they termed "underprivileged" youth.

Youth-conscious policing then wed police expertise of delinquency's local geography with principles of boy work. Police Chief Robert Harshaw revealed in a 1937 article for *The Canadian Police Gazette* that his "secret" to quelling youth trouble in Nelson, British Columbia, was "knowing your Boy's [*sic*] in your Community."[38] Boy work in the guise of Boy Scout leadership became central to the police mission in Nelson; Harshaw himself sat on the Executive Council of Nelson and District Boy Scout Association, and one of his constables acted as the local scoutmaster of the Fifth Nelson Troops of Boy Scouts. Across the continent in Bridgeport, Connecticut, the local police force formed their own Boy Scouts troop using police officers and veterans of the US Army as scoutmaster and assistant scoutmaster. In this case, police officers targeted a specific neighbourhood – a "slum," according to the US Housing Authority – that they had identified with a delinquency problem. This neighbourhood was, of course, underserviced by the Scouts and most in need of police attention. Boys were selected for this troop in conjunction with the local schools, where teachers identified boys at risk who would benefit most from a police-led club.[39] Formation of this troop was aimed at marginalized boys growing up in an area already identified by police as productive of delinquency. That it recruited from the local schools suggests that it was not directed at those boys who had already dropped out.

In Toronto, pressing delinquency problems that had arisen during the Depression and revealed in a 1938 Big Brother survey led to its police department establishing the 171st Boy Scout Troup. "Gang leaders" from a local downtown school in an area fed by immigration were the first recruited by Inspector Herbert Bolton. The boys were described as filthy, "lacking in respect for the Union Jack," and "a disorganized mob" with "a chip on its shoulder."[40] Describing the boys as a motley crew connects to their visible cultural and racial otherness: three-quarters of them were

African Canadians (or Americans) and eastern and southern Europeans (from Russia, Turkey, Romania, and Galicia). According to the principal of the Niagara Street Public School, "[i]n sportsmanship, in initiative, and in general deportment, there has been appreciable betterment among most and probably among all the boys of this group."[41] For the boys' part, they saw the establishment of a scout troop as transactional; the boys' attitude was summed up as "What are we going to get, and when do we get it?" By early 1939 thirty-two boys had free uniforms – provided by local businesses – and were praised not only for their leadership qualities but for doing light police work in their neighbourhood.[42]

Cleveland's new youth squad brought both a heightened focus on youth crime and a growing involvement of officers in youth clubs. Soaring juvenile delinquency rates in the 1930s prompted the formation of a new Juvenile Crime Prevention Unit of the Cleveland Police Department at the end of the decade. By the mid-1940s, this youth squad was involved in creating and leading boys' and girls' clubs and athletic organizations. Policemen played scoutmasters in twelve of the city's Boy Scout troops. The Cleveland police were also involved in sponsoring Girl Scouts troops and three ball clubs, and facilitating a summer camp for girls and boys from "underprivileged" areas.[43]

Beyond quelling rising delinquency numbers, the police-led club activities were expected to help form positive relationships between the cops and the kids. In the early 1930s, the New York Police Department (NYPD) reported making inroads into the Flatbush (Brooklyn) Boys' Club. A special event, Police Night, apparently helped to convince young people that local policemen were their friends. The NYPD showed up with its band and Glee Club,[44] with the evening's program including drills, calisthenics, jiu jitsu, and boxing. It also gave Deputy Commissioner Henrietta Additon an opportunity to lecture boys on crime prevention.

By the 1940s police-led recreational clubs and activities had gained great momentum across North America. Police organizations were motivated to replace youth's leisure hours spent in spontaneous (read disorderly) street play and to extricate youth from "pirate dens" (makeshift clubhouses that allegedly bred petty criminality).[45] Embracing a leadership role in youth clubs and in organizing sports activities gave officers a chance to reinforce a new set of rules about not just fair play but also a code of liberal morality. In their self-studies of effectiveness, police organizations found they were succeeding. In 1940, a report issued by the International Association of Chiefs of Police's Crime Prevention and Juvenile Delinquency Committee boasted that police involvement in youth clubs had dealt a blow to juvenile delinquency. The report correlated the progress made in delinquency reduction with police involvement in youth clubs in 150 American cities; of those, clearly one-third were entirely conducted or supervised by police officers.[46] Thus by the time the Second World War was underway and delinquency panics dominated the narrative of home-front youth behaviour, police involvement in the Boy Scouts, boys' and girls' clubs, and the like, had become an accepted and recognized part of law enforcement's approach to delinquency.

A "Pal" to Youth: New York City's Police Athletic League

New York City's Police Athletic League (PAL) is likely the best-known and longest-running crime prevention program directed at youth in North America. This initiative followed the establishment in 1930 of an official Crime Prevention Bureau (CPB) and its embrace, at least superficially, of the child-study movement and police-led sports activities.[47] The Crime Prevention Bureau produced the Juvenile Aid Bureau (JAB) in 1935, and in 1936, its youth recreation wing officially became PAL. A dedicated office in the NYPD amenable to the crime prevention turn in policing is largely responsible for the establishment of PAL; as told by PAL officers and contemporary observers, its story is more sentimental, conjuring the kind-heartedness and initiative of empathic individuals on the force who were committed to neighbourhood children.

The official implementation of a PAL network – across Manhattan, the Bronx, Staten Island, Brooklyn, and Queens – in the 1930s marked the culmination of earlier efforts to resolve the delinquency problem with ad hoc sports solutions. Antecedents included the temporary Junior Police program of the 1910s that conscripted youth into mimicking police hierarchy while providing games and military drill exercises to occupy them. In the same decade, safety concerns about children playing in the streets inspired Police Commissioner Arthur Woods to help develop the "play streets" movement. Focusing on areas with especially high residential density and little green or communal space, such as the area below 14th Street, Woods advocated closing one hundred city blocks to traffic during the summer of 1916 to give children a place to play: "The children … have simply got to be taken care of … the sooner we get them off the streets and out from under the wheels of vehicles just so soon will the street accidents begin to go down."[48] But safety was just one part of the urgency surrounding play streets; they also served to organize young people's play in specific areas under constant supervision, so that they would avoid getting into trouble, and helped "reduce tensions between police officers and youth."[49] Working with the Parks and Playgrounds and Neighborhood Associations, the commissioner helped to spark a movement that would become central to the Police Athletic League's mission. For its part, the NYPD claimed to be addressing the needs of disadvantaged children by providing structured play.

PAL was officially recognized in 1936 but its clubs date to the early 1930s. Its origins in that decade lay in the makeshift innovations at the hands of crime prevention officers. The NYPD annual reports are full of stories in which destructive juvenile gangs were successfully redirected to church basements, community centres, and formerly vacant lots for supervised recreation and old habits gave way to a new competitive spirit that was channelled through sports.[50] In the early 1930s, a crime prevention officer led the way to creating a sports league for boys in his precinct. He observed that boys who had little access to proper recreation played ball in the street, "breaking windows, shooting craps on street corners, maintaining pirate dens in vacant houses and otherwise making a nuisance of themselves."[51] The officer came up with the idea that the boys simply needed an alternative, so he organized them into a Twilight Baseball League with eight teams. He solicited equipment, a field, and materials from local businesses and organizations, all of which seemed happy to participate in this community effort to get the kids off the streets. They contributed dirt for the field and lumber for the seats, and a local newspaper agreed to publish the scores. With a large group of captive boys, the police officer didn't just play ball. He took the opportunity to lecture the kids about self-care and proper behaviour, brought in community faith leaders to address issues of morality and religion, and called on businessmen to give job advice.[52] This first year ended triumphantly with the championship game played at Ebbets Field, home to the Brooklyn Dodgers. This initiative took on a kind of lore – a lone police officer does right by the kids in his neighbourhood and becomes the mortar that holds the working-class community together and leads it to Ebbets Field, all the while combatting delinquency without bullying or formal correction tactics.

This 1930s origins story does several things very well. It reveals the aims, purpose, and success of police-led athletic clubs, it shows how big-hearted and creative the ordinary patrolmen could be, and it demonstrates how police (as opposed to sociologists, church leaders, and social reformers) could effect positive community change.[53] This involved condemning youthful self-directed leisure as "misdirected play" and as easily replaceable by supervised sports.[54] PAL's history tends to revolve around the actions of patrolmen who wanted to both fill the desperate need for leisure activities in "marginal and transitional" areas of New York City and to bring order to restless urban youth on their beats. Confronting a situation in which youth's homes were "crowded and disorganized," which forced them into poolrooms and onto the street, policemen sought to challenge youth's presence in public and spatially manage them. Starting in 1933, Police Commissioner Mulrooney further brought youth into the police sphere by offering them membership cards in a ritualized celebration of the close fraternity of children and police.[55] As an argument and advertisement for police community action with youth, the origins narrative helped recreation in the form of PAL to become a feature in crime prevention programs.

The elaborate recreation program of JAB's PAL reflected contemporary expertise on the importance of the child's environment as a measure for future success and was also a product of its time. Those "transitional" areas of New York City in which children had few or no public spaces in which to play besides the streets were signs of economic depression and social dislocation. Neglected by municipal administrations, these communities were dotted with abandoned buildings and lots rather than playgrounds and parks. High unemployment of boys, according to Henrietta Additon, deputy police commissioner and head of the Crime Prevention Bureau from 1931 to 1934, caused them to "congregate on street corners ... [and] drift into delinquency."[56] Associating these neglected and impoverished areas with incipient delinquency was an effective strategy for reform. In 1936, the year that the PAL was officially formed, 520 workers hired through the Works Progress Administration (a New Deal agency that focused on public works projects) turned vacant lots and buildings into recreational sites for youth.[57] That year, PAL boasted seventy-seven summer and forty-four winter recreation centres and "play streets," nine field days, fifteen outdoor boxing shows, and eight sports tournaments involving hundreds of teams.[58] Over the course of the late 1930s, all of these numbers would swell.[59] By 1940, fourteen youth centres (four in Manhattan, eight in Brooklyn, one in the Bronx, and one in Staten Island) had been opened and named after fallen police officers. This practice of memorializing police officers did double duty in paying tribute to officers in their districts and reminding youth of sacrifice and honour. In an era when the city was financially strapped, it was critical that PAL programs be cost-neutral; private funding and volunteer labour were critical to its success. The Education and Recreation Departments of the Works Progress Administration supplied personnel until 1942, when those workers were replaced by paid recreation employees.[60]

If self-reported numbers can be relied upon, the demand for PAL opportunities was extremely high. Youth heard about the programs from police officers on local radio stations like WNYC and WBNX, and PAL representatives eventually made appearances on television shows.[61] Publicity stunts, like the balloon drop from the Empire State Building announcing PAL Week in 1936 featuring heavy weight champion Jack Dempsey and New York Governor Alfred E. Smith, helped to capture city-wide attention.[62] The helium-filled balloons were filled with a free membership card, saving the lucky recipient the ten-cent fee. Governor Smith took the opportunity to reflect on his youth – a time when the "waterfront was the only place where youngsters could find recreation" – and to commend the police for deterring crime by "surrounding boys and girls with recreational activities of a character-building nature."[63] Anyone under the age of twenty-one could join. In its first year, 34,407 took out memberships, with the total number participating at various games reported to be 3,963,673.[64] Within a year, the number of memberships had doubled to 74,281; by the end of the 1940s, 300,000 boys and girls were card-carrying members and had signed up for organized "fun."[65] Young people were especially drawn to the sports, from baseball to paddle tennis, but also to the list of recreational clubs: arts and crafts, aquatics, dancing, dramatics, lectures and discussion, library, motion pictures, nature study, music, newspaper, quiet games, storytelling, street games, and so forth.[66] The play streets remained especially popular in summer with the street "showers," when the fire hydrants were turned on and streets closed to traffic.[67]

Through PAL, police work with children expanded. In 1938, Fox Lair, the PAL camp for "underprivileged" boys of New York City opened. Each year, hundreds of boys attended camp for over three weeks, although the camp was suspended during the war. In 1947, it moved to the Adirondacks with an explicit program of rehabilitating and rescuing youth. Each year, a Police Athletic League Day brought thousands of children to a sponsored event at Coney Island amusement park, and countless youth attended professional baseball and hockey games as well as circus and rodeo shows for free. The police ran radio programs directed at young people, who were given opportunities to participate on air and gain instruction in performance and the technical aspects of broadcasting.

Through its recreation wing, the Police Athletic League, the JAB aspired to greater breadth by "reaching nearly all children" with elaborate sports and leisure programs.[68] Although much of the focus was on boys' sports teams, girls also had access to basketball teams, swimming lessons, and the like.[69] In 1936, five hundred girls participated in a field day at Central Park.[70] In the self-reporting on PAL programs, race is conspicuously absent; in fact, Police Commissioner Arthur W. Wallander publicly insisted in 1946 that no race or colour lines were drawn in PAL's activities.[71] The images of children enjoying PAL activities, which were meant to be advertisements for fundraising, suggest that a racially diverse group of youths partook.

The fact was, PAL simply did not reach all neighbourhoods. In 1939, PAL opened the Robert H. Holmes Youth Center in Harlem, named for the first black patrolmen to be killed in the line of duty.[72] Through the 1940s, studies of rising juvenile delinquency rates, youth gangs, and racial tension revealed that inadequate recreational facilities for youth persisted in the most transitional and poor communities. The Bedford-Stuyvesant area of Brooklyn (with a majority African American population), "Little Spain" (a Puerto Rican area of East Harlem), and the increasingly Puerto Rican Boulevard-Prospect area of Bronx, for example, experienced higher delinquency rates, more policing, and a dearth of PAL sites in the 1940s, despite the organization's million-dollar fundraising campaign.[73]

Evidence of PAL's success in subverting delinquency is anecdotal. The police reported, for example, that boy gangs – mostly petty thieves caught stealing fruit or robbing vending machines – were steered into boys' clubs, "where they had the use of a swimming pool, gymnasium, playroom, and a library," and were supervised by a crime prevention officer. In the case of the young gang members who stole from vending machines in order to afford the movies, the crime prevention officer regaled them with cautionary tales of what happens to boys "who go in for a life of crime." This officer taught them jujitsu and, apparently, convinced them to want to be policemen when they grew up.[74] Aware that youth were attracted to the PAL initiative for its "entertainment value" in the absence of alternatives, the JAB insisted that its actual success lay in being a "long range weapon leveled at delinquency."[75] Despite the rise in youth crime and gangs in the 1950s, the adage that recreation facilities would prevent crime persisted and, in fact, became all the more entrenched, with the exception of some high-profile doubters. In 1944, Mayor Fiorello La Guardia railed against the idea that recreational centres for youth could solve the city's delinquency problem, accusing parents of not doing their jobs in raising their children.[76]

PAL began in the high-delinquency precincts of the city in the 1930s, but by the 1940s its community centres and programs covered the city, with important exceptions as noted above. The PAL remained a central part of the JAB, although it was separately incorporated in 1945 with a board representing government, industry, labour, and professional interests. It grew in these decades with the benefit of donations and small membership dues. In 1948, it started publishing a newspaper, *The Pal*, originated by the PAL Youth Council, an organization that represented all youth centres.[77] In 1949, it signed on volunteer doctors to provide medical examinations for all boys and girls belonging to the youth centres, and a dental unit was organized the following year.[78] By the early 1950s, PAL looked like a social service agency designed for, in NYPD Commissioner William O'Brien's words, "every underprivileged child [in the city]."[79] However, their definition of "underprivileged" closely resembled that of "troubled" kids. From the beginning, the JAB used PAL as a destination for those kids who ended up on its "trouble list" of wayward youth who showed "tendencies" toward delinquency.[80] The baseball league expanded beyond sports to include a wide range of physical activity and leisure pursuits and had a presence in youth centres throughout the city. While directed mostly at boys, who were seen as the main instigators of trouble, PAL programming continued to attempt to attract girls, too. PAL officers would brag that hundreds of thousands of boys and girls experienced "wholesome play" under "proper supervision."[81] Through the late twentieth century PAL continued its "beat on the streets"; an example of the delinquency prevention–supervision nexus is the establishment in the 1970s of the American Double Dutch (skipping) League by African American officers who sought to regulate black girls' verbal and physical play by making it an "authentic sport for girls."[82] In the early postwar years PAL had become a model for other cities to follow; it was a major player in the Inter-City Police Committee on Youth Activities – a site for the exchange of information on pre-delinquency work, the PAL method, and organizing inter-city sports tournaments that would continue to this day.[83]

Montreal's Police Juvenile Club

In early August 1955, Trans-Canada Air Lines marked the occasion of its new Montreal–New York City route by facilitating an international exchange of boy members of the cities' police athletic clubs. Acting as ambassadors of the Montreal Police Juvenile Club (PJC), five Montreal boys flew to New York City to meet five members of the New York City PAL, who then returned to Montreal with them. Accompanied by PJC head Ovila Pelletier and Deputy Police Director Pacifique Plante, the Montrealers spent two days in the city, meeting the mayor and the police commissioner and visiting the United Nations, Coney Island, and the Empire State Building. Photographed next to the new turbo-prop plane for the publicity stunt, the Montreal boys were impeccably dressed in their gold and blue police juvenile club sweaters. The boys were chosen for their good behaviour, demonstration of leadership, and sports acumen, and for embodying disciplined adolescence in an era known for high delinquency. The Canadian press focused on the only boy of colour in the Canadian contingent, thirteen-year-old Randy, who claimed the "biggest thrill was visiting the United Nations."[84] Membership clearly had its privileges, especially for these boys. The story of international "trade" in boys' club members formed part of an enduring counternarrative to alleged ungovernable postwar delinquents and the equally ignominious Montreal Police Morality Squad.

As the police athletic club exchange of 1955 suggests, Montreal paralleled New York City's efforts by using sports as a means to prevent delinquency. Unlike New York City, which was more circumspect about such efforts to reduce juvenile crime, Montrealers were relatively uncategorical about the police club's great success in reducing delinquency. As we saw in chapter 2, during the Depression a radical shift in rhetoric (followed by practice) targeted not simply delinquency but latent juvenile criminality. Focusing on pre-delinquents, as they were sometimes called, the Montreal youth squad proposed schemes to reach marginalized youth, by teaching them to respect authority, to reject delinquency, and to exercise their idle minds and bodies. This multi-pronged approach involved greater surveillance of youth hangouts, a centralized citywide program for the administration of arrested juveniles, and a new network of police clubs for youth.

It was the sports solution to the problem of wayward kids in the guise of the Police Juvenile Club that became the pièce de résistance of Montreal's youth-conscious policing. As Pelletier remarked in 1949, "boys are in prison today because we did not have these clubs [before now]."[85] Ovila Pelletier started the Police Juvenile Club of Montreal in 1947, likely benefiting from the earlier US examples and conceptual-ized from the start as a broad network of clubs and athletic activities run by the police youth squad and supported by public fundraising efforts. The clubs would be non-denominational but include strong spiritual and moral messages. These groups put boys in direct regular contact with young athletic male officers, putative paragons of public spiritedness and moral fortitude. According to the press, Montreal's declining delinquency rates in the 1940s resulted from this substantive and innovative program.

Pelletier told the origins story this way. One day, three boys were arrested for stealing sports equipment from a department store. Since the youngsters were first offenders and had stolen the items in order to play hockey, Detective-Captain Pelletier took a special interest in their case. He was concerned that they were being brought up in large families that could ill afford to provide them with what he considered responsible and healthy leisure pursuits, much less expensive sports equipment. Pelletier decided to take these boys under his wing and redefine them not as a gang of thieves, but as a hockey team. In 1945, the youth squad began an experiment: gather seventy-five boys "from the streets," known for their stubbornness and resistance to rules, and make a sports club. Over the course of twelve months, only one boy slid back to his old ways; the rest were reformed.[86] With these astonishing results, Pelletier approached the Police Athletic League for recruits to help broaden the club.[87] Channelling boys' excess energy had long been a goal of community boxing clubs and the like; now the police offered similar opportunities. This "sports solution" demanded a high degree of child deference to police (such as a willingness to wear police colours rather than gang colours), acquiescence and acceptance of the hierarchy of power and authority, and undoubtedly coercion.

Motivation for the clubs came from the context of high wartime delinquency. Between 1941 and 1944, the number of juvenile delinquency cases rose 45 per cent, and almost a fifth of those incarcerated in the city jails were juvenile delinquents, a scandalous fact that Ovila Pelletier would later use when raising money for his PJC.[88] These crime statistics suggested to observers that during wartime youth was both out of control and more policed, yet the discourse concerning juvenile delinquency in the immediate postwar period emphasized the need for compassion and prevention strategies. Police involvement in boys' leisure activities in Montreal was heralded as the panacea to the wartime rise in juvenile delinquency. It also reflected a broad shift in attitude toward the treatment of minor delinquent acts from severe punishment to rehabilitation. Delinquents became "innocent victims" of the times and of their parents. One 1950 publication argued that all kinds of homes produced wayward children, for in "good homes" they are indulged and treated severely, and in impoverished ones, the overcrowding, exposure to drink, "sexual anomalies," and "absence of faith and Christian principles" resulted in maladjusted youth.[89]

To combat delinquency, the authors of the *Montreal Police Juvenile Guide* advocated character building through organized leisure activities, especially physical training and sports, a position reminiscent of earlier discourses: sports and games "create good habits of energy, courage, good will, that will remain through all the life."[90] A variety of opportunities existed for city youth to become active: the municipal playgrounds programs in the city parks, the Boy Scouts and Girl Guides programs, and boys' clubs, for example. Participation kept both boys and girls busy so "evil desires have no chance to germinate ... their moral [*sic*] is high and their body develops normally."[91] Sports were similarly expected to foster teamwork and eliminate class and cultural differences that drove youth animosities off the playing field. Using hockey as a prime example, the *Guide* tells the story of Roland, who, in playing a game, wants to score not only for himself. He has learned to be a "true sportsman," with self-control and "to work unselfishly for the benefit of the team," so he passes to Peter and they share the victory.[92] It was the PJC's goal of teaching respect for authority and discipline that made it popular with police agencies and the community.

The establishment of PJCs in 1947 added another layer of organized youth leisure to the city's offerings. Many of the city's youth clubs were parish-based or denominationally organized and arranged along linguistic and religious lines (for example, the YW/YMCAs and Catholic or parish youth groups). The PJC stands out in Montreal for initiating recruitment of members regardless of religion or language.[93] The secular programs offered a new site for boys' socialization where boys would learn to trust each other and police officers. Ovila Pelletier hoped to foster "better understanding between youngsters and policemen" and to get boys to ally themselves with the force.[94]

Scattered around the city, the PJC provided boys aged ten to seventeen years of age with leisure-time activities, especially the opportunity to play on hockey, volleyball, basketball, and softball teams.[95] In the summer, the PJC operated softball teams that participated in the city parks leagues. Policemen volunteered as coaches for volleyball, track and field, football, and rugby. Under the supervision of policemen, it was hoped that team members would gain guidance and instruction in these sports, embrace team spirit, and at the same time develop a sound appreciation of the friendly neighbourhood policeman. Free equipment was issued, although boys playing hockey had to purchase a team sweater that sported the Police Juvenile Club logo and the Montreal Police Department flag.

By 1949, there were an astonishing 42,000 members of the PJC; by 1954 the PJC comprised 80,000 members.[96] That year, there were 160 teams, including football, volleyball, basketball, and hockey as well as classes in boxing, self defence, and music. In an attempt to keep boys' leisure hours structured, membership included free admission to professional sporting events. In the late 1940s, as many as 10,000 kids annually attended Montreal Royals (baseball) games for free as members of the PJC. After almost fifteen years, Julien White of the Delinquency Bureau reported that the PJC ran 548 sports teams with 9,638 players. These included 196 hockey clubs with 3,528 players, 182 baseball clubs with 3,276 players, 86 softball clubs with 1,548 players, 40 floor hockey clubs with 600 players, 23 basketball clubs with 345 players, 12 lacrosse clubs with 216 players, 5 football clubs with 125 players, and 4 volleyball clubs with 60 players.[97]

The sports solution was an expensive proposition and required both popularity with youth and acceptance from the public. An executive committee of the PJC included members of the bench, a mayor, the police chief, and one of the city's most important entrepreneurial leaders, John Molson.[98] Fundraising therefore became a central part of the PJC's mission. Sports equipment and venues were costly, but so were delinquency and criminality.[99] In 1949, Pelletier launched his ambitious $125,000 fundraiser for his city-wide club system.[100] While he failed to reach that amount, he did raise $72,000 and free radio spots. The fact that boys wanted to play sports and the Juvenile Morality Squad under Pelletier had a solid reputation in the press helped the fundraising campaigns. Eventually, it would become an independent corporation under the Delinquency Prevention Bureau.[101]

Young people obtained admission to the PJC through free but mandatory membership. Boys were solicited to join Police Juvenile Clubs through radio broadcasts in both English and French and by word of mouth and visit their local police station for membership cards. Membership demanded that the boy or girl take a pledge to "be a good sportsman and be at all times a good law-abiding citizen."[102] Membership required that the young behave "honourably"; failure to follow the honour code could result in the retraction of membership. A juvenile court appearance was another cause for membership cancellation.

Through the PJC the police focused on making the point that staying out of trouble had its rewards. Boys were also offered membership as an alternative to juvenile justice measures. Reporting from the streets of Montreal, a Swiss newspaper ran the story of a gang leader called Archie. This youth and his band of "little rascals" attacked a corner grocery store, smashing the front window. At the sight and sound of breaking glass Archie fled the scene, only to be stopped in his tracks by a police officer. According to the photo story, this officer did not take him to a cell but rather to a "welcoming place" where there were boys his own age. Rather than prison or even a scolding, gang leader Archie was given a membership card to the Police Club for Boys.[103]

Despite its disciplinary function, the Montreal Police Juvenile Club was also an expression of 1950s liberal democratic values. The discursive framing of the Club's goals – training for citizenship through popular recreational participation, removing the material and financial barriers to organized sport, and promoting egalitarianism and ethnic and religious inclusivity – speaks to its liberal values and the emerging welfare-state context.[104] As Shirley Tillotson's study of the public recreation movement in post–Second World War Ontario illustrates, state-funded recreation in the 1950s aimed "to develop a subjectivity that encompassed both a submission to the constraints required of a liberal citizen (tolerance, avoiding violence) and also a passion for participation in community life."[105] Achieving and maintaining membership in the PJC was meant to produce a sense of belonging to youths who had suffered during wartime and the early postwar disruptions.

In practice, the PJC was popular but exclusionary. First, it barred membership for youth who were in conflict with the law – those who had been arrested and convicted under the Juvenile Delinquents Act. In the self-promotional coverage of the clubs and boy work, emphasis was placed on bringing together French- and English-speaking boys as a way to communicate the clubs' powerful approach to what was described as racial harmony. Longtime "racial" tensions referred to the antipathy between French Catholics and English Canadians. Because the PJC was non-denominational, Pelletier and others argued, it functioned as a bridge between the two solitudes. Boys of colour were not featured in the visual and textual coverage and promotion of the PJC, except in the rare case of Randy, the boy who was selected for the exchange with the New York City PAL. Montreal's large allophone communities (those whose first language was neither French nor English) were also under-represented in the news stories and promotional materials about saving youth with sports. Jewish, Italian, and Polish youth from the working-class areas of the city may have readily played sports, choosing to identify with one of the two major language groups and allowing their ethnic difference to fade. In the 1960s, the chief of police who let the PJC decline argued that "traditional" groups of youth shunned marginalized members, suggesting that race and cultural difference were policed by the boys themselves.[106]

Because male delinquency dwarfed female cases by about five to one, the focus on girls' participation in athletic activities was muted, although not absent. The *Montreal Police Juvenile Guide* insisted that keeping girls' leisure hours organized was also essential to producing good citizens. Swimming was highly recommended for being "feminine," while tennis and volleyball benefited the girl by improving her health and constitution.[107] The vast majority of money and effort was directed at traditional sports and male leagues – football, hockey, soccer, and basketball.

Nonetheless, the PJC experiment was judged a great success in the media. The press was particularly impressed with the idea that the PJC allowed boys to play their "favourite" sports for free and that club membership helped form good citizens, taught respect for authority, and relieved intercultural tensions of Montreal youth – among French, English, Catholics and Protestants.[108]

Boys themselves were likely attracted to the PJC because it meant access to spectator sporting events as well as participatory team sports. Thousands of youths, for example, received free admission with their cards to see the Montreal Royals baseball team at the Delorimier Street Stadium or to the Montreal Forum to see hockey games. Clarifying children's responses to the emergence and expansion of child-friendly policing and the municipal forces' "good works" with youth is vexing. The degree to which they absorbed the overall message about police being new friends remains for further research. Certainly, Ovila Pelletier made big claims about its success, which was broadcast widely, including a 1954 National Film Board short on the Juvenile Clubs for Boys.

The sports solution drew some criticism. In late 1948, the umbrella organization Montreal Council of Social Agencies (MCSA) took note of the police organization's advances into the field of juvenile delinquency prevention. Since 1921 this agency had been concerned with studying and alleviating Montreal's social problems, including delinquency. A number of representatives of welfare agencies in the city petitioned the MCSA to examine the efficacy and value of the Juvenile Delinquency Prevention Bureau, especially its Police Juvenile Club. While undoubtedly biased as a source, the report on the Delinquency Bureau does provide us with some interesting details about, and limitations of, the practice of delinquency preventive programs.[109]

The MCSA's report was the result of "careful study" of police work and "correspondence with leading authorities in United States welfare organizations."[110] Concerning the "tours of inspection," the report stressed the vital role played by the police in making rounds through adolescent hangouts. The street patrol also seemed to conform to the role the police were supposed to be playing in making sure youth obey municipal regulations. This work apparently led to a decline in the number of youths coming before the juvenile court, "allowing the time of the Judges and the Juvenile Court staff to be spent on more serious cases."[111]

The Juvenile Morality Squad's role in making decisions about whether to take a child home or to the court gained a negative review from the report writers and the city's juvenile court. The problem, as the social agencies saw it, was that a minor offence could mask a larger familial or social problem in the home, one that the officers were not equipped to see. These cases required "an expert" in child psychology.[112] The report took issue with the JMS's assertion that its officers were handling cases more effectively than the juvenile court, and by implication its cast of experts. The Police Juvenile Clubs were also not given a positive review. Too often the boys were encouraged to develop a taste for spectator sports where there was little supervision. The report writers estimated that while the clubs had thousands of members, only five hundred to six hundred boys actually participated in physical activity. As well, the literature from across the United States (Boys' Clubs of America, National Probation and Parole Association) on the issue suggested that the police clubs for boys duplicated already established sporting clubs and gymnasiums. Perhaps the most telling critique was the report's claim that police were in fact not equipped for such prevention work because they were not social workers.

Ultimately Pelletier and his colleagues prevailed in the media. With numbers of delinquents declining in the late 1940s and into the 1950s, it appeared that the police were doing their job in creative fashion. Despite the social agency's concerns about the new directions of policing in the late 1940s, the Prevention Bureau continued with its mandate. It enlisted the media to advance its position. In 1954, the National Film Board of Canada's weekly television series, *On the Spot*, featured an episode on the Montreal Police Juvenile Clubs. In this news short, Pelletier proudly demonstrates how his PJC had quelled the "serious and tragic problem" of juvenile delinquency. Replete with images of boys happily focused on table tennis, volleyball games, and the like, the uncritical documentary provides ample evidence of the success of the police in preventive care for children Essentially, disciplined white youth eagerly tell the interviewer that the sports solution worked.

When Detective Inspector Ovila Pelletier died in 1958, he was honoured for his work with youth. Within a few years, he would be memorialized in ways that directly connected to the PJC experiment

4.1   Parc Ovila Pelletier. Photo by author.

(see figure 4.1). Each year a trophy in his name was awarded to civic-minded girls and boys.[113] The PJC did not last a decade after Pelletier's death. In 1965, the process to dismantle Pelletier's legacy began as the city administration set up a Parks Department and a reorganized youth section of the police force embarked on a new approach to policing youth. *La Presse* reported that, with the end of the PJC, Montreal would see the end of a positive force in the city, in which those less fortunate got to play sports and learn to "become men and good citizens."[114]

Conclusion

Following the Second World War, boys' "promiscuous shooting" of small-bore rifles presented "a difficult and perplexing problem" for North American communities and especially for police departments. Rifles in the hands of "uninformed and untrained juveniles" amounted to an "extremely dangerous situation," according to a 1952 report in the *Police Chief News*. Some jurisdictions were rife with juvenile shooting accidents, including fatalities; yet confiscation was pointless, given the high demand for and ready supply of guns. Such a situation had prompted the Maryland State legislature to present "drastic" firearms bills that, according to Chief of Police Marcus H. Miles of Sparrows Point, Maryland, would be "bad, in that they will forbid all firearms to the public."[115] Rather than clear the streets of firearms, Police Chief Marcus thought it better to educate youth about proper respect for and handling of weaponry. In collaboration with the local YMCA and Boy Scouts, this local Maryland police department offered rifle instruction at police facilities, employing police as instructors. Rifles and ammunition were secured from the US Army, as were charters for a Junior Club from the National Rifle Association of America. By 1952, the Sparrows Point Police Department ran eight rifle clubs with more than three hundred boys in training. Over the course of the five years of the clubs' operations, Chief Miles bragged, promiscuous shooting had disappeared, no club boy had been found delinquent, and relations between the police and youth had "never been better." He pointed to how some youthful graduates demonstrated the connection between club membership, rifle instruction, and citizenship by signing up for the armed services and serving their country.

Predicated on environmentalist ideas, crime prevention programs like PAL and PJC were designed to provide young people with alternatives to unsupervised street play. The PAL system was first and foremost a crime prevention scheme that was directed at incipient criminality and criminals, or young people whose lack of access to "proper" recreation made them vulnerable to anti-social behaviour. The notion that sports and leisure activities could have a remedial effect on latent delinquency held powerful currency in the early twentieth century.

Playing coach to youth was readily accepted as an effective police strategy. A *Canadian Police Gazette* reporter noted what had become axiomatic in the mid-twentieth century: "Much of the juvenile delinquency problem would be eliminated in most cities if the police officers and the youth ... were closer friends."[116] What better way to become friends? Police-led clubs focusing on skill development, such as rifle shooting, and especially sports and recreational activities became sites for "breaking down barriers between the kids and the police." Young people and their apparent need for recreational engagement allowed the police to reinvent themselves as central to citizenship campaigns and to counter the negative images polices held surrounding corruption and abuse of power.

Some boys undoubtedly benefited from police efforts to offer them the possibility of learning and playing a sport. Happy, white, sporty youth played well in the media. Boys who fought each other over cultural divides on the streets found a positive outlet for aggression on the hockey rink. The generation that came of age at mid-century might have embraced Pelletier's idea that cops are not to be feared or reviled but looked up to, and they may have given up unsupervised street culture in exchange for a spot on a team. Yet some of these youths were likely more instrumental than that would suggest, bending police rules in order to both play sports and foster a commitment to peer group that existed by its own rules. The PJC may have facilitated youth gang cohesion by excluding some and by the obvious overrepresentation of white boys in the clubs' work.

CHAPTER FIVE

Traffic Tragedies:
Police, Children, and Safety
in the Age of Automobility

In the midst of a public panic over the apparent rise in child sex slayings in 1956, Toronto's police chief relativized children's vulnerability. Since 1928, Chief Constable John Chisholm claimed, Toronto had experienced *only three* child sex murders. The heinous nature of these crimes had exaggerated the actual threat posed to children, he observed, obscuring a more common and persistent hazard to childhood: the traffic accident. Over those same twenty-eight years, 350 children had died on the city's streets in tragic encounters with cars, trollies, and trucks.[1] In the postwar era, the Canadian media declared accidents the "greatest child killer of them all": every year some two thousand Canadian children under fifteen years of age were killed "accidentally" by automobiles.[2] Chisholm had reason to know these numbers because traffic accidents during the golden age of the car had become a far too common feature at the intersection of police work and baby-boom childhood. Urban police forces, long involved in enforcing traffic laws and responsible for forensic accident investigation, dramatically expanded their roles beyond regulation and control of automobiles toward educating potential victims. This educational function helped establish law enforcement firmly in childhood, the safety apparatus of modern cities, and, not coincidentally, in North American schools.

The automotive revolution that transformed North American society in the early twentieth century has been the subject of scholarly debate for decades. While arguments persist about the nature and implications of automotive society, most agree that the automobile ignited a profound social, cultural, and physical transformation of cities and the surrounding countryside.³ Such widespread and thorough change had many unintended consequences. including the reordering of the relationship between children and law enforcement. Childhood and policing were fundamentally altered by the rise of car culture, and by the middle decades of the twentieth century the car accident imbricated the two in unprecedented fashion.

The perils of motorized society presented the police with an opportunity to recast its relationship to youth. The need to curb the rise in automobile-related child accidents drew police into the spaces of childhood and the creation of new subjectivities, including the "traffic officer" and the "school safety patrols." The focus on the causes of preventable child death helped put local police forces in a positive light. Rather than simply being an instrument of discipline and correction, law enforcement now also promised to keep young lives safe. By undertaking their new role in the safety industry, police officers helped identify the victims of accidents – children – as the source for their prevention. In exchange for safety, wisdom, and protection from injury and possibly death, police expected children to incorporate the rules and regulations governing public space, accept that roads were for cars, and develop a new respect for the law. Becoming part of the solution to the traffic problem gave children access to a mid-century citizenship that involved preparedness, obedience to authority, and conformity to automobility.

At mid-century, traffic safety campaigns pointed to the high cost and folly of children's inability to comprehend the risks associated with roads and cars, and municipal police forces redoubled their efforts to rectify the problem. Equipped with the stories and statistics of child accidents, police safety materials offered stern and shocking messages about the hazards of childish imprudence that emphasized the positive role of the policeman as a vital friend to youth.

Local police forces effectively challenged children to prove their competency in the modern world and gave them responsibility to govern themselves. By means of school patrols, a highly organized peer regulation system, children assumed authority over others. Originating in the decades prior to the Second World War, school patrols grew in prominence in the postwar period. Dressed up in uniforms, sporting the accoutrements of authority, and charged with controlling fellow students' behaviour in the streets, safety patrollers became junior traffic cops.

Turning to the middle decades of the twentieth century, this chapter
examines a time when risk was less associated with industrial modernity's newly mechanized world in the shape of trains, trams, and the
workplace, but rather with the school and the streets. As accidents began
to claim more children's lives than diseases, the safety movement rapidly
spread to focus on prevention and children's responsibility. Containment
was sought, although not in the way late twentieth-century parents
would seek it by "demobilizing children" with fenced playgrounds and
chronic chauffeuring.[4] Rather, safety would be accomplished through
peer regulation, surveillance, and an overall intensification of police
presence in schools and childhood. In this particular moment, we see the
police forces continue their attempts to reach children directly through
circumventing or interrupting the parent–child relationship, along with
instilling values and practices that emphasized competency as a key
element of mid-twentieth-century citizenship training for youngsters.[5]

When Streets Became "Plague Grounds": Children and the Rise of the Automobile

Although the twentieth century was optimistically called the Century of
the Child, it could as easily have been named the Century of the Car.[6] As
the century began, the automobile remained a prerogative of the wealthy,
and horse-drawn vehicles dominated urban streets; within a generation, the automobile had put the horse out to pasture and unleashed a
profound transformation of urban society. Numbers hint at the depth
of this dramatic cultural change. For example, in turn-of-the-century
Ontario, registered automobiles numbered in the hundreds; by the end
of the 1920s they totalled in the hundreds of thousands,[7] the horse had
all but disappeared from large centres like Toronto and Montreal.[8] By
mid-century across North America, the middle class had embraced the
automobile, and it increasingly became accessible to and necessary for
working-class families.

The proliferation of automobiles in the early decades of the century
sparked both celebration and rage. For some, passenger vehicles offered
unprecedented freedom and ease of movement, an iconic sign of
technological progress and modernity. Automobiles also made streets
unpredictable and dangerous, however. As it forged a place in urban
North America, the car brutally ran over traditional understandings

and uses of the streets, leaving behind environments ill prepared to accommodate it.[9] Rules of the road that made sense in a non-motorized setting were woefully inadequate for the speed and volume of car traffic. A lack of signage and poorly engineered roads created chaos. In addition to congestion and confusion, motorists maimed and killed pedestrians, passengers, and themselves. In short, as American historian of technology and traffic Peter D. Norton writes, "Old street uses plus new automobiles equaled disaster."[10]

Not only did the automobile destabilize former social constructions of the street, it fostered a crisis in major US centres between 1915 and 1930.[11] The motor death toll climbed steadily each year of the new century, culminating in the 1920s, when automobile accidents took the lives of 200,000 Americans.[12] In much of urban Canada, the pattern was similar; by the 1910s, the streets became a space to be feared as accidents and injuries mounted. In smaller cities like St John's, Newfoundland, this transformation began with the Second World War, when Canadian and US military personnel brought the automobile revolution to the island, causing "traffic problems," or more to the point, a new threat to life and limb.[13] Newfoundlanders were not alone in experiencing the advent of motorized streets as an invasion.

In urban centres across North America, motorists appeared to target pedestrians, especially young ones. In 1924, a Canadian newspaper noted that in a small, industrialized city outside Toronto, 162 children were involved in car accidents over a ten-month period, forcing the editors to wonder if the streets had become "unhealthy plague grounds, a menace to the safety and sanity of child life."[14] In a four-month period during 1925, nineteen Montreal children died in car or truck accidents.[15] In that same year, seven thousand children perished on US streets.[16] Catherine Cournoyer's study of Montreal children involved in accidents in the first half of the century shows that working-class childhood had gained a familiarity with trains and electric tram systems and their inherent dangers.[17]

As the clash between this modern technology and a youthful public created a rising death toll, city dwellers reacted with fear and fury. Newspapers, with their "gothic … tales of evil drivers and innocent pedestrians," underscored the gruesome nature of child death by automobile, helping define the motorist as a modern-day menace.[18] Urban North Americans reacted strongly to motorists' reckless endangerment

of the public. Some argued for the rights of pedestrians to their traditional use of the streets, while others formed vigilante mobs that directly
attacked drivers in the wake of accidents.[19] Montreal parents portrayed
motorized vehicles in their neighborhoods as unwelcome foreigners
snatching life from otherwise healthy children.[20] The press, coroners,
and police heard the indignant voices of bereaved parents attempting
to make sense of these untimely deaths.

With mounting death on the streets, "safety" became a social problem
of considerable magnitude.[21] The safety movement, according to Viviana
Zelizer, was a key marker of the rise of the "sacred child" concept, which
had arisen in the wake of declining infant death rates and the official
end of child labour. As subsequent histories of childhood and childrearing have argued, this new emotional landscape generated heightened
expectations of children's invincibility in the face of disease and the
chaos of urban centres.[22] The pricelessness of children and a growing
intolerance for their preventable deaths spurred the establishment of
National Safety Councils and school programs that emphasized safety
vigilance in the home, school, and on the streets.

Before examining the mid-twentieth-century safety movement to
which urban police forces contributed, we must understand its origins
earlier in the century. The automobile safety problem galvanized an
organized response from associations that had sprung up around other
sites and technologies that imperilled the vulnerable, such as industrial
workers. In early twentieth-century urban centres like New York City
and Montreal, vehicles, including horse-powered ones, trains, streetcars,
trams, and, increasingly, automobiles, annually claimed the lives of
hundreds if not thousands of people, many of them children.[23] In the
US, private street railway companies organized public safety education
initiatives directed at lowering the accident rates involving trains and
trams. The "Safety First" movement of the 1910s built on the pamph-
lets and lectures of these initial campaigns, with Safety Days, Safety
Weeks, and the introduction of safety lessons in school curricula.[24]
The National Safety Council, founded in the US in 1913, for example,
turned to the traffic safety problem late in the decade, launching an
education campaign directed at schoolchildren, teachers, and parents.
The American traffic safety movement in the 1910s featured a collective and public approach to accidental child death; it included broad
educational campaigns in the nation's schools and public memorials

to the "child martyrs" of modernity that sprung up in New York City in the 1920s.[25]

Canadians moved in the same direction. In the 1910s, Arthur Gaboury, of the Montreal Tramways Company, brought together representatives of urban electric transportation companies from across North America to discuss the issue of accidents. From this meeting came a local education campaign aimed at curbing the rise of tramway accidents.[26] Following Gaboury's organizing, the Canadian National Safety League was founded in 1917 and the Quebec Safety League was formally established in 1923, both designed to prevent accidents at work, in the home, and on the streets. Local officials representing police departments, public health offices, city councils, and business elites led safety organizations, which operated with volunteers. Public education consisted of safety lessons distributed through the media with messages to targeted groups, such as schoolchildren. Safety leagues, alongside local police forces, organized North American school patrols in the late 1910s and throughout the interwar period. Decades after his initial safety organizing, Gaboury stated that the success of the campaign proved that it was possible to prevent tramway accidents locally.[27]

In Canada and the US, children learned about traffic safety through the public school system. By the early 1930s, most American schools offered safety instruction; children might also have heard safety messages through radio broadcasts.[28] The central message of these campaigns, delivered on posters, in cartoons, and the like, emphasized the dire consequences of failing to approach the streets with caution. Crude slogans like "Better belated than mutilated," "Slow your pace or lose your face," "Better to see cars than stars," and "Go slow with your feet or be dead meat" similarly warned children of the dangers of everyday life.[29]

Safety league pioneers came to arbitrate the contest over public space that had led to high child traffic casualty rates. While they might have advocated measures that kept automobiles out of children's path, they chose the opposite: to designate the streets too dangerous for children. They amplified the sentiment that streets were being redefined as unacceptable spaces for children. This discourse around children's access to public space incorporated ideas from middle-class reformers, who advocated for playgrounds in the late nineteenth century and sought to "clean" the city streets of working-class and "rough" children. The *Hamilton* (Ontario) *Times* declared in 1918 that "Playgrounds are becoming more a necessity than ever ... [as] the automobile and the motor truck have driven the children off the streets."[30] Urban police forces responded to child traffic deaths and unruliness on the streets by arresting young people, which Zelizer describes as the "criminalization of children's play."[31] In Montreal, where traffic accidents similarly made daily headlines in the interwar period, the city's coroner began to insist that the city take measures to prevent children from playing in the streets, in what Zelizer and Cournoyer call the domestication of childhood.[32] By the 1920s, traffic safety meant the entrenchment of the idea that the street was dangerous and children's presence there was problematic.

By the 1930s, a shift had occurred. Control typified this new paradigm of traffic safety, Norton summarizes, where "pedestrians lost their innocence" and children became responsible for their own safety.[33] For the moment, it appeared that the initial efforts of the traffic safety movement had succeeded, as the US child accident rate declined precipitously. Anger toward the motorist for the 1910s and 1920s slaughter of children receded, and according to some scholars the domestication of childhood had succeeded.[34] Children's right to play in the streets had been challenged by the automobile and the children had lost, in the name of their own protection.

A key part of this new paradigm involved the careful manipulation of the automobile's reputation and place in North American society. Auto manufacturers and automobile clubs, like the American Automobile Association, sought to emphasize the benefits of the car, despite its role in causing injury and death. Highway experts sought to "reconcile safety with speed," suggesting the possibility of eliminating death on the roads.[35] Ford advertisements in Canada called its 1924 model a "modern Magic Carpet" and "friend of childhood" because it could transport young people away from the dangers of the urban street.[36] Automotive interests joined the safety industry in the 1920s, pouring money into promoting the motorcar alongside the dutiful, safety-conscious child. With this interest group entrenched in safety education, gone were safety posters of "limp little corpses." They emphasized, rather, the positive side of rules and regulation.[37]

At the same time, the "moral drama" of the street contest between youngsters and cars no longer presented children as innocents or drivers as culprits. As traffic accidents became part of the daily news, children were blamed and parents held responsible.[38] Much had changed since the Ontario premier argued for pedestrians' rights on the roads in 1910: "It is not the pedestrian who must get out of the way of the automobile[,] but the automobile must get out of the road."[39]

Across North America, the contest over public space would continue. With the sharp rise in the number of children born in the baby boom, cars continued to threaten young people. The domestication of children remained an incomplete ideal that followed the contours of class and privilege. In an era known for the successful eradication of many childhood illnesses, a seemingly new "epidemic" loomed over mid-century childhood.

Automobility + Baby Boom = Carnage

Despite the establishment of an extensive safety movement prior to the Second World War, traffic tragedies persisted. Such accidents exposed the "illusion of safety" that a well-organized and highly visible traffic safety industry had created in earlier decades.[40] In the middle decades of the twentieth century, North American society became more automobile-centric, not less, and across the century into the next, motor vehicles continued to be the leading cause of child injury and death.[41] The simultaneous surge in both numbers of children and motor vehicles in urban North America increased the possibility for the injury and death of young people.

The relative affluence of the early postwar period encouraged two parallel developments: the baby boom and the mass purchasing of cars. As the baby boomers became toddlers and reached school age, Canadians, like their neighbours to the south, embraced the positive economic times by buying cars and ushering in the automobile's "golden era."[42] "Automophilia," as historian Christopher Dummitt calls the postwar embrace of car culture, transformed cities, spurring urban and suburban growth, car-based family leisure time, the rise of powerful car-centred lobby groups (car companies and automobile associations), a reinvigorated safety industry, and expanded government bureaucracies tasked with the proliferating roadways.[43] Both hallmarks of the late 1940s and 1950s, automobility (the organization of a culture around the car) and the baby boom combined to produce social life that was dominated by cars and kids.[44] The eradication of childhood diseases in mainstream society further secured a general sense of the good life. Yet baby boomer children and motor vehicles collided in these decades, resulting in traffic tragedies that pierced the postwar promise of peace and security.

At the beginning of the Second World War, there were under 1.5 million motor vehicles registered in Canada. At war's end, car ownership still remained elusive in Canada, where there was only one passenger car per ten people – half the American rate. Yet by 1953, half of Canadian families enjoyed car ownership,[45] with registrations doubling to over three million.[46] Canada had become a motorized nation.

New subjectivities – primarily masculine and youthful – arrived with automobility. The "good driver" indicated a responsible, capable, modern man; the "hot rodder," a rebellious youth striving for attention and respect; and the jaywalker a pedestrian lacking the know-how and sophistication required of the new rules of the road brought by the automobile revolution.[47] Under automobility, it wasn't only drivers who were defined in relationship to the car, as Sarah S. Lochlann Jain argues. Everyone was. "The allure of the automobile became a powerful force in disciplining the possibilities for human action in relation to networks of technologies (roads, suburbs, car payments, and Buicks), while also producing new subject positions attached to car-coded behavioral requirements (drivers, drive-in waitresses, and pedestrians)."[48] As passengers and future drivers, children were the chief beneficiaries of postwar automobility; at the same time, they were also vulnerable pedestrians susceptible to the hegemonic presence of cars on North American streets.

Although baby boomers, especially middle-class ones, might have been "born at the right time," they hardly lacked immunity to the dangers of car-oriented society. The overall number of road accidents more than kept pace with the growth in automobiles and population. In Vancouver, reported car crashes climbed, as table 5.1 indicates. And while being a passenger in a postwar automobile was dangerous, children were especially vulnerable as pedestrians. In the late-1950s Vancouver, cars struck 250 children, three to five fatally, each year.[49] By the mid-1950s in other centres such as Toronto, injuries by motor vehicle numbered over one thousand annually while fatalities could run as high as sixteen.[50] Montreal was particularly dangerous. At the beginning of the 1950s, children's automobile deaths annually numbered between 24 and 29, and child pedestrian injuries climbed to above 1,400.[51] Although these

Table 5.1 Reported car crashes, injuries, and deaths, Vancouver, 1940–70

Date	Reported auto accidents	Number injured	Deaths	Population*
1940	3,009	1,504	23	275,833
1950	8,163	2,145	47	344,833
1960	10,261	3,264	31	384,522
1970	18,068	5,359	40	426,256

Source: City of Vancouver Archives, Vancouver City Police Department, Annual Reports, 1940–1970. *Population for City of Vancouver, 1941, 1951, 1961, 1971.

numbers of traffic injuries and fatalities pale in comparison to the slaughter of children on American city streets in the 1910s and 1920s (about which Zelizer has written),[52] postwar North American society was not complacent about child death.

Although cars and kids were considered a bad mix in the postwar era, the former did not become the pariah of earlier decades. Rather, the "enemy" of children became the accident, not the automobile. In this discursive sleight of hand, the car represented the good life, somehow divorced from its real and present danger to children and other pedestrians.[53] Beginning in the late 1940s, child health experts remarked that the disconcerting problem of accidents lay in the shadow of a lowered childhood disease rate. Childhood accidents became a major public health issue in the mid-twentieth century, and as Mona Gleason has shown, this crisis produced the "public child," a new identity around which discourses of blame and new safety practices emerged. Thus another of automobility's subjectivities – the "accident child" – was born.

In women's magazine *Chatelaine* and public health journals, accidents in childhood replaced disease as the biggest threat to young people. Dr Elizabeth Chant Robertson, writing in *Chatelaine* throughout the postwar period, offered her (aspiring) middle-class female readers an overview of the recent changes in the well-being of their children. In 1949, she triumphantly declared that antibiotics like penicillin and streptomycin now provided physicians with the capacity to save young lives from life-threatening illnesses. Yet, rather than celebrate a medical breakthrough, her articles emphasized that a new danger followed children virtually everywhere: the home, the school, and the street. Accidents, she claimed, had become the most common cause of childhood death.[54] Motor vehicles were consistently responsible for about one-third of all accidents. The new child-killer was the accident. [55]

By the 1960s, accidents were known as "the twentieth-century disease."[56] Canadian nurses and doctors emphasized that accidents had become a public health issue, being responsible for more deaths than any single disease. The challenge was to reduce the annual child death toll of two thousand lives.[57] The orientation of child medical expertise was to establish the significance of accidents ("More children die annually from accidents than from the ten leading infectious diseases combined") and also to assert the preventable nature of most accidents.[58]

Vancouver's high rate of traffic injuries involving children in the late 1950s prompted an epidemiological study of child pedestrian accidents by the Department of Preventive Medicine at the University of British Columbia (UBC) in 1960. In drawing conclusions from his study of accidents involving 749 children over three years (1958–1960), Dr Read found an "epidemic" of traffic accidents in certain areas of the city related to causal environmental factors such as overcrowding, a lack of playgrounds, relatively high density on-street parking and traffic, and a lack of parental supervision.[59] When compared with the control child, the "accident child" experienced a "disruptive family life" with younger mothers who worked and absent fathers.[60] The study also showed that boys and younger children of both sexes (aged three to seven) were particularly susceptible to serious injury. Read and his colleagues explained that this was because of boys' "impetuous and venturesome" nature.

Blaming parents, historian Mona Gleason argues, was typical of public health officials. UBC's child traffic accident study pointed to a daily failure to oversee children's play, which happened on the sidewalks and streets, and to the fact that children as young as five years of age crossed streets alone while on errands.[61] Strikingly for the researchers, "the parents did not seem to accept their role in [the accident's] etiology."[62] Taking an extreme view, *Chatelaine* columnist Dr Chant Robertson wrote that "parents deserve the blame" in as much as 75 per cent of accidents.[63] Dr Chant Robertson was ahead of her time in insisting that playing ball in front of the house was too dangerous for children and the answer to accidents lay in a "completely fenced in backyard." She advocated a penned-in or domesticated childhood in her parental advice columns from 1949 through 1960. Yet blaming parents was only one trend in safety discourse: postwar safety actors, including the police, also attributed blame for accidents on the child, or at least directed safety education at children so they might be held responsible for their own well-being.

According to Imperial Oil health care worker Dorothy J. Guild, accident prevention would be most successful if the child were "immunized" with safety. More characteristic of the era's approach to child development, Guild advocated disciplining children around safety issues. Ninety per cent of child accidents could be avoided, reported Quebec's women's magazine *La Revue Moderne* in 1953, arguing that well-trained *children* can prevent accidents. In contrast to Dr Chant Robertson, who would have children demobilized by fences, this position advocated discipline around safety issues and instilling a sense of responsibility for one's own safety and that of others.[64]

Police, Traffic, and Safety

As the automobile transformed North America at the beginning of the twentieth century, it profoundly changed police work. North American police's initial approach to increasingly automobilized urban areas did not begin with safety concerns so much as the need to impose order where motorized vehicles had created chaos.[65] Philadelphia originated the first traffic squad in 1904, followed by New York City in 1907.[66] Peter D. Norton argues that police forces in major US cities chose a "fundamentally conservative" approach to the rapid introduction of automobiles in the first two decades of the century. This approach, focused primarily on enforcing traffic codes and intersection control, was wholly inadequate to the scale of change brought about by the motor age. Thus, the police developed a reputation for both impeding progress (by imposing low speed limits) and initiating ineffectual safety measures (by implementing limited traffic intersection control).[67] By the 1920s, plenty of motorists were being found in violation of traffic law, but the enforcement approach did little to quell the disorder and arrest the rising casualty rate as drivers tended to ignore or plead ignorance of traffic rules. Early US safety reformers therefore looked elsewhere to reduce the carnage caused by the advent of the car, as several scholars have noted, leaving law enforcement peripheral to the safety campaigns sweeping North America. A fundamental shift occurred by mid-century, as traffic safety became, for the most part, a police responsibility.

In the interwar decades, automobile traffic reoriented police activities and reshaped officers' reputations and relationships with the public, including children. As a new system of traffic regulation developed slowly from the turn of the century, law enforcement officers' jobs were increasingly oriented around traffic offences and vehicle inspection. This new role pitted officers against drivers. In combination with the apparent inability of police to stop accidents, the growing surveillance of drivers made the "police the potential enemy of a large percentage of the adult population."[68]

Canadian cities responded to the traffic problem in similar ways, with local police working in piecemeal fashion at a solution. As historian Greg Marquis has noted, the Chief Constables' Association of Canada aimed at implementing uniform speed limits across the country, but only in 1934 did it form a permanent traffic committee.[69] Following guidance from the International Association of Chiefs of Police and American traffic expertise coming from Northwestern University's Traffic School, Canadian police departments focused on standardizing accident reports, and advocated mechanical checks and inspections and education for drivers. In 1930s Toronto, the police department's annual report noted that the city had been designed prior to the surge in motor traffic, resulting in untenable congestion and a high accident rate.[70] Through that decade, the local police department's traffic squad focused on reducing the threat automobiles posed to the public by enforcing the rules of the road and improving drivers' comprehension of the city. They cited motorists for violations of the Highway Traffic Act (including reckless driving), annually sending more than twenty thousand drivers to court; performed on-the-spot checks of motor vehicles, especially concerning brakes; mounted traffic signs; endorsed automatic traffic signals; and kept careful note of traffic statistics.

Although thousands of Toronto drivers were cautioned on minor traffic infractions, the police were not able to turn the accident rate around as fatalities persisted. In 1935, Toronto recorded 5,323 traffic accidents, with 3,087 injuries and 39 pedestrian deaths. In 1936 Toronto's civic administration began to pressure the police department to reduce the traffic menace. With financial support from the Automobile Chamber of Commerce and the Ontario Motor League, the Toronto police department emphasized safe driving as the solution to the traffic casualty problem through the Toronto City Police Safety and Accident

Prevention School that opened in 1937.[71] Yet the injury and fatality rates from accidents continued to climb.

Child safety received minimal consideration from local forces, even though getting to and from school required youngsters to share the nation's increasingly car-congested roadways. Despite police insistence that the protection of children was an "important duty"[72] and that the supervision of schoolchildren crossing Toronto streets "receive[d] careful and active attention," too few officers and budgetary constraints hampered good intentions.[73] Instead, only the most dangerous crossings were covered; less than half of the city's schools had school crossing supervision in the 1930s.[74] "Full protection" of children remained elusive due to a shortage of officers. At the same time, in Nova Scotia, law enforcement officers, acting in their community outreach role and perhaps expressing their sense of futility in controlling the motorized roadways, went door to door to warn parents to keep children "out of the way of traffic."[75]

While the police's relationship to traffic problems began with enforcement of traffic rules and vehicle inspection, accident prevention programs, especially child safety education, would come to predominate urban forces' efforts starting in the latter 1930s. This move helped to expand their public profile and improve their reputation with traffic-weary citizens and parents. This shift involved new levels of expertise. In the interwar period, Canadian officers began to take courses at Northwestern's Traffic Institute, with the first Canadian graduating in 1937.[76] The Traffic Institute, begun in 1933, became an important North American training ground for accident investigation and eventually safety. It churned out a new kind of officer: the "scientific traffic officer," who could audit accidents, speak the language of traffic engineers, remain fair to drivers, and talk to children about safety. In the 1940s, Canadian police chiefs were encouraged by their national organization to pursue National Safety Council materials on traffic.[77] In "Order Out of Chaos," Daniel Marc Albert suggests this professionalization greatly increased police prestige and helped temper the negative reputation of local cops.[78] Anecdotally, by the 1950s, the traffic cop in "one of the world's nastiest traffic cities," Toronto, became a "symbol of hate and fear," suggesting a continuing resistance of drivers to the imposition of order.[79]

Working to instill safety consciousness in Toronto, the Traffic Division of Safety and Accident Prevention Bureau launched a massive educational campaign in 1939. Traffic safety officers spoke on the city's radio stations and showed safety films and gave lectures in schools, churches, and clubs; to publicize their good works they distributed safety data and booklets to the press.[80] By 1940, the police reported reaching 29,000 schoolchildren. In 1946, these efforts were redoubled with the establishment of the Toronto Traffic Safety Council.[81] Together, the Toronto police and the Council broadened the public education campaign. In the 1950s, the Montreal Police Department's Bureau de la Prévention des Accidents delivered 120 lectures to 97 schools in one year, reaching almost 63,000 students.[82]

If police officers were to lecture in the schools, traffic safety education required that they develop child consciousness. This fact was not lost on police forces, who knew well the advantages of having good relations with children and their parents. Helping to protect schoolchildren, Toronto's Chief Constable noted, "has created an atmosphere of friendship, trust, and cooperation between child, parent, and the police."[83] Importantly, work in the schools served to "break [...] down the fear that children at one time had for a police officer."[84]

Underneath the elaborate safety education programs that gave police officers access to elementary schoolchildren lay an assumption about the nature of children and their place in the social hierarchy. Although early twentieth-century cops often blamed accidents on bad drivers and faulty vehicles, children were now blamed for their own traffic casualties. "Children should be got into the habit of remaining on their own side of the street," stated a 1935 article on "Saving the Kids," in the *Canadian Police Gazette*. In 1950, J.P. Bickell, Ontario's Registrar of Motor Vehicles, pronounced that children's "carefree actions and lack of awareness of traffic dangers cause accidents that even the most careful drivers cannot avoid."[85] Being "impulsive" led children to endanger their own lives. Whether it was because of children's thoughtless approach to the street or a sense of hopelessness about truly taming traffic chaos, Canadian law enforcement began to equip children with the appropriate reaction to real bodily threat.

As police became safety educators in the middle decades of the twentieth century, the age of child protection transitioned into an age of preparation.[86] In the words of safety activists in Montreal, the aim was to have "safety inbred into the very fiber of [children's] being."[87] Being prepared meant learning to be fearful, cautious, and competent in evaluating risk. The appropriate sensory and emotional response to being on the street could be learned in the body, as Joy Parr posits in her history of the senses and twentieth-century technological change: "safety" became dependent on "well honed, unconsciously held reflexes."[88] Making children aware of street hazards and helping them to develop quick reflexes in their environments became the centrepiece of safety education. Reflexes would improve with safety consciousness, according to child experts. The ability to adapt to street hazards and obey legitimate authority became critical to child safety (not the eradication of cars or even the use of bike lanes and helmets). Traffic safety officers and other safety reformers recognized that given children's need to get to school on busy streets and the impossibility of fully protecting them, the answer was preparedness – a child inculcated with a consciousness of risk and an embodied response to it.

Didactic Sudden Death: The Police Go to School

As law enforcement organizations took to schools to impart traffic safety, they used both the carrot and the stick to get children to obey rules of the road. The safety messages insisted on children internalizing those rules and complying with new forms of authority, such as peer traffic patrols. By the early 1950s, automobility and police traffic safety campaigns ensured that when it came to accidents it was children (and their parents) who were to blame for being in the wrong place or acting against their own best interest. The high stakes – the lives of children – and the unrelenting pace of automobile hegemony, help to explain the resurgence in this period of what I call didactic sudden death messages. Police both used and starred in films with dramatic lessons; this safety practice was a form of pedagogy that used death and dead children to teach a consciousness of the daily dangers they faced.[89] While its method involved threatening children, that was not its purpose: the necropedagogical project in this instance held out the reward of citizenship for those who learned and obeyed.

Didactic sudden death messages are those visual and textual messages that used the brutality of traffic accidents to sway the public: in our case, young people.[90] Consisting of chilling depictions of "real life" – or, in this case, real death – these images were intended to provoke strong reactions among viewers and lead to a transformation in attitude and behaviour. By bearing witness to the deadly consequences of inattention to rules, the child was meant to identify with the victim and be scared into better behaviour.

Didactic death messages, made popular in children's literature in the nineteenth century, apparently faded with a cultural shift in Western childrearing toward death denial and fear avoidance.[91] Historians of childhood have asserted that in the mid-twentieth century child experts rejected fear as a didactic strategy for protecting children from witnessing the dying and death of loved ones. The urgent need to have children follow traffic rules and also protect them from the emotional knowledge of death influenced the visual materials developed for schoolchildren. Yet the relationship of cars to children opened an opportunity for fear of death to persist in the twentieth century. Frightening children, therefore, was not new when these images began to circulate in high volume in the 1950s. But instead of the Bible, nursery rhymes, and fairy tales, it was now films, photos, and police classroom visits that were used to frighten children. Anthropomorphized objects replaced children in these films, carefully abstracting any child death. The script, however, remained the same: a life expunged, a child to blame.

Following the Second World War, instructional school films evolved into social guidance and mental hygiene films. In didactic fashion, these films covered a range of material about appropriate morals and manners and presented hypothetical situations involving allegedly ordinary youth.[92] Didactic sudden-death images and films were similarly prescriptive. Using the drama of sudden-death imagery, they accomplished what the best educational films did: stimulate and motivate students. In this case, they used fear to effect change in behaviour and attitude toward authority.

The images and films containing didactic sudden death foreshadowed the highway safety film that was introduced to North American audiences in the 1950s and became prolific a decade later. Often heavy-handed, school shock cinema traded on the trope that reckless teenage behaviour led to deadly consequences. Introduced to teenagers to scare them into safe driving, highway safety films dropped audiences into countless scenes of actual fatal accidents, where respect for the dead was superseded by the need to educate the living. In his *Mental Hygiene Classroom Films*, Ken Smith declares the first educational gore film to be *Safety or Slaughter* (1958), produced by Ottawa filmmaker Budge Crawley. Crawley was first to use real accident scene footage.[93] Even more dramatic, the half-hour 1959 *Signal 30* – named for the Ohio State Highway Patrol's code for dead body at the scene of an accident – was filled with both stills and film footage of bloody accidents on the turnpike.[94] *Signal 30* sold well, and the US National Safety Council honoured it.[95] So powerful and influential was this genre of film that some have argued it opened the door to escalating screen violence in 1960s Hollywood, when suspense and fear were maximized and gory death was anxiously anticipated.[96] The generation of teenagers exposed to these educational yet gruesome "safety films" in the late 1950s and 1960s had first been exposed to didactic sudden-death images in elementary school.

Didactic sudden-death images differed from the highway safety films in several ways. They targeted a younger cohort and parents. Both teens and children were blamed for causing accidents, but only the latter were depicted as unknowing, while their older siblings behind the wheel were seen as willful. In the end, these films were not gory and rarely revealed the bloody mess of traffic accidents. Rather, their haunting power rested in presenting the senseless end to young lives in the midst of happy, innocent circumstances, like going to school or playing ball with friends.

Law enforcement played a leading role in didactic safety messages. Police officers worked to reduce children's fear of state authority, even while employing it. This goal of affective change mirrored a transformation in attitude in the fields of medicine and psychology toward the use of fear as a disciplinary method. As Peter N. Stearns argues, the 1920s in the United States was a turning point in the banishment of fear in children's lives. Childhood expertise in that decade drew on the findings of behavioural psychologists who emphasized fear avoidance and a rejection of the previous century's belief that confronting fear was an important part of emotional development.[97] Whereas in the nineteenth century, courage was considered the product of conquering childhood fears, in the twentieth century, child experts advised that a fearful childhood resulted in social and emotional difficulties later in life, including juvenile delinquency. By the 1940s, fear aversion had settled into North American culture, evident in parenting magazines and the transformation of children's literature and other media in which fear was downplayed.[98] The effect of assessing fear as a negative emotion in childhood led, according to Peter Stearns and Timothy Haggerty, to dramatic changes in children's culture.[99] Yet these efforts to diminish fear in childhood could not cover up the challenges of living in anxious times.

If Stearns and Haggerty are correct – that this transition to the happiness imperative and reduction of fear as a disciplinary tool occurred by mid-century – how do we explain fear-mongering through didactic images of instant death? The insecurities of the Cold War were reflected in approaches to children, where obedience to authority and conformity of behaviour were paramount. This apparent contradiction was not a contradiction at all: happiness and security would only follow demonstrated evidence of compliance to rules. Police instrumentally used children's fear and got away with it because the stakes were so high. The complete surrender to automobility meant that the danger to children would not be reduced except through modification of children's behaviour.

Didactic sudden-death images were produced by coroners, police officers, and professional photographers and placed in magazines for adult viewing. *First Day of School*, for example, was published multiple times in police magazines in 1949–50. It showed a sudden-death drama involving a boy, his bicycle, and their tragic encounter with a truck. Despite, or perhaps because of, its shocking subject matter and the brutal reversal of the first-day-at-school narrative, this image won first place in an annual traffic safety photography contest.[100] (See figure 5.1.) The photo of the death of an apparently healthy child portrayed the ordinary quality, ubiquity, and randomness of traffic accidents. *I Fell Out of Mommy's Car* is another award-winning photo intended to shock the population into changing their obliviousness to endangered childhood. This insensitive, blunt commentary – a toddler lying motionless in the street next to a car – matches the monotone narration of later highway safety films that were often sarcastic and rather unnerving. Other common images included accident scenes of limp and injured children, young witnesses, and panicked adults. In popular women's magazines like *Chatelaine* images were more suggestive: a haunting triumvirate of car, ball, and child headed for a collision; or a post-accident scene of car, downed bicycle, and shadow.[101]

The Canadian film industry, especially the National Film Board (NFB), produced its share of educational films featuring young death. The Board had begun as a government information and propaganda tool during the Second World War, but in the postwar period, films depicted the

5.1   "First Day of School," *Police Chiefs News* 17, no. 1 (January 1950): 7.

return to peacetime and Canadian attitudes for a new era. As Brian J. Low has noted in his history NFB *Kids*, postwar films featured happy children in idyllic surroundings. Yet, by the 1950s, NFB films acknowledged the era's uncertainty and the challenges besetting children and families under a precarious peace.[102] Learning the lessons of accepting authority underscored many films. A short informational film from the early 1950s called *Policewomen*, which was shown in movie houses before the feature film and was directed at the entire family, is a case in point. Launching an argument about the importance of policewomen to neighbourhood policing, the film shows a boy on a bike felled by a car and his limp body carried away by the police. (See figure 2.3.) In this case, the filmmaker's point was that Montreal's policewomen were essential to the contemporary working-class environment, where children's reckless street play could use a woman's influence. Unmistakably promoting policewomen's work, the film both teaches lessons about the boy's bad behaviour and alleviates parental anxiety.

Most films produced for children avoided using real dead children. For example, *Look Alert, Stay Unhurt*, was produced by the NFB in 1955 and directed by Gordon Burwash, who made sixty NFB films, many of

5.2   *Stay Alert, Stay Unhurt*, National Film Board of Canada, 1955.

them belonging to the mental hygiene and social guidance genre. *Look Alert, Stay Unhurt* was a twelve-minute film that featured a friendly but authoritative policeman giving advice to Ted, a boy who, in attempting to join his friends in a game, runs across the road into the path of an oncoming car, narrowly escaping serious injury or death. (See figure 5.2.) The driver of the car insists that the policeman arrest young Ted for being "a menace to the streets of Toronto." Though not under arrest, Ted is placed in the back of the police car and taken to the local police station to be taught a simple lesson: "roads are for cars." Once there he is shown how accidents can be avoided if he observes safety rules. The officer tells the cautionary tales of others who were not quite as lucky as Ted. The camera shifts to a re-enactment, where two girls are walking their dolls in carriages on the sidewalk. One girl crosses the street between two parked vehicles and a car crushes her stroller. Her doll's head lies cracked open on the street, delivering the message to viewers about what might have happened to the girl, and, by extension, to Ted. The policeman next turns to a file of actual accident photos, and while the camera eye does not focus on the most graphic images, shock and fear transform Ted's face as he views image after image. The camera shows one of the

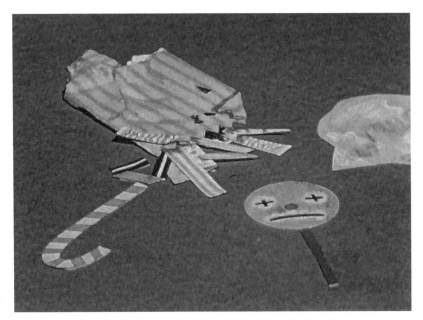

5.3   *One Little Indian* ©1955 National Film Board of Canada, all rights reserved.

photos in which a child is lying in the street to the horror of adults and
children who witness the accident. The policeman explains: "All this
pain and tragedy all because children are careless."[103] Ted walks free from
the police station once he has grasped the gravity of what might have
happened, and learns the "don'ts" of traffic safety: "Don't cross except at
a green light; Don't play in the streets; Don't cross around parked cars."
Having been instructed in the right way to be a competent child, Ted
happily goes about his day, rejoining friends in street play. Equipped
with this knowledge, he can take to the roads in a safe manner. These
skills were not about demobilizing Ted and his friends.

Many of the NFB safety films follow a similar narrative. In these films
the children witness what can happen when rules aren't followed, they
register fear and admit to having learned a lesson, and can now get on
with their happy childhoods. The NFB's *One Little Indian* (1955) won
awards for both filmmaking and safety.[104] This fifteen-minute film features
an animated puppet and follows an Indigenous boy on his first visit
to the big city. It reflects the postwar efforts to integrate Indigenous
history and culture into the Canadian national narrative and is a forum
in which, as Joan Sangster writes, "primitive, strange, and alien behavior

5.4   *One Little Indian* ©1955 National Film Board of Canada, all rights reserved.

[of Indigenous peoples]" is "contrasted to white Canadians who were modern, rational, progressive, and technologically advanced."[105] The Native boy is a crude representation of the pre-modern person who is ignorant of city life, traffic rules, and automobiles. His is a world untouched by automobility. In the film the boy, called Magic Bow, is in town to perform his Native skills for city folks through an act in the rodeo.[106] Prior to his performance, he sets out to explore the urban scene. Even though he has magic powers, he is bewildered by the traffic. He wanders down the street, where he comes across a candy store and buys himself a sucker; this sucker is anthropomorphized as a smiling friend. Since Magic Bow is not familiar with traffic lights, he walks into the street against a red light, and tragedy ensues. In this case, the boy survives, but the sucker does not, not unlike the girl's doll in *Look Alert, Stay Unhurt*. (See figure 5.3.) Magic Bow experiences two more incidents of failing to observe basic safety rules and finds himself in front of a police officer, who sets him straight. These lessons are so profound for him that he integrates the modern lessons of traffic safety into his rodeo performance and thanks his new friends for the help he receives. (See figure 5.4.) *One Little Indian* makes several things clear: that traffic tragedies are caused

5.5   Elmer the Elephant

by unknowing children and that part of becoming modern is to know that one is responsible for keeping oneself safe and out of harm's way.

Not only did police play avuncular yet stern guidance officers in National Film Board instructional films, they also became part of the elementary school and high school experience. In Canada, municipal police forces were also responsible for instituting a national icon, Elmer the Elephant. (See figure 5.5.) Toronto's mayor apparently decided traffic safety needed a mascot for children after visiting Detroit, Michigan, in 1946, where that city's boy mascot made an impression.[107] In 1947, a Winnipeg-based Disney artist redesigned Elmer, crafting the safety mascot in the image of Dumbo (1942); by the mid-1950s, Elmer became the safety mascot in as many as fifty communities worldwide. In the 1950s, policemen arrived at schools with a stuffed Elmer to demonstrate that an elephant never forgets the safety rules. In 1954, police officers visited 166 Toronto schools and awarded seventeen of these mascots for schools that maintained an accident-free record for the year.[108] In 1955, the Toronto chief constable reported in 1955 that "every school" received a six-foot Elmer pennant that was flown on the school flagpole. As long as the school was accident free, Elmer would fly high. When an accident occurred, police officers visited the school and lowered Elmer before the entire student body. The elephant remained lowered in symbolic death until a month passed with no accident.[109] While Elmer softened the police image and the message of potential death on the roads, Elmer was a constant visual reminder of child injury and possibly death.

"Small-Fry Constabulary": The Safety Patrol Movement

Elmer's insistence on rote memory work around traffic rules helped teach schoolchildren about how to behave in their motorized environment. Yet no campaign was more effective in enlisting children in the safety enterprise than the school safety patrols. Often begun by motor clubs (and continued by the local Canadian Automobile Association [CAA] and the American Automobile Association [AAA]) and managed by schools and municipal police traffic officers, the safety patrol systems across North America not only helped reduce the injuries and deaths of school-age children, they helped transform the relationship of police to youth. A system of peer regulation and reward found deep and lasting popularity with young people.[110] As observers and police officers commented, the school safety patrols did far more than help children to cross busy roads. A system based on conformity to rules and regulations and the daily rituals of obedience to state authority appealed to youngsters, for the promise of a narrow but sure path to citizenship and inclusion, and to city administrations for costing nothing.

School safety patrols had their start in 1922 as the brainchild of Charles M. Hayes, president of the Chicago Motor Club, to control the threat the automobile posed to children. The campaign came to Canada in the following decade. Although cars also endangered children outside of their journeys to and from school, it was felt that this daily pilgrimage of the nation's youth could at least be made safer. Importing the idea from the United States, Winnipeg's Patrol Sergeant Fred Barnes launched Canada's first major school safety patrol system in 1936.[111] The idea quickly spread to other mid-sized cities like Calgary, Edmonton, Vancouver, and Victoria and many towns such as Sault Ste Marie and Windsor, Ontario.[112] Police departments helped initiate patrol systems and co-operated with school boards and principals of individual schools and automobile clubs. Origin stories often include a first-hand account of child trauma or a near-accident involving a motorized vehicle. This program of police-directed self-regulation gained favour, for example, in Vancouver after automobiles claimed the lives of two schoolchildren in 1935.[113]

Where school patrols caught on, their numbers climbed during the postwar era. In Vancouver, a 1936 experiment involving three schools expanded during the war: in 1943, the safety patrol system oversaw 10,536 students crossing safely at 29 intersections, helped by 638 school-boy patrols. Within a decade, Vancouver had more than 2,000 boys from grades four to eight working the school crossings.[114] Edmonton and Calgary school patrols numbered over 2,000 by the 1960s as well.[115] In the 1950s, Calgary had a waiting list of children hoping to become safety patrols, which speaks to the coveted nature of these positions.[116] In the first decade, the patrol system was the prerogative of boys, but the Second World War opened up positions for girls. By the 1950s, most cities had gender diversity in the ranks of these junior crossing guards. Cultural and class diversity was also evident, although not much discussed by the media that covered the school patrol programs. Images from the 1950s and 1960s depict African- and Asian-Canadian boys working as patrollers,[117] while in 1963 Edmonton's eleven-year-old Pauline DeHaas, a girl from a "poor family," not only was a patrol girl but was also selected to represent Alberta at the CAA School Patrol Jamboree in Ottawa.[118] In the late 1960s, the Calgary City Police Department organized a group of students from the Sarcee Indian First Nation who were enlisted to oversee the loading and unloading of school buses.[119]

From the outset patrollers worked key intersections near the schools, morning, lunchtime, and after school, leading groups of schoolchildren across the street, raising a hand or a stop sign to oncoming traffic.[120] The fact that children were sometimes in busy streets commanding traffic would become controversial, although the safety record countered the negative commentary about schoolboys and girls using their bodies in this way. When cars failed to obey their traffic-calming gestures, the safety patrols were instructed to take down licence plate numbers and a report them to the police.

The popularity of the patrol system likely stemmed from the power and considerable responsibility associated with the job. The uniforms also helped. To distinguish themselves from other students and to make them visible to drivers, patrols were decked out with accoutrements of authority: a Sam Browne style white belt (a thick leather belt that included a strap or bandolier across the right shoulder, modelled after a nineteenth-century British soldier), special badges, white caps, and stop signs. These items indicated authority and were apparently happily donned by proud patrollers. Playing the role of safety patrol boy or girl also came with rewards not accessible to other students. Patrollers were acknowledged on local radio programs, invited to tour police stations, and celebrated each year at picnics, parades, and rallies organized in their honour.[121] As these junior-crossing guards helped tens of thousands of children to cross safely at intersections, police forces, automobile clubs, and school boards congratulated themselves on a system in which children saved children's lives. A 1952 article on the Calgary patrol recounts the heroism of an eleven-year-old girl: faced by an oncoming truck sliding into the intersection where she was leading a group of her fellow students, this girl "with the coolness of a veteran at traffic direction ... spun around and hurled herself at the children, knocking them out of the way."[122] It is not hard to see why the patrol programs were popular and why patrollers were celebrated as providing a "safe and happy future" to thousands of other schoolchildren.[123]

The tremendous success of the safety patrols was touted by those in charge of the patrols, who often pointed to their "remarkable record of safety."[124] Vancouver could boast in 1960 that it "had not one" seriously injured child from the time the patrols started in 1935 to the present;[125] in 1969, the Calgary police traffic division reported thirty-two years of "accident-free" service.[126] At a time when "every third accident victim was a child" according to the police media, these statistics did indeed seem revolutionary as the site of accidents moved away from the school zones.[127] To be clear, children were still being injured, just not near the schools.

Elementary and junior high school safety patrols helped reinforce the ongoing professionalization of police work. The new category of officer who was responsible for traffic obtained professional training and skills to deal not only with traffic circulation and accidents but also with managing a new army of fourth- to eighth-grade recruits. Police officers across North America competed for scholarships to Northwestern University's Traffic Institute and forged new avenues for relations with local schools, school boards, and the like.[128] The training of juvenile crossing guards fell to the traffic constable, who instructed them in safety rules, showed them how to control their peers, and told them when to call a police officer.

As traffic squad Sergeant Bob Moffat claimed in 1952, the school patrol was the "best public relations scheme the police force in Calgary has ever embarked on."[129] Equipped with greater safety knowledge than their parents had, children were able to "criticize dangerous procedures" taken by parents. School patrols also helped the children realize that "the policeman is their best friend."[130] In the 1950s, the patrols were acknowledged as "splendid training for children in the meaning and use of authority."[131] Student patrols were "a very special type of person" with a "keen eye, good co-ordination, personal neatness, the ability to accept orders and carry them out diligently and without hesitation." A connection was also made between safety co-operation and a reduction in juvenile delinquency.[132] The patrols also had the benefit of inscribing in its young volunteers an appreciation for policing and power. Called a "small-fry constabulary," schoolboy patrols were likened to junior officers who would provide future officers for local forces. Not only did schoolchildren learn an appreciation for safety, but they also embraced the idea of police work. The *Canadian Police Gazette* ran the photo of twelve-year-old Kenny Cobbs, a school patrol boy from Vancouver, who proudly posed next to two traffic officers who sized him up for a spot on the city's police force. (See figure 5.6.) He was not alone in this dream of translating a stint with the school safety patrol into a career with the police: Jack O'Neill, interviewed in 2002 long after he retired from the Calgary police force, recalled that his patrol work taught him "accountability, responsibility, dedication, and life-saving skills … and a chance to be part of something important."[133] He fondly remembers the officer who trained him in 1940, and he was so in awe of the respect conferred upon him that he sought out policing as a profession.

Not all police departments supported the idea of a child volunteer–based safety patrol. Toronto and Montreal did not implement such a service; other cities that eventually used safety patrol programs also debated their merits. Detractors across the country listed several problems with the system: the improbability of children succeeding at the job; a concern that it effectively turned children into "scabs," depriving adults of jobs; and the issue of the danger posed to the juvenile crossing guards and the corresponding question of liability. In the 1930s, directing

SCHOOL PATROL BOY KENNY COBBS, will soon be tall enough to join the city force. Anyway, that's the ... of Constable I. A. L. Simons and Constable McKinnon, who are in charge of Vancouver ... patrols.

5.6   School patrol boy Kenny Cobbs. *Canadian Police Gazette* 30, no. 7 (September 1955): front cover.

traffic was considered a "man's job, not a 10 year old child's respons-ibility,"[134] and children were considered unsuitable for policing traffic, since their testimony would be considered unreliable.[135] In Toronto, the chief constables discussed schoolboy patrols in their annual reports, and while a broad safety campaign was inaugurated in the late 1930s, and they supported the idea of such patrols, the school board rejected it for the heavily trafficked downtown area. In 1946, Toronto's school crossing guards were implemented, using not children but part-time volunteer adults.[136] Both Montreal and Toronto used adult crossing guards, except in outlying areas where schoolchildren were organized into patrols. This system was also seen as imperfect: adults were expensive, unlike children, and volunteers were unreliable. Calgary's Safety Patrol Committee reported in 1967 that in its investigations of best practices for traffic safety around schools, older male crossing guards had been responsible for the molestation of children, which was "more frequent than one might suspect."[137]

Safety patrol programs spread across Canada from the mid-1930s onwards and were part of the postwar school system. These programs were at times organized and run by traffic constables, who themselves had been specially trained for new conditions prompted by the rise of the motorized society. Police lauded the school patrol boys and girls, who, in turn, seemed to embrace the power over peers that the badge earned them. The school patrol program represented a new path to leadership for young Canadians, one that had important lessons of obedience and reward for their compliance. The fact that no deaths occurred where patrols escorted schoolchildren makes it easy to evaluate this intervention into childhood in positive terms. Yet the patrols were part of an expansion of police authority in schools, as we will see in the coming chapter, that emphasized that a good child was a disciplined one who would act on behalf of the police. Children flocked to safety patrol programs, absorbing the lessons for a safe and happy childhood and gaining knowledge of hierarchical power relations. These children helped solve the "twentieth-century disease" (motor vehicle accidents), but they also were conscripted to police themselves and each other and did not challenge the desirability and danger of automobility. In fact, the school patrols helped to undergird the automobile's dominance by making its threat appear diminished.

In a now-ironic conclusion, research into children and car accidents led the University of British Columbia's Dr Read and his team to imagine a future society in fifty or one hundred years in which the automobile and childhood would not collide because the pedestrian "will be completely dissociated from the automobile: Not only will the pedestrian traffic hazard be eradicated, the community will be more peaceful and the opportunity for recreation will be greatly increased."[138]

Conclusion

Vehicular injury and death – car "accidents" – emerged in the early twentieth century as a new threat to childhood. As car culture came to characterize mainstream urban North American society in the middle decades of the twentieth century, traffic fatalities and injuries became part of the fabric of modern life. The normalization of accidents perversely followed the automobile's ascendance.[139] As this trend coincided with the decline of childhood diseases, public focus turned to the danger the automobile posed to childhood. This recognition led to a subtle but persistent cultural transformation around safety, risk, and responsibility.

In the early part of the century, parents, municipal authorities, citizen groups, schools, and automobile clubs generated a safety movement dedicated to halting industrial modernity's devastating toll on children's bodies. Municipal police forces and public health officials joined this campaign and led the movement by mid-century. Law enforcement agencies evolved to address the growth in traffic and accidents by developing expertise in controlling traffic and accident forensics and establishing specific divisions and officers responsible for implementing rules based on this new knowledge.

Imbued with power and knowledge from their role as the civic authority responsible for dealing with accidents and public death, police officers circumscribed children's access and use of public space in the name of controlling traffic and the consequent casualties. As chief arbiters of relations between kids and cars, local police, especially as traffic overseers, constructed themselves as a vital force in the campaign to end the tragic confrontations between the two. As a link between children and modern street life, officers made their way into North American schools, narrowed the gap between themselves and children, and played a principal role in the twentieth-century safety movement.

As police moved into the realm of childhood in the era of accident prevention, the traffic officer at once befriended baby boom children and struck fear in them, using pedagogical programs to ensure young people understood what was at stake. Both real and rhetorical child traffic injury and death betrayed the fiction of postwar peace and security that was supposed to be the prerogative of suburban childhood. On the surface, cautionary tales that used young death pointed to the dangers of modern society; the deeper meanings point to children's vulnerability and mortality, which had profound metaphoric traction in the late 1940s and 1950s: a temporal landscape shaped by Cold War fears and a heightened desire to live the North American dream.

Looking at the mid-twentieth-century safety movement reveals the discourses and practices that helped shape a new youthful subjectivity – that of the citizen-child – one based on new levels of competency and peer regulation in the years when automobility was in the process of becoming entrenched. Children learned that getting to school was a risky but necessary venture; police and even elephants held the key to responsible and happy childhood; rules and regulations needed to be absorbed; and, when necessary, some children could wield power over others in the name of safety. In turn, the 1970s tendencies toward containment of childhood and the growing demobilization of children in the late twentieth century directly challenged this competency paradigm.

Epilogue: Police and Schools

In 1958, Detective Inspector Ovila Pelletier, head of Montreal's youth squad, died suddenly at the age of fifty-six, prompting a public appraisal of the police department's impact on young people and juvenile delinquency. The Montreal press lauded the work of this career policeman for bringing international acclaim to the squad's innovative and effective approach to the youth problem.[1] In the mid-1930s, lacking specific training in youth work, Pelletier inaugurated the city's first youth squad; in the 1940s, he oversaw its growth and initiated a major crime prevention program, including the extremely popular Montreal Police Juvenile Clubs (PJC).[2] Effusive about the youth squad's transformative work, a chorus of voices praised Pelletier and his delinquency-fighting colleagues as "a positive, energetic force for good among the city youth."[3] Pelletier's influence on the city's young people was nothing short of monumental, the press declared, for he helped instill in youth a new attitude toward police and authority: "for thousands of young Montrealers it [the word "cop"] has come to mean 'friend.'"[4] Laid to rest in 1958, Pelletier would be remembered as "ami des jeunes" (a friend to youth).

Such resounding acclaim for the youth squad's historic impact is hardly surprising given the massive undertaking by Pelletier and his colleagues to implement the youth turn in Montreal's police services. Pelletier had built a substantial and centralized department of youth officers that exercised city-wide control over delinquents and incipient delinquency. With each development – new offices and a centralized bureaucracy, the hiring of women, name changes signalling crime prevention strategies, and the establishment of the Police Juvenile Clubs –

6.1   Parc Ovila Pelletier, Montreal. Photo by author.

Pelletier constructed and amplified his successes through the media, seemingly capturing the public's imagination. Known for tackling the "corruptors of youth" in the 1940s and reversing the rising tide of delinquency in the postwar period, Pelletier would be best remembered for creating the Police Juvenile Clubs in Montreal. Fittingly, when city hall memorialized him, it renamed a children's playground at Ontario and Bennett Streets in the city's east end in his honour. His practice of rewarding young people for "proficiency" in various activities and demonstrable moral conduct was memorialized with an annual ceremony in which "Ovila Pelletier" trophies were awarded to civic-minded girls and boys.[5] (See figure 6.1.)

Youth squad work would evolve after Pelletier's death. In 1965, the PJC board of directors decided to terminate their programs as the expansion of city parks service and parish recreational institutions made their role in youth club activities redundant.[6] This did not mean an end to crime prevention, though, as the sixties moral panic over transgressive youth behaviour emboldened a new generation of officers to find a way to reach pre-delinquent teens. In the late 1950s and '60s police and school administrators associated the rise in teen trouble with gangs, drugs

and alcohol usage, youth hangouts, and runaways. These issues were
not unique to Montreal – they were ubiquitous in teen culture in this
era. Specifically prompting the city's youth workers to action were the
leather-jacket gang problem of the late 1950s and the "goofball" (barbit-
urate) drug problem of the early 1960s. As Montreal's mayor, school
boards, and police department discovered that the use of barbiturates
and amphetamines had penetrated high schools, the youth squad devised
a program to enter students' lives.[7]

Montreal's sixties version of the youth squad, the Youth Aid Section
(Section à l'Aide à la Jeunesse) inaugurated a new crime prevention unit
consisting of police-educators that placed officers in schools, a version of
the School Resource Officer (SRO) programs that expanded dramatically
in the later years of the twentieth century. Through the traffic safety
campaigns, as seen in chapter 5, police officers had begun a practice
that gave them purposeful roles in elementary and secondary schools,
and not incidentally, access to young people. The police-educators
program, and others like it elsewhere, expanded this access, normalizing
the place of law enforcement in schools. Like community policing that
became popularized at the same time, getting police officers to reach
young people in school through educational programming superficially
marked a positive use of police authority while increasing the reach and
influence of state authority over students. By the close of the century,
however, the punitive turn would make the presence of police in North
American schools controversial.[8]

Since the 1960s the police presence in North American schools has
grown exponentially. The systematic placement of law enforcement
officers in schools was in part a reaction to the belief that educational
institutions were rife with discipline problems and disorder, appearing to
threaten student safety. The much-publicized shootings in high schools
in the 1990s, especially in Littleton, Colorado, and a copycat act in Taber,
Alberta, reinforced the idea that security of students could not be left
to school administrators. In turn, the police presence in schools has
resulted in critiques about the over-policing of youth, the abrogation
of their rights, and an obsession with securitization in society.[9] The
recent controversial police presence in schools follows a half-century
effort by police organizations to bolster police legitimacy through
modifications in their relationships to youth. The groundwork was laid
from mid-century onwards to allow police access to both schools and

childhood. School visiting schemes, SROs, police-educators – like their more repressive counterparts of the 1990s and 2000s – emphasized a deep penetration of youth spaces and culture by "youth-oriented" officers and sought to instill respect for and fear of law enforcement. The earlier programs, however, which could be legitimately called police visiting schemes, were born in an era of rising awareness of civil rights and thus at least acknowledged youths' rights and attempted to persuade young people to "keep straight." Police visiting schemes at mid-century, unlike today, were about safety, not securitization.

The Growth of the Police Presence in Schools

Sociologists and criminologists who are interested in the contemporary police presence in schools pay little attention to how officers got there, assuming it was a new solution to a contemporary problem. Early experiments in assigning officers to schools include Indianapolis Public School Police (est. 1939), the Los Angeles School Police Department (est. 1948), and the School Resource Officer program in Flint, Michigan (est. 1950s).[10] These first programs were part of a larger plan to control delinquency (and by extension adult criminality) by focusing on pre-delinquents and forming independent relationships with children so they would honour and obey police power. As this book has shown, it was in the early to mid-twentieth century that municipal police forces – or small groups within them – developed a kind of community policing that targeted young people. This involved a new form of expertise on youth, held traditionally by social scientists, that insinuated police into the juvenile justice system. As youth squads were formed, new demands of professional training required officers to take post-secondary courses, if not degrees, in social sciences directed at building an academic expertise in youth work.

Under the umbrella term "crime prevention," police became youth conscious and committed themselves to youth work, a trend that emerged in the interwar period and gathered steam through mid-century. Conceptually a crime prevention strategy insisted on examining the provenance of criminals, which would open the door to scrutinizing the childhoods of gangsters and other criminals. In pursuing the cause of criminality police looked to the social, economic, and cultural environments in which criminals were raised for specific sources of bad behaviour. The pursuit of incipient delinquency or pre-delinquents helped make crime prevention look like social service work, as police officers monitored youths' social venues and spaces, and offered them enticements to join police-directed recreational activities.

Police athletic programs for youth heralded youth-conscious policing. Between the 1930s and the 1960s, hundreds of thousands of young people joined police athletic leagues and social and cultural clubs, and took advantage of membership in police youth club opportunities to attend local sporting events and amusements. This popular development was propelled by the belief that such a movement could remedy incipient delinquency that, if left unchecked, would become tomorrow's adult crime wave. In cities like New York and Montreal, comprehensive sports and cultural programs became a major answer to the panic over delinquency rates and youth gangs.[11] Organizing children's play on the streets became necessary with the rise of automobility and the threat of delinquency among "idle" youth, leading to police intervention in public spaces.

The safety movement, as we saw in chapter 5, involved teaching children to avoid the common dangers and accidents of modern society, especially around traffic. Drawing on the safety movement that had emerged earlier in the century, police involvement in eliminating childhood accidents came in the form of instruction about the rules and regulations of, and respect for, state authority. Police officers, equipped with safety rules and forensic accounting of accident causation, employed threatening messages of sudden death to teach children the dire consequences of the failure to obey authority. By the mid-twentieth century, despite the real risk to children posed by traffic, the safety industry, including the local police, did not advocate the containment of children, at least not in the way late twentieth-century parents would seek it by "demobilizing children" with fenced playgrounds, strict school-leaving policies, and chronic chauffeuring. Rather, childhood safety meant peer regulation, surveillance, and an overall intensification of police presence in childhood.[12] Compliance to authority held out a specific reward: the promise of a safe, happy, and active childhood.

Since adolescents came of age in schools, it would follow that police needed to coordinate with their administrators and insinuate themselves into the classroom. Formal police school liaison schemes emerged in the postwar period. In the United Kingdom, for example, beginning with a pilot project in Liverpool in 1949, many cities developed police liaison schemes and "police weeks" that brought together teachers, social services, and youth club leaders to help prevent delinquency.[13] As historian Louise Jackson illustrates, these were aimed at keeping juveniles out of court and establishing strong ties with youth and a caution system.[14] A variation on the liaison schemes, school resource officer programs spread through northern North America during the postwar era. Montreal's experiment in this regard became an important model in the late 1960s.

Montreal's *Policiers-Éducateurs*

Prevention-oriented police work in Montreal was reinvigorated in the 1960s as juvenile delinquency rates shot up, baby boomers became adolescents, and the spectre of teenage drug use loomed.[15] Jean-Paul Gilbert, the first police department director (1965–70) to hold a university degree in criminology, advocated making youth work central to 1960s policing. Difficult to ignore was the fact that one-third of the city's 1.2 million citizens were minors.[16] Youths were growing up in a decade of dramatic social and political change, Gilbert told the press: "The sociological changes have created great confusion, great restlessness, on the part of the young … Often they do not know which way to turn. It is up to us to help them."[17] Armed with a master's degree in criminology, and referring to Émile Durkheim's sociology of law, he spoke of the naturalness of adolescent conflict with authority, the arbitrariness of who got labelled a delinquent, and the normalcy of crime in contemporary society. Gilbert called on parents, schools, and the public to help with crime prevention and "indifference to crime and those who commit it."[18] For its part, the Montreal youth squad, called the Youth Aid Section, once again attempted to triumph over this North American delinquency trend by introducing what they called a "new initiative" in policing; this time it would involve a broad educational plan to implement the spirit of Gilbert's message.[19]

Drawing on the example of Liverpool, England, Gilbert reoriented the Youth Aid Section. Whereas the police juvenile clubs had previously fulfilled a need in the city, Gilbert felt a new approach was needed. Police coaching and recreational organizations under the PJC left sixties youth feeling uninspired and "straightjacketed," Gilbert argued, and, worse, mainstream teens who did join rejected other young people who exhibited any difference (of dress, language, or behaviour), defeating the goal to create an inclusive neighbourhood experience.[20] The new methodology was aimed at schools and youth as students would fill an important gap in citizenship education. As teachers, police could influence the next generation, imparting critical life lessons about law, order, and safety.

The *policier-éducateur* program (called the Police Educational Patrol or simply police-educator in the anglophone press) comprised public panels directed at parents, students, and the public. They included Judge Marcel Trahan of the Social Welfare Court; Viateur Ravary, director of the Catholic School Commission (CECM); Philippe Lapointe, psychologist with the CECM; and Detective Captain Russell Trépanier, head of the Youth Aid Section.[21] The actual educational patrol consisted of youth squad officers, who visited classrooms and, reminiscent of Pelletier's rhetoric, implored youth to see them as friends who had come to chat. Framing delinquency as a resolvable problem that affected the entire social body, Trahan and his colleagues sought out an audience with parents and teachers while police-educators attempted to win the hearts and minds of youth.[22] Within months of the launch of the pilot project Montreal's crime prevention success made headline news both at home and abroad.[23]

In 1965, Sergeant Claude Labelle, a liaison officer with the Social Welfare (juvenile) court, was asked his opinion on the escalating juvenile delinquency rates. In recounting his nine years of experience with youth in trouble with the law, he pointed out how processing adolescents through the court system for petty crimes shamed and traumatized them and ultimately turned them against law enforcement and into likely recidivists.[24] He also noted a long-standing complaint of police officers that children were primed to become delinquents in part because of the negative attitude toward the police held by parents: adults passed on to their children, he argued, "a false image of the police, as bêtes noirs" and regularly threatened their children with police discipline.[25] But what youth needed was a thorough understanding of criminal law and municipal bylaws so as to avoid getting into trouble.[26] Thus, by the mid-1960s, calls again went out to replace police "repression" of youth with outreach, and for youth-oriented officers to bypass the courts in the case of minor offenders.[27] Labelle, conscious of whose shoulders he stood on, remarked that he was indeed a disciple of Ovila Pelletier.[28]

Labelle's plan to reach young people brought police to youth-dense spaces. This time the focus was not restricted to the playing field, park, or bowling alley, but also to the schools. This method would bring the law into the lives of teens but also to a younger cohort that could be warned of the dangers facing youth today. Labelle proposed that police-educators would have four years of university-level criminology training, as well as intense police training with youth. His plan was to make the police-educators as fundamental to the school system as the school nurse service, career counsellors, and school chaplains. For him, the addition of police in schools would make for a thoroughly modern educational system.[29] Confronted by a rising student population and the growing complexity of youth problems, school administrators in Montreal made room for police-educators in schools across the city.

The police-educator job description was rooted in crime prevention models that had been around since the 1920s. Labelle himself described the work as helping boys to become men.[30] These officers aimed to counsel and guide young people; to motivate and model good behaviour; to promote the role of police in society; and to inform youths of the current dangers of contemporary society. Highly ambitious and optimistic, these school liaison officers sought to prevent the emergence of the next generation of delinquents, help them recognize the errors of their ways, and vastly improve the reputation of police in the city.[31] The goal of this education in the matter of law, he thought, could be done without paternalism, hypocrisy, threats, or condescension; rather, in close keeping with 1960s sensibility, Labelle's method was to "dialogue" with youth and earn their trust and respect. The result would be better police relations with the public. Indeed, the major reasons for engaging in this kind of work with youth was to impress upon youth respect for law enforcement.

Sergeant Labelle's pilot program was established in 1966. To begin, he isolated a cohort that he felt could most benefit from his message. Directed at eighth graders – thirteen-year-old boys and girls – in the city's working-class and immigrant districts (Mile End, Ville Émard, Point St Charles, and Saint Henri), his lessons in law and criminology helped young people to define crime and delinquency, to avoid committing either, and develop a consciousness of their own behaviour and attitudes. While informing students how to stay out of trouble he also incorporated cautionary tales about what happened to youth who go bad.

Labelle's educational lessons reflected a highly gendered perspective on young people and a popular psychological perspective on the roots of adolescent crime. Hinting at a moral panic familiar to the 1950s, Labelle talked about how eight-, nine-, or ten-year-old boys were ignorant about homosexuality and needed information – from him – to be "armed against" such men.[32] Teenagers, he told them, were prone to "impulsiveness," and adolescence for them was an age of turbulence, peer pressure, and group identification when boys (their real target) discovered girls and girls "discovered love." Importantly, it was a time when young people tried to demonstrate that they were not children, which brought them into contact with dangerous situations. Boys were pressured into proving their maturity by stealing hubcaps, breaking antennas on cars, and shoplifting from department stores. For boys, adolescence introduced the appeal and danger of gang membership. Labelle outlined the psychological makeup of gangs and how to watch out for the so-called leaders, who tended to intimidate the others, getting them to act out in ways they might not otherwise have done.[33] In the Catholic school system, schools were often divided by sex, enabling Labelle and the other police educators to address delinquency and teenagers in gender-specific ways.[34]

The youth squad defined teenage girls as a problem because "men started to notice them." Defining girls as prey for "undesirables" was hardly new in the 1960s, but the increase of incidents of sexual assault involving runaways and teenage girls who hitchhiked caught the attention of the Youth Aid Section. The police educator therefore tried to convince girls of their vulnerability and the threat posed by their mobility. Like the traffic safety messages, these lessons ventured into necropedagogy, as the police-educator attempted to scare girls straight. In these cautionary tales, girls' hitchhiking habits caused their demise. In case the story was not vivid enough, the thirteen-year-olds were shown an image of a dead runaway's body that was eventually found in the woods.[35]

In eight months Labelle visited 258 classes and spoke with more than 5,800 students.[36] The pilot project then ballooned. Within two years, nineteen policemen were touring schools and having contact annually with 13,000 students. (Policewomen worked with the Catholic School Board on truancy cases and Captain Mongeau of the youth squad planned to have them visit girls' schools for safety lessons.)[37] By late 1969 Labelle suggested that since its inception the police-educators had met

more than 500,000 Montreal schoolchildren. The press regularly celebrated their innovations and diversity orientation, including the work of
Officer Jean-Guy Wong, who addressed young Chinese Canadians and
helped "raise the esteem of police work in the eyes of that community."[38]
While Labelle started with the Catholic School Commission schools,
Constable Gordon Reid worked the Protestant School Board institutions. Through 1967 the city's school boards had formally integrated
these programs into their curricula, and within two years fifteen police
stations had sent officers for formal police-educator training. By the end
of the decade, officers were giving twenty-five-minute lectures for nursery
school students, forty-minute lectures to elementary school classes, and
hour-long sessions with high school students and meeting with parents
in the evenings.[39] Labelle also hosted radio programs answering youth's
questions. In 1968, he appeared on a local television station where he
discussed such pressing topics as alcohol, drugs, and delinquency.[40]

As illegal drug use among teenagers became more apparent, Labelle
modified his lessons to students to include the harmful effects of the
decade's drug craze. He told his colleagues that youth today found in
drugs a "new religion," a trip, and a way to get away from family and
school.[41] In late 1968, the Catholic School Board of Montreal (CECM)
approved the contents of the lessons for Labelle and colleagues, such as
the course on prevention of hallucinogenic drug use in schools."[42] His
approach was to be straight with the students: demystify the vocabulary
of drugs and how to identify them. Using images, he taught them to
recognize speed, LSD, and heroin. His message, though, leaned heavily on cautionary tales – as opposed to a "dialogue" or conversation.
Labelle outlined the seriousness of drug crimes and how this vice could
enslave youth.[43]

In early 1969, youth officers claimed responsibility for the 17 per cent
decline in juvenile delinquency and for having revised the city's police
reputation as beloved advisers to young people. This school liaison
scheme in the context of 1960s youth activism and unrest caught global
attention, especially in the French-speaking world. In November 1967,
France's prime minister sent representatives of the Ministry of Sports to
Montreal find out how to deal with youth problems.[44] Representatives
from Gabon, Tunisia, and Haiti followed suit. The Quebec press quoted
international guests' amazement at the kind of positive relationship the
young people had with police "compared to the hostility witnessed at

home."[45] In 1970, at an international congress on juvenile delinquency held in Versailles, France, Labelle and colleagues plugged their work: "The delegates were amazed not only ... with an in-school educational program, but also that it was accepted by school authorities and the students themselves."[46]

How did the youth respond? The students were not asked to vote on this program per se, but those surveyed in the early years of the program found the officers amiable; 80 per cent of students claimed that after the school liaison officers' visit they considered the youth squad officers like friends.[47] Likely some felt alienated by law enforcement moving into their schools. Here, too, the media spun this positively – the Montreal newspaper *La Patrie* suggested that grade ten girls who had just heard an hour-long discussion about law, drugs, and delinquency asked for more instruction and time.[48] The frank talk about teenage behaviour (and likely their own vulnerability) was "indispensable" – that delinquency in their minds was subjective and he (Claude Labelle) helped clarify what exactly was being policed. "He gave us a lot to reflect upon," one student told a reporter, "unlike when our parents talk." The implication was that Labelle could reach teenagers in a way that eluded parents; he understood their milieu – the gangs, the drugs, the dangers, and the consequences.[49] Students seemed to be fascinated by straight talk on the effects of drugs and had many more questions. The report concludes that this program is urgent.[50] Yet not all police educators were as popular as Labelle. Eventually the school boards would find that students responded negatively to police authority and in the 1970s pronounced the police educators' efforts a failure.[51]

For police departments this innovation permitted a way to not only control crime but also influence the public's attitude toward police work. The police-educators became the solution to rising delinquency rates, youth alienation in turbulent times, and heightened antipathy toward the police. By directing their efforts at kids in school the officers had a captive audience for their message and their presence, which was welcomed by school administrations as it served to reinforce adult authority. The press coverage emphasized how teaching young people about the law and getting them to know their local officers could help steer them to a course free of trouble. This strategy could be seen as an exercise in developing liberal citizenship and competency: a youth armed with the knowledge of legal rights (and wrongs) was one ready to grow up and participate in society. Ultimately the program normalized the presence of law enforcement in elementary and high schools. Students in high-delinquency districts likely felt the police-educator as an invasion and threat rather than an opportunity to become part of the community.

Our Times: The Armed Presence in Schools

Placing police officers in schools became a popular feature of community policing from the 1960s onwards. In Canada, school liaison programs maintained similar goals to those of the 1960s police-educators in Montreal: crime prevention education, investigation of criminal offences, the "elimination of barriers between youth and police," and the promotion of law enforcement work.[52] By the 1990s, these program officers also performed the role of safety auditor and educator, coach, and club adviser.[53] In both Canada and the United States juvenile liaison officers and SROs could be caught between an older model of assertive and tough policing and the avuncular and sympathetic youth-oriented approach. This tension – the paradox of protection – underscored crime prevention schemes across the century. As Alfred J. Kahn noted in the 1950s in his assessment of police work with youth in New York City, police officers were trained to *deter* crime and delinquency and *enforce* the law, muddying their role in prevention schemes.[54] By the 1990s US schools, unlike the majority of their Canadian counterparts, turned many SROs into armed guards, emphasizing enforcement in the name of child protection. Toronto's recent SRO program, that seems to have followed the US model, has been controversial since its inception in 2008, with complaints that it promoted the school-to-prison pipeline and discriminated against racialized youth.[55]

Criminologists suggest that violence in American schools was still relatively rare in the 1980s and '90s but that school shootings gave the impression that it was everywhere and out of control. Student violence performed in dramatic and shocking fashion at the Columbine High School massacre of 1999, in which fifteen students died, exacerbated heightened public anxiety over school safety everywhere. Columbine solidified what sociologist Randall R. Beger calls a "climate of fear" in which student safety became an impossible goal and justified "drastic measures."[56] To quell the rising tide of anxiety public officials and schools turned to an augmented police presence in schools as a quick fix.[57]

Throughout the 1990s the police presence in schools followed several models and expanded dramatically in both Canada and the United States. According to Na and Gottfredson, in 1975, principals in only 1 per cent of US schools reported police stationed at schools; by 1997 principals in 22 per cent of schools reported having a police officer protecting their schools.[58] Also by 1997, there were almost ten thousand school resource officers (a.k.a. local police officers) in public schools.[59] In a 2007 survey of students aged twelve to eighteen, 69 per cent said they had police officers or security guards in their schools.[60]

In the name of keeping students safe, the police presence in schools has meant a more repressive approach toward young people. School resource officers conduct a number of duties including patrolling school grounds, searching lockers, and generally taking over disciplinary roles that teachers used to fill. They also arrest students who are in violation of the rules and the law. Most remarkably, they constitute an armed presence in schools that supersedes the authority of the principal and other school authorities.[61] The police presence has been accompanied by an increase in security measures – including surveillance cameras, metal detectors, and search and seizure – to the point where criminologists refer to schools as "prison-like" environments. The vast majority of schools require guests to sign in and students are forbidden to leave at lunchtime.[62] Criminologists argue that the widespread use of police officers and technological surveillance in schools has facilitated the link between school and the criminal justice system and can be seen as part of the turn toward mass incarceration.[63] Not surprisingly, then, the school is participating in prison-like discipline, training "lower income and minority youths [to become] habituated to treatment that many are bound to eventually experience in prison."[64]

Beyond the strict control of access, Hirschfield suggests that the police-in-schools program was part of an overall "criminalization of school discipline," meaning that what used to be dealt with by the school – student discipline – was now falling under the purview of the police. The informal handling of student discipline by teachers and administration may have been far from ideal, but with the police presence, students learn early to mistrust authority and also that they are not trusted; this alienation is linked to misbehaviour.[65] US courts have facilitated this development by granting police and school officials more authority to conduct searches of students, whose Fourth Amendment rights (protecting them from the extended arm of the law in public schools) are being abrogated.[66]

The recent proliferation and normalization of the police presence in schools was predicated on an old binary in the discourse around the nature of youth: being at once endangered and dangerous. This recent securitization of schools is just the latest in a series of moral panics that youth are out of control and require a broad and thorough response from the state. The nineteenth-century emergence of child welfare and juvenile justice reform similarly operated around anxieties about children, who were constructed as either vulnerable or vicious; in the latter part of the century this reform produced new institutions (reform schools and juvenile courts). The special institutional categorization based on age focused on rehabilitation – teaching the vicious and vulnerable to better adapt to societal norms. The municipal police did not embrace this age-specific treatment for wayward youth and instead hung on to its crime control mission (and thereby effectively repressing youth). It was not until the 1930s that the municipal police became integrated into the juvenile justice apparatus and made a youth-conscious turn. With the rise of youth-conscious policing – in the guise of youth squads and friendly officers – police officers paved the way for entering schools and becoming embedded in childhood and adolescence.

Notes

Introduction

1 Goluboff, *Vagrant Nation.*
2 Wojcik, "Coplay Council Favors Teen Curfew," *Morning Call* (Allentown), 2 September 2015, 6.
3 In the seventeenth and eighteenth centuries, legal practice followed political determinations that deemed the child incapable of reasoned consent and not the legal equals of adults. In the nineteenth century children were further understood in more age-defined ways, with the rights of minors circumscribed by their dependent status within the family. See Brewer, *By Birth or Consent: Children, Law, and the Anglo-American Revolution in Authority*; Grossberg, *Governing the Hearth*; Chudacoff, *How Old Are You?*; for Quebec see Joyal, *Les enfants, la société et l'état au Québec, 1608–1989.*
4 Canada raised the age to twelve in 1983.
5 Schlossman, *Transforming Juvenile Justice*, introduction.
6 Sutherland, *Children in English-Canadian Society* (1976; repr., 2000).
7 Schneider, *In the Web of Class.* For arguments about the class bias in juvenile justice, see Platt, *The Child Savers* (1969; repr., 2009).
8 I was influenced by delinquency studies that stressed the development of juvenile justice institutions (laws, courts, and reform schools) in the context of a child-saving reform ethos or on the class, gender, and racial biases of the new court systems. See Platt, *The Child Savers*; Ryerson, *Best Laid Plans*; Schlossman, *Love and the American Delinquent*; and Sutherland, *Children in English-Canadian Society.*

9   Donzelot, *The Policing of Families*; Cox, *Gender, Justice, and Welfare*;
    Hogeveen, "'The Evils with Which We Are Called to Grapple,'"
    37–68; Iacovetta and Mitchenson, "Delinquent Girls, Working-Class
    Parents, and the Family Courts," in *On the Case*; Myers, *Caught*; Odem,
    Delinquent Daughters; Sangster, *Girl Trouble*; Trépanier and Quevillon,
    "Garçons et filles: la définition des problèmes posés par les mineurs
    traduits à la cour des jeunes délinquants de Montréal (1912-1950)," in
    Bard et al., eds., *Femmes et justice pénale*.

10 See Wolcott, *Cops and Kids*.

11 For an overview see Fogelson, *Big-City Police*; Hahn and Jeffries, *Urban
    America and Its Police*; Marquis, *The Vigilant Eye*; Garland, *The Culture of
    Control*.

12 Garland, *The Culture of Control*, 32.

13 Wolcott, Introduction.

14 This reform – sometimes called the professional era of policing – dates
    in the US from 1900 to 1960. See Walker, *The Police in America*; and
    Marquis, "Policing the Urban Age," in *The Vigilant Eye*.

15 Cohen, *Visions of Social Control*.

16 Grant, *The Boy Problem*; Carrigan, *Juvenile Delinquency in Canada*.

17 Marquis, *Policing Canada's Century*, 184–5.

18 Ibid., 185.

19 Potter, *War on Crime*.

20 The role of the beat cop as community hero or enemy has been
    addressed by police historians. See Walker, *The Police in America*;
    Umbach, "Introduction," *The Last Neighbourhood Cops*.

21 Sidney Katz, "Why Do We Hate the Police?," *Maclean's*, 30 August 1958,
    9–11, 38, at 9.

22 Schneider, Agee, and Chronopolous, "Dirty Work: Police and
    Community Relations and the Limits of Liberalism in Postwar
    Philadelphia," 1–9.

23 Katz, "Why Do We Hate the Police?," 38.

24 Field and Syrett, eds., *Age in America*; Chudacoff, *How Old Are You?*; on
    adolescence see Comacchio, *The Dominion of Youth*.

25 On the state response to modern childhood, see Lindenmeyer, *A Right
    to Childhood*.

26 Constable E.R. Moore, "Understand That Juvenile Delinquent," RCMP
    Quarterly 11, no. 2/3 (October 1945 and January 1946), 129.

27 Cohen, *Visions of Social Control*, 218–19.

28 Maxine Davis, "The Cop Appeals to the Kids," *Saturday Evening Post*, 29 April 1944, 28, 96–7. About 1,200 boys had signed up according to the article. About 300 girls were also involved but their activities were not mentioned.

29 Police presence in playgrounds and schools helped create what Michel Foucault referred to as the disciplinary society, which featured constant oversight and control. Burchell et al., eds., *The Foucault Effect*.

30 The punitive turn in Canada can be tied to the Young Offenders Act 1984, the panic over violent youth in the 1990s, and the 2003 Youth Criminal Justice Act. See Marquis, *Policing Canada's Century*, 181–2.

31 Jackson with Bartie, *Policing Youth*, 2.

32 Flamm, *Law and Order*, 14–17.

33 "Delinquency Wanes Here: Bureau Chief Cites City Improvement," *Montreal Star*, 2 February, 1956; "J'ai joué à la veste de cuir," *Le Petit Journal*, 5 February 1956; "The Black Jackets: Hanging Around, Boys Gradually Drawn into Gang," *Montreal Gazette*, 2 February 1956.

34 Garland, *The Culture of Control*, 28.

35 Marquis, *The Vigilant Eye*, 67.

36 Appier, "'We're Blocking Youth's Path to Crime:' The Los Angeles Coordinating Councils during the Great Depression," 191.

37 Umbach, *The Last Neighbourhood Cops*.

38 Agee, "Crisis and Redemption: The History of American Police Reform since World War II," 1–10, at 3.

39 Bush, *Who Gets a Childhood?*; Ward, *The Black Child-Savers*.

40 Hinton, *From the War on Poverty to the War on Crime*, 123; Bush, *Who Gets a Childhood?* chapter 5.

41 Proceedings of his speech: Jean-Paul Gilbert, "Origine et justification du policier-éducateur," *Police Jeunesse* (Montreal: Graph-o Pier, 1970): 19–34, at 23.

42 "Help Minority Youth," *Montreal Gazette*, 12 December 1988.

Chapter One

1 "Want Police Work Made a Profession," *Municipal Review of Canada* (September 1938): 8.

2 "Boys' Gold Medal Goes to Valentine," *New York Times*, 5 April 1945, 25.

3 Garland, *The Culture of Control*, 30–2.
4 Deputy Police Commissioner James B. Nolan, "New York Crime Prevention Work," *Canadian Police Gazette* 22, no. 5 (August 1947): 1.
5 The *Municipal Review of Canada* was a compendium of articles gathered from across North America on municipal issues including crime. It frequently printed articles supporting this direction of police practice: see "Cities Can Cut the Costs of Crime," *Municipal Review of Canada* (September 1937): 20 (from the *Michigan Municipal Review*).
6 Potter, *War on Crime*.
7 Early juvenile justice historiography emphasizes how the child savers and child welfare advocates asserted an emergent middle class–based construction of proper childhood in their mission to rescue the "waifs and strays" of industrializing American cities. Platt, *The Child Savers* (2009 [1969]); Mennel, *Thorns and Thistles*; and Schlossman, *Transforming Juvenile Justice*.
8 Early historiography on childhood emphasized how state formation and child welfare were integral: see, for example, Sutherland, *Children in English-Canadian Society*; Rooke and Schnell, *Discarding the Asylum*; Comacchio, *"Nations Are Built of Babies"*; Joyal, ed., *Entre surveillance et compassion*. For the US see Grossberg, *Governing the Hearth*.
9 Ward, *The Black Child-Savers*, 11.
10 Ibid., conclusion. Ward stresses the efforts of the African American child savers to replace Jim Crow juvenile justice with a racially inclusive system.
11 Wolcott, *Cops and Kids*; and see, for example, Mitrani, *The Working Class in American History*.
12 Platt, *The Child Savers*; Tanenhaus, *Juvenile Justice in the Making*; Myers, *Caught*.
13 Wolcott, *Cops and Kids*, 127.
14 Fogelson, *Big-City Police*, 86–7.
15 Houston, "'The Waifs and Strays' of a Late Victorian City," 131.
16 Baldwin, "Nocturnal Habits and Dark Wisdom," 593–611; Gilfoyle, "Street Rats and Guttersnipes," 853–82; Romesburg, "Wouldn't a Boy Do? Placing Early-Twentieth-Century Male Youth Sex Work in the Histories of Sexuality," 367–92; Hogeveen, "The Evils with Which We Are Called to Grapple," 37–68.
17 Gilfoyle, "Street Rats and Guttersnipes," 865; Stansell, *City of Women*.
18 See Stansell, *City of Women*; Poutanen, *Beyond Brutal Passions*; Gilfoyle, *City of Eros*.

19 Gilfoyle, "Street Rats and Guttersnipes," 870.

20 For overviews see chapter 8, "Save the Child," in Mintz, *Huck's Raft*, 154–83; Sutherland, *Children in English-Canadian Society*; Joyal, ed., *Entre surveillance et compassion*.

21 Ward, *The Black Child-Savers*.

22 Wolcott, *Cops and Kids*, 20; see also Monkkonen, *Police in Urban America, 1860–1920*; Harring, *Policing a Class Society*.

23 Wolcott, *Cops and Kids*, 22–3.

24 Ibid., 27.

25 Gilfoyle, "Street Rats and Guttersnipes," 869–70.

26 In most jurisdictions, juvenile delinquency was a broad designation that included minor offences only juveniles could commit as well as violation of laws. Serious criminal acts could trigger a transfer to adult court. Media and experts still used the term juvenile "crime" especially when referring to criminal acts committed by young people, even if they would be labelled juvenile delinquents.

27 Schlossman, *Love and the American Delinquent*; Ryerson, *Best Laid Plans*.

28 Wolcott, *Cops and Kids*, 120.

29 Ibid., 122–4.

30 "Spanked the Kids," *Canadian Police Gazette* 10, no. 10 (January 1936).

31 Constable E.R. Moore, "Understand That Juvenile Delinquent," RCMP *Quarterly* 11, no. 2/3 (October 1945 and January 1946): 128.

32 Wolcott, *Cops and Kids*, chapter 4.

33 See Myers, *Caught*; Hogeveen, "'The Evils with Which We Are Called to Grapple;'" Platt, *The Child Savers*; and Schlossman, *Love and the American Delinquent*.

34 Marquis, "The Police as a Social Service in Early Twentieth-Century Toronto," 335–58.

35 "Toronto Policewomen to Patrol Downtown," *Montreal Gazette*, 1 August 1942, 11.

36 "Police Will Establish Metro Youth Bureau," *Globe and Mail*, 16 January 1959, 4; "Youth Bureau's Task," *Globe and Mail*, 13 April 1959, 7. The original bureau comprised four policewomen and three policemen. By the late 1960s, Inspector Fern Alexander headed the bureau, having joined the force (one of three policewomen in 1952). "Police to Give CAS Names of Potential Troublemakers," *Globe and Mail*, 23 July 1969, 8.

37 Potter, *War on Crime*.

38 Fass, *The Damned and the Beautiful*; Comacchio, *The Dominion of Youth*.

39 Appier, "'We're Blocking Youth's Path to Crime,' 190–218, at 196–7.
40 "Cities Can Cut the Costs of Crime," 20.
41 "Protests the Lash," *Canadian Police Gazette* 6, no. 1 (April 1931): 22.
    "There is unfortunately more romanticizing of degenerate gunmen than
    is good for the youth of the present day." The unidentified journalist was
    rejecting Minister of Parliament J.S. Woodsworth's complaint about the
    use of the lash on a sixteen-year-old "robber."
42 J. Edgar Hoover, "Age and Crime," *Canadian Police Gazette* 11, no. 9
    (December 1936): 30–1.
43 "Cities Can Cut the Costs of Crime," 20.
44 Ibid.
45 Mrs E.T. Sampson, "The Youth of Today," *Municipal Review of Canada*
    (August–September 1939): 19.
46 Ibid.
47 C.A. Wylie, "The Problem of Unemployed Youth," *Municipal Review of
    Canada* (October 1939): 11.
48 Nolan, "New York Crime Prevention Work," 1.
49 New York Public Library, New York City, *Annual Report of the Police
    Department* (1931), 117.
50 Frederic M. Thrasher, "The Lower West Side Crime Prevention Program,
    New York City," 49.
51 Sheldon and Eleanor Glueck, "Introduction," in *Preventing Crime*, 6.
52 Thrasher, "Lower West Side," 49: Thrasher suggests using the term
    "incipient delinquent" to describe children growing up in areas such
    as New York's Lower West Side, which was known for its immigrant
    character and poverty but also its "crime-breeding" blocks and lack of
    recreational facilities.
53 Glueck, "Introduction," in *Preventing Crime*, 7.
54 Ibid., 6.
55 Ibid., 7, quoting Charles S. Thompson.
56 Ibid., 5.
57 Appier, "We're Blocking Youth's Path to Crime," 192.
58 John Kidman, "Crime Prevention in Wartime," *Municipal Review of
    Canada* (June 1943): 17.
59 Ibid.
60 Nolan, "New York Crime Prevention Work," 1.
61 His accomplishments were transformative: he demanded more and

extensive training and education of officers, sought out the latest technology for investigative police work, and created what we might associate as the modern police force. Wolcott, *Cops and Kids*, 128–9.

62 Elisabeth Lossing, "The Crime Prevention Work of the Berkeley Police Department," 237–63, at 239.

63 Wolcott, *Cops and Kids*, 130.

64 Lossing, "Crime Prevention Work," 241.

65 Ibid., 240.

66 Ibid., 242.

67 Ibid., 244–5.

68 Ibid., 245.

69 Appier, "We're Blocking the Youth's Path to Crime," 195.

70 Lossing, "Crime Prevention Work," 247.

71 Ibid., 249.

72 Wolcott, *Cops and Kids*, 128–31. See also Lossing, "Crime Prevention Work," 237–63.

73 Lossing, "Crime Prevention Work."

74 See Wolcott, *Cops and Kids*; Edward J. Escobar, *Race, Police, and the Making of a Political Identity*.

75 Lossing, "Crime Prevention Work," 258.

76 A.P. Woollacott, "Junior G-Men of Canada," *Maclean's*, January 1939, 14–27; Comacchio, *Dominion of Youth*, 201.

77 Kahn, *Police and Children*, 12.

78 New York City [Mayor's Committee on Juvenile Delinquency], "Report on The Juvenile Aid Bureau and the Prevention of Crime and Delinquency," 5 June 1944, 2.

79 Glueck, "Introduction," in *Preventing Crime*, 15.

80 Kahn, *Police and Children*, 12.

81 Ibid., 12.

82 Ibid.

83 Wolcott, *Cops and Kids*, 94; Kahn, *Police and Children*, 12. Junior Police were the precursors to the Police Athletics Leagues; welfare lieutenants were established in 1915–16.

84 New York City, "Report on The Juvenile Aid Bureau," 3; Nolan, "New York Crime Prevention Work," 1.

85 New York City, "Report on The Juvenile Aid Bureau," 2.

86 Ibid.

87 The latter began as the Philadelphia Training School for Social
    Work 1908 and is now the School of Social Policy and Practice of the
    University of Pennsylvania. See "Miss Additon Made Crime Bureau
    Head," *New York Times*, 12 October 1930, 22.

88 Ibid.

89 Ibid.

90 "Drive on Wayward Planned," *New York Times*, 25 November 1930, 27. She
    repeated this point at the 1933 Annual Congress of the American Prison
    Association and emphasized that her bureau was turning boys from
    crime to athletics. "Crime Deterrent Seen in Probation," *New York Times*,
    11 October 1933, 26.

91 "Rise in Child Crime Laid to Depression," *New York Times*, 4 December
    1932, 8.

92 Kahn, *Police and Children*, 13.

93 In the 1930s, she served on the Motion Picture Research Council, which
    examined the "influence of motion pictures on the health, attitude and
    conduct of children and adolescents." "Hibben Heads Motion Picture
    Research Group to Lead Campaign Next Fall for Better Films," *New York
    Times*, 25 July 1932, 17.

94 "Rise in Child Crime Laid to Depression," 8; "Urges Single Court for
    Family Cases," *New York Times*, 4 November 1932, 21.

95 "166 City Play Sites Urged by Police," *New York Times*, 20 June 1933, 21.

96 Ibid.

97 "Anti-Crime Bill Signed by Walker: Mayor Signs Bill Making Prevention
    Unit Permanent Part of Police Work," *New York Times*, 17 June 1931, 22.

98 New York City, "Report on The Juvenile Aid Bureau," 3.

99 According to the Police Department's Manual of Procedure (article 10
    Section 14), the JAB "shall be responsible for a) planning and placing
    into operation measures for the prevention of delinquency in NYC b)
    helping to secure adequate social treatment for juvenile delinquents and
    wayward minors." Quoted in New York City, "Report on The Juvenile
    Aid Bureau," 2; "[Report of] The Juvenile Aid Bureau of the New York
    City Police Department and the Police Athletic League," 1 September
    1943, 5.

100 Quoted in New York City, "Report on The Juvenile Aid Bureau," 3.

101 Ibid., 5.

102 Ibid., 4.

103 Nolan, "New York Crime Prevention Work," 4.

104 For a discussion of how juvenile justice of the early twentieth century reflected white supremacy see chapters 4 and 5 of Ward, *The Black Child-Savers*. Hinton's *From the War on Poverty to the War on Crime* locates juvenile "(in)justice" mechanics in the 1960s and '70s but clearly during the Great Migration discrimination was already underway. Hinton, *From the War on Poverty to the War on Crime*, chapter 6.

105 "Police Plan Lists of Wayward Boys," *New York Times*, 4 August 1936, 21.

106 "5,000 Put on Truant List," *New York Times*, 5 August 1936, 17.

107 Kahn, *Police and Children*, 14.

108 New York City, "Report on The Juvenile Aid Bureau," 7.

109 Ibid.

110 Schlossman and Sedlak, "The Chicago Area Project Revisited," 398–462.

111 As William Bush explains, protected childhood had been on the agenda of reformers since the early nineteenth century; a century of policies and programs followed, yet the result was "abject failure." Bush, *Who Gets a Childhood?*, 5.

112 Lossing, "Crime Prevention Work," 252.

113 Wolcott, *Cops and Kids*, 127.

114 Nolan, "New York Crime Prevention Work," 4.

115 Reprinted as "The Children's Friend," *Canadian Police Gazette* 11, no. 5 (August 1936): 23.

Chapter Two

1 Brodeur, *La délinquance de l'ordre*. For a discussion of the anti-vice campaigns and official inquiries into police corruption, see Lapointe, *Nettoyer Montréal*.

2 Turmel, *Police de Montréal, historique du service*, 152.

3 Ibid., 207; Before the Second World War, the police budget was under 6 per cent of the municipal budget, rising to over 8 per cent by 1954. Ibid., 206.

4 The bureau was located on Craig Street, now rue Saint-Antoine.

5 "La protection des jeunes à Montréal," *Le Devoir*, 28 August 1948; "L'Évolution du Bureau de la Prévention de la Délinquance," *Montréal Matin*, 11 March 1952. "Youth Aid Section, MUCPD, History," Service de Documentation, Service de Police Communauté Urbaine de Montréal, n.d., ca 1977; Consultation Régionale sur les Relations Communautaires Région Est, "Historique de la Section Aide à la Jeunesse," Service

de Documentation, Service de Police Communauté Urbaine de
Montréal, 1980.

6　Archives Municipales de la Ville de Montréal, Département de Police,
Personnel File, Ovila Pelletier 104-03-04-00, "Statement of Ovila Pelletier
an applicant for appointment as policeman of the Police Force of the
City of Montreal," 26 September 1922.

7　Montreal was known in the 1940s and 1950s as the "wide-open" city
where vice and corruption were tolerated until a series of citizens'
committees fought back. See Kuplowsky, "A Captivating 'Open City'";
Straw, "Montreal and *The Captive City*," 13–24; Weintraub, *City Unique*.
On police corruption, citizens' committees, and official inquiries, see
Lapointe, *Nettoyer Montréal*; Turmel, *Police de Montréal, historique du
service*, vol. 2: 187; and Brodeur, *La délinquance de l'ordre*. L'enquête Caron
(1950–53) indicted police tolerance of gambling establishments and
brothels. During the 1960s Police Chief J. Adrien Robert instituted a
plan for change, encouraging university courses and degrees for officers
and attempting to clean up police comportment in response to the
negative public image.

8　Marquis suggests that police services in Canada were "monopolized by
dominant ethnic groups." Marquis, *The Vigilant Eye*, 188. "Why No Ethnic
Police?," *Montreal Gazette*, 4 July 1979.

9　Turmel, *Police de Montréal*, 199.

10　Myers, *Caught*; and Myers, "Embodying Delinquency," 383–414.

11　Det.-Sgt. A.O. Pelletier, "Campaign Ahead to Stamp out Juvenile Crime,"
Revue des Agents de Police / Constables Review 1, no.1 (February 1946): 12.

12　On parental blame see Gleason, *Normalizing the Ideal*.

13　Sidney Katz, "It's a Tough Time to Be a Kid," *Maclean's*, 15 December
1950, 7.

14　See Marquis, "The Police as a Social Service in Early Twentieth-Century
Toronto," 335–58.

15　Archives Municipales de la Ville de Montréal, Département de Police,
Annual Reports, 1930s.

16　On the child protection and welfare movement in Canada see Jones
and Rutman, *In the Children's Aid*; Joyal, *Entre surveillance et compassion*;
Sutherland, *Children in English-Canadian Society*.

17　Archives Municipales de la Ville de Montréal, Département de Police,
Personnel File, Julien White [Secretary of the Delinquency Prevention
Bureau], letter to the Comité des Greffs, Syndicat des Fonctionnaires
Municipaux, 30 January 1948. In this letter, he recounts the history of the

Juvenile Morality Squad. He suggests this began in 1934, although Ovila Pelletier claims in print that it started in 1935 and 1936. Officially, the JMS is mentioned in the Police Department Annual Reports in 1941.

18 Pelletier, "Campaign Ahead to Stamp out Juvenile Crime," 12.

19 Comacchio, "Dancing to Perdition: Adolescence and Leisure in Interwar English Canada," 5–35; Myers, *Caught*, 64–70.

20 For an overview of the policing of labour see Marquis, "Policing Class Conflict and Political Dissent to 1970," in *The Vigilant Eye*, 95–132.

21 "Juvenile Delinquency in Montreal," *Canadian Police Gazette* 14, no. 3 (June 1939): 10–11.

22 Ibid., 10–11.

23 Ibid.

24 Archives Municipales de la Ville de Montréal, Département de Police, Personnel File, Ovila Pelletier, letter from Judge Arthur Laramée to Director Fernand Dufresne, 19 November 1942, 2.

25 Freedman, "'Uncontrolled Desires': The Response to the Sexual Psychopath, 1920–1960"; Jenkins, *Moral Panic*.

26 Bibliothèque et Archives Nationales du Québec, à Montréal, Fonds de la Cour des Jeunes Délinquants de la Cité de Montréal/Montreal Juvenile Delinquents' Court (hereafter MJDC), Dossier 2282-2292, 1940. The theatres mentioned in this case, the Crystal and the Midway, appeared in other cases involving adult men and young boys; in MJDC, Dossier 606, 1941, a fourteen-year-old boy and his ten-year-old friend were witnesses in a case against a thirty-five-year-old man who gave them money in exchange for manual and oral sex, all of which allegedly occurred at his workplace. The older boy admitted to attending the theatres and being involved in masturbating men and having oral sex with them there.

27 MJDC, Dossier 2287, 1940.

28 "Juvenile Delinquency in Montreal," 10–11.

29 MJDC, Dossiers 8987, 8988, 8989, 8990, 9003, 9004, 9007, 1945.

30 Juvenile Delinquents Act, S.C. 1908, c.40, 1929 revised (Canada).

31 Pelletier, "Campaign Ahead to Stamp Out Juvenile Crime," 12.

32 Miriam Chapin, "Boys' Clubs Run by Police Cut Down Delinquency," *Saturday Night*, 5 April 1949.

33 Chief Constable Walter H. Mulligan, "Molestation of Children," *Canadian Police Gazette* 22, no. 10 (January 1948): 1. Differences between the two charges included penalties: the maximum penalty for the former, a federal Criminal Code offence, was six months. Several of the men in the above case received sentences well in excess of six months.

34 Senior Crown Prosecutor Irenée Lagarde, "Rape and Similar Offences,"
    Revue des Agents de Police / Constables Review 1, no. 9 (October 1946):
    32–45, at 40.

35 Roderick Haig-Brown, "Problems of Modern Life and Young Offenders,"
    Saturday Night, 28 May 1955, 9–11, at 9.

36 Juvenile Delinquents Act (Canada). Article 33. "(1) Any person, whether
    the parent or guardian of the child or not, who, knowingly or willfully,
    (a) aids, causes, abets or connives at the commission by a child of a
    delinquency, or (b) does any act producing, promoting, or contributing
    to a child's being or becoming a juvenile delinquent or likely to make
    any child a juvenile delinquent, is liable on summary conviction before a
    juvenile court or a magistrate to a fine not exceeding five hundred dollars
    or to imprisonment for a period not exceeding two years, or to both.
    (2) Any person who, being the parent or guardian of the child and
    being able to do so, knowingly neglects to do that which would directly
    tend to prevent the child being or becoming a juvenile delinquent or
    to remove the conditions that render or are likely to render the child a
    juvenile delinquent is liable on summary conviction before a juvenile
    court or a magistrate to a fine not exceeding five hundred dollars or to
    imprisonment for a period not exceeding two years, or to both."

37 For example, Pelletier investigated the case of a grandmother who
    abused her granddaughter in MJDC, Dossier 1343, 1940; in another
    case, a woman with five children under the age of eight was judged
    "amoral" for receiving men while her husband was institutionalized for
    tuberculosis (MJDC, Dossier 657, 1939). In other cases, witnesses described
    minor girls being exposed to commercial sex exchanges and being
    pressured to participate. See MJDC, Dossiers 6610 and 7394, 1944.

38 "Dr. Watson's Corner," *La Revue des Agents de Police / Constables Review* 3,
    no. 2 (February 1948): 59.

39 MJDC, Dossier 4023, 1943, J.E.A. Marcotte, M.D., "Psychiatric Examination
    Report," 11 June 1943, Arthur L.

40 MJDC, Dossier 2038, 1942, Judge Robilliard, Summary, Simeon L., 5.
    The judge fined him $300 plus court costs, deciding that he had indeed
    committed the offence and was "un être dépravé, pervers, corrumpu."

41 MJDC, Dossier 1035, 1939, Édouard L. Judged incapable of understanding
    the gravity of his actions, the accused was sent to the Bordeaux Hospital
    for the Insane. MJDC, Dossier 3350, 1943, Robert V. fined $40 (or three
    months in prison) plus court costs.

42　MJDC, Dossier 2398, 1942. The judge in this instance sentenced the man to two years less a day (the maximum sentence under article 33), then sent his paperwork to the federal authorities, who proceeded with deportation.

43　"Un garçon de 9 ans est assassiné à la montagne," *La Patrie* (Quebec), 26 February 1945, 3. "Garçonnet assassiné à la montagne," *Montréal Matin*, 26 February 1945, 5.

44　"Police Hold 3 Possible Suspects in Search for Mountain Murderer," *Montreal Gazette*, 28 February 1945, 13.

45　"Police Follow Hundreds of Tips in Search of Benson Boy Slayer," *Montreal Gazette*, 3 March 1945, 13.

46　"Police Hunt Machinist in Kidnap-Murder," *Montreal Gazette*, 2 August 1954, 1.

47　See Jenkins, "Age of the Sexual Psychopath, 1935–1957," in *Moral Panic*; and Chenier, "Criminal Sexual Psychopathy: The Birth of a Legal Concept," in *Strangers in Our Midst*.

48　Gleason, *Normalizing the Ideal*, 82.

49　"Dr. Watson's Corner," *La Revue des Agents de Police / Constables Review* 1, no. 2 (February 1946): 15. Doctors examining adults and youth for the juvenile court also used the term "inverti." See for example, MJDC, Dossier 1392, 30 September 1947, Report of Dr. Emile Legrand, 20 October 1947.

50　See case of Thomas R., MJDC, Dossier 208, 13 February 1946; Report of the probation officer, 12 April 1946. This equation was common in the 1930s and '40s when the law on criminal sexual psychopaths began to change. See George, "The Harmless Psychopath," 225.

51　Translated from the French by author. MJDC, Dossier 1392, 1947, Report on Benoît B., Émile Legrand, 20 October 1947.

52　MJDC, Dossier 1904, 1948, probation officer report.

53　Robertson, "What's Law Got to Do with It? Legal Records and Sexual Histories," 161–85; Romesburg, "'Wouldn't a Boy Do?': Placing Early-Twentieth-Century Male Youth Sex Work into the Histories of Sexuality," 367–92; Maynard, "Horrible Temptations," 191–235.

54　Robertson, "Shifting the Scene of the Crime," 223–42, at 240.

55　Ovila Pelletier, "Allocution" (speech, Annual Convention of the Association des chefs de Police et Pompiers de la Province de Québec, Chicoutimi, Que, July 1946), 8.

56　Translated from the French by author. MJDC, 1947, Dossier 1333, two boys aged eleven and fifteen; probation officer's reports, 17 September 1947.

57 MJDC, Dossier 65, 1948, Probation officer report, 15 March 1948; Report from the Clinique de l'Aide à l'Enfance, Dr D. Voghel, Médécin-Psychologue, 16 March 1948; and Dr A. Pilon, Psychiatre, 16 March 1948.

58 MJDC, Dossier 208, 1946.

59 Ibid.

60 Pelletier, "Allocution."

61 Zoe Bieler, "The Cops Who Change Diapers," *Maclean's*, 15 January 1952, 22–4.

62 Service de Police Communauté Urbaine de Montréal, "Youth Aid Section, MUCPD, History," Service de Documentation, MUCPD.

63 Of the six girls involved, the records indicate that three (MJDC 8988, 8989, 8990) were given three-year sentences to the Maison de Lorette reform school.

64 Fishman, *The Battle for Children*; Keshen, *Saints, Sinners, and Soldiers*; Myers, *Caught*.

65 Gilbert, *A Cycle of Outrage*, 14.

66 Fahrni, "The Romance of Reunion," 187–208.

67 See the *Canadian Police Gazette* and the *Canadian Police Bulletin*, both of which contained myriad stories of postwar delinquency problems and reproduced US, British, and Canadian press articles on delinquency.

68 Gerald Zoffer, "Underworld Evils Breed Juvenile Delinquency," *Saturday Night*, 12 January 1946, 6–7, at 6.

69 Ruth Hobberlin, "Why Blame Comics, Movies, Etc., for the Young's Delinquency?," *Saturday Night*, 16 November 1946, 28.

70 Gilbert, *Cycle of Outrage*, 27; Keshen, "The Children's War: 'Youth Run Wild,'" in *Saints, Sinners, and Soldiers*, 194–227.

71 Pelletier, "Campaign to Stamp Out Juvenile Crime," 12.

72 John McLeish, "Youth Problems in Wartime," *Municipal Review of Canada*, 39, nos. 7–8 (July/August, 1942): 7.

73 "'Teen-Age' Unrest Held Due to War," *Montreal Gazette*, 22 January 1941, 5; Myers, *Caught*, 70–5.

74 "Inquiries into Juvenile Crime Indicate Films' Beneficial Effect," *Montreal Gazette*, 11 March 1944, 6.

75 Keshen, *Saints, Sinners, and Soldiers*, 204.

76 Reproduced from *Survey Midmonthly* in *Revue des Agents de Police / Constables Review* 1 no. 2 (March 1946): 2.

77 "Juvenile crime has become a veritable plague not only in Montreal, but in all large cities of the world," wrote medical-legal expert Dr Rosario

Fontaine in 1946, "La criminalité juvénile, *Revue des Agents de Police /
Constables Review* 1, no. 2 (March 1946): 2. Montreal police officer Ovila
Pelletier described youth-oriented commercial leisure spots as "centres
of infection." Pelletier, "Campaign to Stamp Out Juvenile Crime," 12.

78 Gilbert, *Cycle of Outrage*, especially chapters 10 and 11; Schneider,
Vampires, Dragons, and Egyptian Kings.

79 "La criminalité chez les jeunes est devenue un terrible fléau de nos
jours," *La Presse*, 19 October 1945, 5.

80 Julien White, Letter to the Comité des Griefs, 30 January 1948, 2.

81 Police Department annual reports often refer in English to the Juvenile
Prevention Bureau.

82 O.-A. Pelletier, "Le B.M.J [editorial]," *Revue des Agents de Police /
Constables Review* 1, no. 2 (March 1946): 1 and 23.

83 Pelletier, "Allocution," 14.

84 Doris Hedges, "The Citizen and His Child," *Municipal Review of Canada*,
41, no. 3 (March 1944): 6. See also Delinquency Prevention Week,
advertisement.

85 Pelletier, "Campaign Ahead to Stamp Out Juvenile Crime," 12.

86 City of Montreal, Police Department, *Annual Reports*, 1942 and 1944.

87 As summarized in the interview in "L'évolution du Bureau de la
prevention de la délinquance," *Montréal Matin*, 11 March 1952.

88 Bieler, "The Cops Who Change Diapers," 22–4, at 23.

89 *The Times* (Fort Frances, ON), reprinted in *Canadian Police Gazette* 11, no.
8 (November 1936): 35.

90 *La Revue des Agents de Police / Constables Review* 3, no. 4 (April 1948): 36;
Canadian Police Gazette 25, no. 3 (June 1950): 4; *Canadian Police Gazette*
29, no. 3 (May 1954): 20; *Canadian Police Bulletin*, September 1947; and
Canadian Police Bulletin 23, no. 3 (June 1948).

91 Bieler, "The Cops Who Change Diapers," 22–4.

92 Ibid., 23.

93 "Policewoman," *Canadian Police Gazette* 21, no. 4 (July 1946): 9;
"Policewomen Serve Well," *Canadian Police Bulletin*, September 1945, 13.

94 "Want Policewomen," *Canadian Police Gazette* 13, no. 10 (January
1939): 20. Regarding the campaign by the Local Council of Women to
augment the female police force.

95 "Lady Cops as Crime Busters," *Canadian Police Gazette* 21, no. 6
(September 1946): 11.

96 "Policewomen Serve Well," *Canadian Police Bulletin*, September 1945, 13.

97   "Policewoman," *Canadian Police Gazette*, 21, no. 4 (July 1946): 9.

98   Jean Short, "Canada Needs Police-Women," *Municipal Review of Canada of Canada* 42, no. 1 (January 1946): 11.

99   Ibid., 11.

100 Ibid., 12–13.

101 Library and Archives of Canada, Local Council of Women Fonds, MG 28, I 164, vol. 7, file 7-1, "Women's Patrols," copy of motion indicating "deep concern" about lack of patrolmen and therefore protection to citizens, and advocating the hiring of policewomen, 17 May 1944; "Letter to the editor from Mrs. Percy Jacobson, Chairman on Social Behaviour," *Montreal Daily Star*, 11 April 1945.

102 Bibliothèque et Archives Nationales du Québec à Montréal, Local Council of Women Fonds, Annual Reports and Yearbooks, Report of the Social Behaviour Committee, 1946–47 and 1947–48, 56.

103 "9 of 109 Women Qualify for Police," *Canadian Police Gazette* 21, no. 10 (January 1947): 29.

104 Archives Municipales de la Ville de Montréal, Département de Police, Personnel File, Claire Chabot, Cité de Montréal Commission du Service Civil, "Occasions d'emploi permanent, 20 Policières (bilingues)," 6 July 1946. On general qualities of policewomen see Bieler, "The Cops Who Change Diapers," 24.

105 Myers, "Women Policing Women," 229–45.

106 "First in 25 Years: Youth Work Challenges Montreal's Newest Policewoman," *Montreal Gazette*, 20 March 1972.

107 Chabot, Cité de Montréal Commission du Service Civil, "Occasions d'emploi permanent, 20 Policieres (bilingues)."

108 "Hire 25 Women," *Canadian Police Gazette* 20, no. 11 (February 1946): 13.

109 "Montreal Policewomen," *Canadian Police Bulletin*, June 1947, 8; "Hire 25 Women," 13.

110 "Montreal Policewomen," *Canadian Police Gazette* 21, no. 10 (January 1947): 25.

111 "Montreal Policewomen," June 1947, 8.

112 Ibid., 25.

113 Ibid., 8.

114 Bieler, "The Cops Who Change Diapers," 23.

115 Marguerite Cloutier, according to her daughter, found shoes for children on her beat. "La policière pionnière: Marguerite Cloutier-Blouin (1921–2014)," *La Presse*, 8 February 2014, 11.

116 Ibid.

117 Cover [with Claire Chabot and Ida Hache], *Revue des Agents de Police / Constables Review* 3, no. 6 (July 1948), also 17 [Claire Chabot, Marguerite and Regina Cloutier, Ida Hache, Mary Elm], and 19.

118 "City Policewomen Look After the Children's World," *Montreal Gazette*, 30 January, 1968. Still on the force, Claire Chabot was interviewed for this article.

119 "La prevention du délit juvenile à Montréal," *Le Devoir*, 11 March 1952.

120 Bieler, "The Cops Who Change Diapers," 23.

121 "Police Women [of Montreal]," *Municipal Review of Canada* 46, nos. 11–12 (November/December 1950): 3; This message was repeated in the National Film Board short film *Guerre à la délinquance: des policières montréalaises*, which is available in the collection *Coup d'oeil*, no. 37 (Eyewitness in English).

122 Bieler, "The Cops Who Change Diapers," 24.

123 "Juvenile Delinquency Topic," *Northern Beacon* (Lake of Two Mountains), 30 January 1958, 1.

124 "Montreal Policewomen," *Canadian Police Bulletin*, June 1947, 8.

125 Policewomen's work in Montreal was featured in a National Film Board short documentary: *Guerre à la délinquance: des policières montréalaises* (National Film Board of Canada, 1952).

126 Bieler, "The Cops Who Change Diapers," 24.

127 "La protection des jeunes à Montréal," *Le Devoir*, 28 August 1948.

128 *Guerre à la délinquance: des policières montréalaises.*

129 "La protection des jeunes à Montréal."

130 Marquis, *The Vigilant Eye*, 188–9. The RCMP finally hired female officers in 1974 but job equality would be an ongoing struggle, as Bonnie Reilly Schmidt demonstrates in *Silenced: The Untold Story of the Fight for Equality in the* RCMP.

131 "Police Juvenile Clubs," *On the Spot* (National Film Board of Canada, 1954).

132 Archives Municipales de la Ville de Montréal, Département de Police, Personnel File, Julien White, Letter to Fernand Dufresne, May 1939.

133 Archives Municipales de la ville de Montréal, Département de Police, Personnel File, Julien White, letter to Comité des Griefs, Syndicats des fonctionnaires municipaux, 10 January 1948, 1–2.

134 Archives Municipales de la Ville de Montréal, Département de Police, Personnel File, Paul-Émile Naud, letter from A. Langlois to L.-A. Lapointe, 31 August 1951; Letter from Executive Committee, City Hall, to A. Langlois, 16 May 1958.

135 Det.-Sgt. O.-A., "Crime and Youth," *Revue des Agents de Police / Constables Review* 1, no 3 (May 1946): 47.

136 Mainstream media commented consistently on the problem of youth gangs and hoodlums: see the 1946 series by Gerald Zoffer in *Saturday Night*; Pierre Berton and C.G. Gifford, "The Beanery Gang," *Maclean's*, 15 December 1948, 12; "How to Punish the Juvenile Hoodlums?," *Financial Post*, 9 June 1951, 11–12.

137 Miriam Chapin, "Boys' Clubs Run by Police Cut Down Delinquency," *Saturday Night*, 5 April 1949.

138 "Police Juvenile Clubs," *On the Spot*, interview with Pelletier.

139 Det.-Capt. A. O. Pelletier, "Delinquency Prevention," *Municipal Review of Canada* 45, no. 3 (March 1949): 13.

140 Chapin, "Boys' Clubs."

141 It is important to remember that Montreal comprised French-Canadian Catholics, and anglophones who might be Irish-Catholic, Jewish, or Protestant. Tensions among these groups were familiar since the conquest of Quebec in 1759.

142 *Montreal Police Juvenile Guide*, no. 1 (November 1950): 79, 81.

143 All numbers derived from: Archives Municipales de la Ville de Montréal, Fonds Département de la Police, *Annual Reports*, 1943–48.

144 *La Patrie Suisse* (Geneva), no. 50, 10 (December 1949).

145 Pelletier, "Crime and Youth," 47.

146 Const. Michael Hayvren, "The Antonians," *La Revue des Agents de Police / Constables Review* 3, no.3 (April 1948): 38.

147 Det.-Sgt. Roland Diotte, President, "Social Committee Report," *Revue des Agents de Police / Constables Review* (November 1948): 38.

148 Archives Nationales du Québec, Québec, E17 Correspondance du Procureur-général, file 1946-2121, Letter from Marcel Trahan to the Assistant Attorney General, Léopold Désilets, 7 February 1946.

149 Archives Nationales du Québec, Québec, E17 Correspondance du Procureur-général, file 1946-2121, Letter from L'Assistant-procureur-général, no date.

150 Archives Municipales de la Ville de Montréal, Département de Police, Personnel File, Paul-Émile Naud, Letter from J.G. Nicholson to Fernand Dufresne, 9 June 1945.

151 Archives Municipales de la Ville de Montréal, Département de Police, Personnel File, Ovila Pelletier, Letter from Arthur Laramée to Albert Langlois, 29 April 1948.

152 *The Policeman*, produced by Gudrun Parker (National Film Board of
     Canada, 1946), 11 min, 42 s.
153 Speech at Mont St Antoine (reformatory for boys), cited by Hayvren,
     "The Antonians," 38.
154 "Youth Aid Section, MUCPD, History," 1.
155 "Le Miracle de Montréal," *La Patrie Suisse* (Geneva), no. 50 (10 December
     1949): 1570–1.
156 "Youth Aid Section, MUCPD, History," 1–4.

Chapter Three

1 Sutphen and Ford, "The Effectiveness and Enforcement of a Teen
   Curfew Law," 57; Hemmens and Bennett, "Juvenile Curfews and the
   Court," 99–121, 100. These articles summarize this position.
2 Hess, Orthmann, and Wright, *Juvenile Justice*, 170. Archives Municipales
   de la Ville de Montréal, Département de Police, *Annual Report*, 1945,
   "Relève de l'action de l'escouade de moralité juvenile – Relève General
   des arrestations effectuées en rapport avec le réglement 1715 – couvre-
   feu," 102. Compare this with 73,897 juvenile arrests for curfew violation
   and loitering in the whole of the US in 2010.
3 "Curfews: Do You Know Where Your Children Are?" *CBC News Online*,
   3 August 2004. According to this report, the Federation of Canadian
   Municipalities and the Association of Municipalities of Ontario claimed
   that most municipalities had curfew laws but that they were not
   generally enforced.
4 Vagrancy laws, as Risa Goluboff, has shown, are a parallel status offence
   that provided police wide discretion for arrests. At mid-century, the
   charge of vagrancy faced a constitutional challenge for its arbitrariness.
   See *Vagrant Nation*.
5 H.L. and R.R.O, "Note: Curfew Ordinances and the Nocturnal Control
   of Juvenile Crime," *University of Pennsylvania Law Review* 107, no. 1 (1958):
   66–101 at 66; Schwartz, "Rights Issue Teen-Age Curfew – A Revival," *Los
   Angeles Times*, 10 August 1985, D1. On Canada see Kelso, *Revival of the
   Curfew Law*, 7; see also "The Curfew," *Globe*, 28 September 1889, 2. This
   statement is attributed to then future President Benjamin Harrison
   in 1884.
6 Kelso, *Revival of the Curfew Law*.
7 Mrs John D. Townsend, "Curfew for City Children," *North American*

Review, December 1896, 725–30, at 727; Baldwin, *In the Watches of the Night*, 191.

8 Beverley Jones, Esq., "The Curfew Bell," *Evangelical Churchman* 22, no. 8 (25 February 1897): 123.

9 "William the Conqueror Ordered General Curfew for England," *Montreal Gazette*, 17 July 1942.

10 Letter to the editor of the *Globe*, signed "A Woman," *Globe*, 11 October 1894, 9; the curfew is referred to as a "dark age proposal" in a letter quoted in Kelso, *Revival of the Curfew Law*, 11.

11 "Curfew," *Oxford English Dictionary* Online (Oxford: Oxford University Press, 2004).

12 Ekirch, *At Day's Close*, 63.

13 Ibid., 61–3.

14 "Curfew Was Rung in the 17th Century," *Montreal Gazette*, 18 September 1942; "Le couvre-feu aux débuts de la colonie," *La Patrie* (Quebec), 13 September 1941. This historical tale was told by the Court House archivist, E.Z. Massicotte. See also E.Z. Massicotte, "Couvre-feu et rondes de nuit," *Bulletin des Recherches Historiques* 36 (May 1930): 266–9.

15 Ekirch, *At Day's Close*, chapter 3 and page 324.

16 Johnson, "It's Ten O'Clock: Do You Know Where Your Children Are?," 327–63; Hemmens and Bennett, "Juvenile Curfews and the Court."

17 Hemmens and Bennett, "Juvenile Curfews and the Court," 100; Baldwin, "Nocturnal Habits and Dark Wisdom," 593–611, at 603.

18 Loewen, *Sundown Towns*.

19 Baldwin, "Nocturnal Habits and Dark Wisdom," 601–2.

20 Ekirch, *At Day's Close*, 65, 329.

21 Joyal, ed., *Entre surveillance et compassion*. This text comments on the emergence of child protection movements in Canada. See also Sutherland, *Children in English-Canadian Society*.

22 "Evils of Street Education," *Globe*, 27 April 1888, 6.

23 Kelso, *Revival of the Curfew Law*, 3.

24 Baldwin, "Nocturnal Habits and Dark Wisdom," 594. See also Davis, *Street-Land*, 62–3 as quoted in ibid., 593.

25 Townsend, "Curfew for City Children," 725–30 at 725.

26 See Baldwin, "Nocturnal Habits and Dark Wisdom." On the history of the night see Ekirch, *At Day's Close*; Schor, *Nights in the Big City*.

27 See also Caldwell, *New York Night*.

28 Ibid., 208.

29 Valverde, *The Age of Light, Soap, and Water*, 130–1.

30 Jones and Rutman, *In the Children's Aid.*

31 Ibid., 51.

32 Valverde, *The Age of Light, Soap, and Water*, 131–4; and, more generally, chapter 6, "The City as Moral Problem."

33 Peter C. Baldwin writes of the response to the growth of nineteenth-century nightlife in New York City: "Night could not be turned into day anywhere, either in the literal sense of illuminating the street as brightly as sunlight, or in the figurative sense of creating an island of virtue in a sea of moral darkness." Baldwin, "Nocturnal Habits and Dark Wisdom," 596.

34 "Author of Curfew," *Fort Morgan Times* (Fort Morgan, CO), 12 June 1896.

35 Townsend, "Curfew for City Children," 727.

36 Kelso, *Revival of the Curfew Law*, 3.

37 "Curfews vs. Playgrounds," *Globe*, 28 September 1903, 4.

38 Ibid.

39 Ibid.

40 Jones, "The Curfew Bell," 123.

41 Kelso, *Revival of the Curfew Law*, 4.

42 Ibid., 3–4.

43 Ibid.

44 Ibid., 3.

45 "Curfews vs. Playgrounds," 4; *Globe*, 4 August 1904, 4.

46 Baldwin, "Nocturnal Habits and Dark Wisdom," 597.

47 On seduction laws see Backhouse, *Petticoats and Prejudice.*

48 "Evils of Street Education," 6.

49 "The Curfew Bell," *Globe*, 3 October 1903, 9.

50 Kelso, *Revival of the Curfew Law*, 7; see also "The Curfew," *Globe*, 28 September 1889, 2. In the *Globe* article, the curfew age is set at "under 16."

51 For example, the *Globe* reported on WCTU petitions in Ottawa ("The Curfew Bell," 7 July 1896, 7), in British Columbia ("Legislation and Politics," 9 November 1896, 6), and in Brandon and Winnipeg (28 May 1898, 19).

52 "Ontario WCTU Meet, 20th Anniversary," *Globe*, 13 October 1897, 2.

53 Ibid. The newspaper was quoting a report from an Ontario WCTU meeting.

54 "The Curfew for Children," *Globe*, 14 September 1894, 4.

55 "The Curfew Bylaw," *Globe*, 11 October 1894, 9.

56   "Couvre-feu aboli dans Caughnawaga," *La Presse*, 19 February 1935.
57   "Ward Three Election," *Globe*, 31 December 1895, 7.
58   Ibid., 7.
59   Kelso, *Review of the Curfew Law*, 11.
60   Ibid.
61   "Cry of the Children," *Globe*, 19 November 1906, 4.
62   Baldwin, *In the Watches of the Night*, 192.
63   "Calls for the Ringing of the Curfew Bell," *Globe*, 22 April 1913, 9; "Want Curfew to Ring in Kingston Again," *Globe*, 12 May 1914, 5; "Quebec Housewives Doing Large Work," *Globe*, 13 October 1917, 11; "Curfew Is Ringing for Windsor Children," *Globe*, 21 August 1922, 1; "Close Cafes at Midnight and Ring Curfew Bell" (Owen Sound), *Globe*, 16 April 1924, 6; "Curfew Enforcement" (Niagara Falls), *Globe*, 13 April 1934, 7; "London Trustees Urge Curfew Law" (London, ON), *Globe*, 27 April 1934, 2; "St Thomas Hints Curfew Law," *Globe*, 18 December 1934, 2; "To Enforce Curfew" (Valleyfield, QC), *Globe*, 13 November 1936, 8; "Curfew to Ring in Sudbury Again," *Globe*, 9 October 1937, 13; "Oshawa Parents Offer 9:30 Curfew as Delinquency Curb," *Globe*, 8 January 1938, 4; "Curfew Wanted" (Halifax), *Globe*, 12 April 1938, 6.
64   Mintz, "The Unfinished Century of the Child," in *Huck's Raft*, 372–84, 255; Tuttle, Jr, *Daddy's Gone to War*; Ossian, *The Forgotten Generation*; Gleason, *Normalizing the Ideal*; Adams, *The Trouble with Normal*; Myers and Poutanen, "Cadets, Curfews, and Compulsory Schooling," 367–98.
65   Keshen, *Saints, Sinners, and Soldiers*, 206, and 203-4; Lewis, "'Isn't This a Terrible War?'," 193-215.
66   On both sides of the border the press commented on the relative "unrest" and "problems" of children and youth. See Myers, *Caught*, 70–5; Keshen, *Saints, Sinners, and Soldiers*; Mintz, "The Unfinished Century of the Child."
67   "Vandalism Presents Problems to Exhibitors," *New York Times*, 17 October 1943, X3.
68   Ibid.
69   Ossian, *The Forgotten Generation*, 102–3.
70   Ibid., 104–5.
71   Keshen, *Saints*, 207. Zoot suits continued to be a form of deviant youth dress in Montreal and were noted in juvenile delinquency cases; for example, Maurice D. and Armand C., Bibliothèque et Archives Nationales du Québec, à Montréal, Fonds de la Cour des jeunes

délinquants de la Cité de Montréal / Montreal Juvenile Delinquents' Court, Dossier 175, 1949.

72 Large US cities like San Francisco and smaller ones like Perth Amboy, New Jersey, set curfew for those under sixteen.

73 "Police Given Orders to Enforce Curfew Measure," *Ottawa Citizen*, 21 November 1942.

74 Library and Archives of Canada (LAC), MG 28, I 10, vol. 49, "Curfew Bylaws in Effect in Canadian Municipalities."

75 LAC, MG 28, I 10, vol. 49, Letter from Charles W. Scott, Police Department, Toronto, Canada to The Canadian Welfare Council, Ottawa, ON, 30 June 1941.

76 "Memorandum Re: Curfew," 21 November 1944, City of Toronto Archives, series 100, file 1351, Juvenile Delinquency and Youth Programs, 1944–1949, box 46705, folio 5. On Toronto youth gangs see Keshen, *Saints*, 208. In Toronto, for example, the Board of Trade supported Alderman Fishley's proposal for a wartime curfew law.

77 "Police Will Establish Metro Youth Bureau," *Globe and Mail*, 16 January 1959, 4.

78 *Globe and Mail*, 5 April 1944. Found in LAC, MG 28 I 10, vol. 49, file 447, Curfew Laws (1941–44).

79 Sergeant Detective A.-O. Pelletier, "Les problèmes de la jeunesse," *Revue des Agents de Police / Constables Review* 1, no. 1 (February 1946): 11.

80 "Pas de couvre-feu pour les enfants de notre ville!," *La Presse*, 6 February 1935; "Curfew Law Issue Discussion Raging," *Montreal Gazette*, 15 February 1935; "Le couvre-feu pour jeunes en notre ville," *La Presse*, 22 February 1936; "Le couvre-feu combattu par des échevins," *La Presse*, 12 March 1937; "Requête en faveur du couvre-feu à Montréal," *La Presse*, 5 March 1937.

81 LAC, Canadian Committee on Social Development (CCSD), MG 28, I 10, vol. 49, 447, Curfew Laws (1941–44). Letter from Police Chief Lepine.

82 Keshen, "Wartime Jitters over Juveniles," 364–6 at 365.

83 *Maclean's*, August 1943, 14.

84 Doris Hedges, "The Citizen and His Child," *Municipal Review of Canada* (March 1944): 5.

85 Ibid.

86 On the moral panic concerning the juvenile delinquency scare during and after the Second World War see Gleason, *Normalizing the Ideal*, 86; Myers, *Caught*, 70–5.

87 "Couvre-feu à 9 h. pour les enfants de moins de 14 ans à Montréal," *La Presse*, 21 May 1942.

88 Ibid.

89 R.P. Archambault, S.J., *Le couvre-feu* (Montreal: L'Oeuvre des Tracts no. 274, April 1942), 8. Archambault was quoting John F. Dalton, Juvenile Court Committee worker.

90 Archambault, *Le couvre-feu*, 9.

91 Ibid., 7–9; interview with John F. Dalton.

92 Ibid., 2.

93 "Le couvre-feu est necessaire, selon le maire," *La Presse*, 21 August 1942, 12.

94 For example, "Approve Curfew Law, Fredericton," *Toronto Daily Star*, 15 July 1942, 2. Children participated in this positive campaign: "Brampton Girls Are All Set to Obey Nine O'Clock Curfew," *Toronto Daily Star*, 19 May 1942, 8.

95 *Charlottetown Guardian*, 27 November 1942.

96 Hedges, "The Citizen and His Child," 6. Hedges is describing the conclusions from Montreal's Delinquency Prevention week, 1944.

97 Archambault, *Le couvre-feu*, 1.

98 Hedges, "The Citizen and His Child," 6.

99 Archambault, *Le couvre-feu*, 4–5; interview with Judge Robillard.

100 "Requête en faveur du couvre-feu à Montréal." Sources for the 1930s curfew debates can be found at the Archives Municipales de la Ville de Montréal, Fonds du Conseil de Ville de Montréal, VM1, series 3, dossier 529, "Couvre-feu" and 3631 and 6842.

101 J.G. Nicholson, "Curfew Law and Child Delinquency," *Municipal Review of Canada* (September 1942): 7.

102 "Le couvre-feu est nécessaire selon le maire," 12.

103 Archambault, *Le couvre-feu*, 2–3.

104 Nicholson, "Curfew Law and Child Delinquency," 7.

105 "Bylaw on Curfew Is Council Feature," *Montreal Gazette*, 2 September 1942, 16.

106 "Le problème insoluble pose par le couvre-feu," *La Presse*, 11 September 1942, 3.

107 Adopted by the Executive Committee of the municipal government on 18 August 1942, and by the Council on 2 September 1942.

108 See, for example, the eleven children brought in by Sergeant Detective Schaffer on 3 and 4 June 1943 (Archives Nationales du Québec à Montréal, Fonds Cour des jeunes délinquants, case 4239, 4 June 1943).

109 Archives Municipales de la Ville de Montréal, Fonds Département de la Police, *Annual Reports*, 1939–49.

110 Ibid.

111 R.P. Valère Massicotte, "La délinquence juvenile et la guerre," *Oeuvre des Tracts*, no. 298, (April 1944): 10–11.

112 "Survey Unfolds Progress in Control Abroad but Worsening in U.S.," *New York Times*, 15 August 1957, 1.

113 "Chiefs of Police Get Juvenile Crime Plan," *New York Times*, 12 September 1956, 1.

114 "Youth Curfew Kept," *New York Times*, 23 December 1956, 18. This permanent law replaced a temporary provision passed two years earlier.

115 "Gang Row Brings Curfew," *New York Times*, 17 September 1952, 33.

116 "Curfews on Teen-Agers Applauded by Police in 6 U.S. Cities," *New York Times*, 2 September 1959, 17.

117 Ibid.

118 "Brampton Girls Are All Set to Obey Nine O'Clock Curfew," 8.

119 "Mob Wrecks Office of Curfew Judge [in Olive Hill, KY]," *New York Times*, 12 July 1943, 10.

120 "Rioting Follows a Common Pattern, *New York Times*, 30 August 1964, 76.

121 "Los Angeles Rioting Is Checked," *New York Times*, 16 August 1965, 1; "Clergymen Seek Peace in Chicago," *New York Times*, 16 August 1965, 18.

122 "Illinois Curfew Enforced," *New York Times*, 29 July 1966, 11.

123 Tu Thanh Ha, "Quebec Teens Fight for Right to Stay Out at Night," *Globe and Mail*, 26 July 2004, A1 and A6.

124 "A Is for Adult Authority," *Globe and Mail*, 5 August 2004, A13.

125 Ha, "Quebec Teens Fight," A1 and A6; A girl interviewed on CBC's *The Current* said it is kids over sixteen who are the real problem. CBC Radio One, interviews on *The Current*, 27 July 2004. *La Presse*'s columnist found that kids at the local high school were not aware of it – and didn't read *La Presse*! – but when told were indignant: Natacha said that 10 p.m. is too early and that she preferred 1 a.m. An incredulous Eric, using a pseudonym, told the reporter, "No one is going to listen to that, fuck off." In an online discussion board, seventeen-year-old Julie, from Huntingdon, rambled on about the unfairness of the curfew but also about the proposed skate park, which she felt served only boys. Michael Skala, a youthful Canadian blogger and former member of the Americans for a Society Free from Age Restrictions commended MLA André Chenail for challenging the curfew law.

126 The story of Huntingdon's curfew summer began in May and continued through August 2004. Most Montreal newspapers (*La Presse*, *Le Devoir*, the *Gazette*) and the visual media (Radio-Canada, CBC), as well as national media sources (*Globe and Mail* and Global Television) reported the issues as they unfolded.

127 "Huntingdon suspend l'imposition d'un couvre-feu," *Le Devoir*, 6 July 2004, A4; Marie-Claude Ducas, "The Mayor Who Thrives on Air," *Globe and Mail*, 6 May 2002, F2.

128 "Huntingdon Bylaw Targets Parents," CBC *News Online*, 3 August 2004; "Huntingdon Mayor Stands by Convictions," *Globe and Mail*, 4 August 2004, A1 and A6.

129 Colleen Simard, "Curfews Won't Save Our Kids," *Winnipeg Free Press Live*, 4 December 2006; Mike McIntyre, "Only 12 Years Old and Already a Killer," *Winnipeg Free Press Live*, 2 February 2009. Audrey Cooper's obituary suggests she was also Aboriginal. Raised by adoptive parents in Ontario, she died in Manitoba and services were organized at the Prairieland Aboriginal Funeral Chapel.

130 Thurman and Mueller, "Beyond Curfews and Crackdowns," in Scott, ed., *Policing Gangs and Youth Violence*, 167–87; Ruefle and Reynolds, "Curfews and Delinquency in Major American Cities," 347–63. See these works for the US case. The YCJA provides no mechanism for generalized youth-specific curfews.

131 Hemmens and Bennett, "Juvenile Curfews and the Court," 119.

132 Valentine, "Angels and Devils: Moral Landscapes of Childhood," 581–99; Collins and Kearns, "Under Curfew and Under Siege?," 389–403.

133 Thurman and Mueller, "Beyond Curfews and Crackdowns," 170.

134 For discussion of late twentieth-century teen violence see Mintz, "The Unfinished Century of the Child," 372–84; Powers, "The Apocalypse of Adolescence," *Atlantic*, March 2002, https://www.theatlantic.com/magazine/archive/2002/03/the-apocalypse-of-adolescence/302449/.

135 Vissing, "Curfews," 63.

136 "The Curfew as a Measure for the Control of Juvenile Delinquency," *Report of the Curfew Committee of the Law Enforcement Students of the Twenty-Third Class of the Delinquency Control Institute of the University of Southern California*, 1970.

137 "Vandalism Presents Problems to Exhibitors," *New York Times*, 17 October 1943, X3.

138 Catherine Mackenzie, "Club for Teen-Agers," *New York Times*, 29 August 1943, SM17.

Chapter Four

1　Gordon R. Sisson, "Police-Sponsored Rifle Club," *Canadian Police Gazette* 27, no. 8 (October 1952): 42; *A Sergeant Sees It Through* (Montreal: Omega Productions, 1954).

2　Brown, "Every Boy Ought to Learn to Shoot and to Obey Orders," 196–226.

3　Ibid., 201–3.

4　"Police Juvenile Clubs," *On the Spot* (National Film Board of Canada, 1954).

5　New York Public Library, New York City, *Annual Report of the Police Department*, 1948, 78. Hereafter NYPD, AR.

6　Deleuze, "Postscript on the Societies of Control," 3–7; on apparatus of security see Michel Foucault's "Governmentality" in Burchell, Gordon, and Miller, eds., *The Foucault Effect*, 102.

7　Bourdieu, "Sport and Social Class," 819–40 at 826.

8　Mills, "Youth on the Streets and Bob-a-Job Week," 112–28 at 114.

9　Matthews, Limb, and Taylor, "The 'Street' as Thirdspace," in Holloway and Valentine, eds., *Children's Geographies*, 54.

10　Grant, *The Boy Problem*, 40.

11　Ibid., chapter 2.

12　Putney, *Muscular Christianity*, 100–1.

13　Grant, *The Boy Problem*, 41.

14　Putney, *Muscular Christianity*, Introduction.

15　Grant, *The Boy Problem*, 41.

16　Ibid., 40.

17　Putney, *Muscular Christianity*, 1–6.

18　Ibid.; MacLeod, *Building Character in the American Boy*; Grant, *The Boy Problem*.

19　Grant, *The Boy Problem*, 49.

20　Ibid., 51.

21　Trepanier, "Building Boys, Building Canada," 45–51; Marr, "Church Teen Clubs, Feminized Organizations?, 249–67; MacLeod, *Building Character in the American Boy*.

22　Originally a Scottish club (1883), it was brought to the US in 1890. Putney, *Muscular Christianity*, 112.

23　Moss, *Manliness and Militarism*, chapters 6 and 7.

24　Trepanier, "Building Boys, Building Canada," 22. See also Hill, "Building a Nation of Nation Builders."

25 Brown, "Every Boy Ought to Learn to Shoot and to Obey Orders," 203–5.
26 Schlossman and Sedlak, "The Chicago Area Project Revisited,"
    398–462, 415.
27 Ibid., 415.
28 Ibid., 402.
29 Ibid., 416–18.
30 Grant, *The Boy Problem*, 132–3.
31 Ibid., 63.
32 "Crime and Youth," *Revue des Agents de Police / Constables' Review* 1, no. 4
    (May 1946): 47.
33 "Y.M.C.A. Aids," *Canadian Police Gazette* 22, no. 2 (May 1947): 8.
34 "Delinquency Curb," *Canadian Police Gazette* 22, no. 7 (October 1947): 8.
35 "Victoria Police Boxing Club," *Canadian Police Gazette* 27, no. 2 (April
    1952): 8.
36 "Juvenile Courts and Rehabilitation," RCMP *Quarterly* (January 1940): 270.
37 Ibid.
38 "Nelson City Police Youth Training," *Canadian Police Gazette* 11, no. 12
    (March 1937): 36.
39 "Boy Scout Problem as Aid in Juvenile Problem," *Police Chief's Newsletter*
    5, no. 9 (September 1938): 5, 9, 6.
40 I thank the anonymous reader of the manuscript for pointing out that
    Bolton, like many Toronto police officers of the era, were British born
    and served in the Royal forces. Their patriotism to the Union Jack can
    be situated in their own reverence for empire.
41 "Police Sponsor Boy Scout Troop: Gang Leaders Become Model Scouts
    under Police Mentors in Downtown Toronto," *Canadian Police Bulletin*
    (March 1940): 7.
42 Ibid.
43 "Crime Prevention in Cleveland," *Police Chief News* 11, no. 10 (October
    1944): 64.
44 NYPD, AR 1931, 106.
45 Ibid., 104.
46 "Editorial Comment," *Police Chief's Newsletter* 17, no. 11 (November
    1940): 8.
47 The Crime Prevention Bureau was established in January 1930 with an
    amendment to the city charter in June 1931 making it a permanent part
    of the NYPD. "Children must be studied," read the Annual Report of the
    NYPD in response to rising juvenile gangs. NYPD, AR 1931, 102.

48 "To Turn Open Lots into Playgrounds ... Police Anxious to Help,"
    New York Times, 11 July 1916.

49 This point is made on PAL's website under "History." http://www.palnyc.
    org/800-pal-4KIDS/History.aspx.

50 NYPD, AR 1931, 103–4.

51 Ibid., 104.

52 Ibid., 105.

53 A similar narrative can be found in John Kiernan, "Sports of the Times,"
    New York Times, 2 September 1932, 13.

54 Alfred J. Kahn, *Police and Children: A Study of the Juvenile Aid Bureau of
    the New York City Police Department* (New York: Citizens' Committee on
    Children of New York City, 1951), 14.

55 "Police Honor Children," *New York Times*, 29 March 1933, 11.

56 Henrietta Additon, "The Crime Prevention Bureau of New York," 229.

57 Kahn, *Police and Children*, 14–15; NYPD, AR 1936, 17.

58 NYPD, AR 1936, 17.

59 NYPD, AR 1938, 37; for example, 154 outdoor recreation sites (play streets,
    playgrounds, play roofs), 70 indoor sites.

60 NYPD, AR 1938, 38; AR 1947, 64.

61 NYPD, AR 1938, 39; NYPD, AR 1948, 80.

62 "Balloons Dot Sky in Drive on Crime," *New York Times*, 6 August 1936, 21.

63 Ibid.

64 NYPD, AR 1936, 17.

65 NYPD, AR 1948, 78.

66 NYPD, AR 1938, 38.

67 NYPD, AR 1947, 65. See photograph on page 64.

68 NYPD, AR 1948, 78.

69 Additon, "The Crime Prevention Bureau of New York," 229.

70 "Balloons Dot Sky in Drive on Crime," 21.

71 "Wallander Denies Police Are Brutal in Negro Arrests," *New York Times*, 8
    August 1946, 19.

72 "Mayor Opens Center for Youth in Harlem, Dedicates Building as
    Memorial to Negro Police Hero," *New York Times*, 28 January 1939, 31.

73 "Eighteenth Precinct Youth Committee," *New York Times*, 11 March 1944,
    17; "Crime Increasing in 'Little Spain,'" *New York Times*, 3 August 1947, 12;
    "Racial Tension up in East Bronx Area," *New York Times*, 24 April 1947, 30.

74 Additon, "The Crime Prevention Bureau of New York," 230.

75 NYPD, AR 1948, 78.

76 "Homes Get Blame for Delinquency," *New York Times*, 2 April 1944, 40. The Mayor flip-flopped on PAL over the course of his career, most often recorded in its favour at fundraising events.

77 NYPD, AR 1948, 80.

78 NYPD, AR 1949, 64; NYPD, AR 1950, 77.

79 William P. O'Brien, "Juvenile Crime Prevention," *Police Chief's Newsletter* 13, no. 1 (January 1951).

80 "Police Plan Lists of Wayward Boys … Prevention Bureau to Use Its Athletic League to Induce Truants to Reform," *New York Times*, 4 August 1936, 21. The lists were created with the help of schools. The following day, five thousand kids were on the list.

81 O'Brien, "Juvenile Crime Prevention."

82 Gaunt, "Dancin' in the Street to ta Black Girl's Beat: Music, Gender, and the 'Ins and Outs' of Double-Dutch," in Austin and Willard, eds., *Generations of Youth*, 272–92, 280–1.

83 NYPD, AR 1947, 65.

84 "Canada–U.S. 'Trade' Police Club Youngsters," *Montreal Star*, 2 August 1955; "Young Montrealers Thrilled by Fabulous Sights in N.Y.," *Montreal Star*, 9 August 1955; "Montreal Boys Visit Kennedy," *New York Times*, 10 August 1955, 51.

85 "Police Juvenile Clubs Credited for 54 p.c. Drop in Delinquency," *Montreal Gazette*, 15 March 1949, 6.

86 This version of events was told by Pelletier to *Le Petit Journal* in 1951. "Nos policiers ont organisé les loisirs de citoyens de demain," *Le Petit Journal*, 21 January 1951.

87 Ibid.

88 *Montreal Police Juvenile Guide*, no. 1 (November 1950): 45. Hereafter MPJG.

89 Ibid., 29–33.

90 Ibid., 93.

91 Ibid., 91.

92 Ibid., 93.

93 It is important to remember that Montreal comprised French Canadian Catholics and anglophones who might be Irish Catholic, Jewish, or Protestant. Tensions among these groups were familiar since the conquest of Quebec in 1759.

94 Pelletier, "Delinquency Prevention," *Municipal Review of Canada* (March 1949): 13.

95 MPJG, 79, 81.

96 "Police Juvenile Clubs," *On the Spot.*

97 "Les 15 ans des Clubs juvéniles," *La Presse*, 29 April 1961.

98 "Nos policiers ont organisé les loisirs des citoyens de demain."

99 "An Effective Weapon against Delinquency," *Municipal Review of Canada* (March 1947): 10–11.

100 "Police Juvenile Clubs Credited for 54 p.c. Drop in Delinquency," 6.

101 "Loisirs et Récréation: Les Clubs juvéniles de Montréal aident les jeunes à pratiquer leurs sports favoris," *La Presse*, 16 April 1957.

102 "Police Juvenile Clubs," *On the Spot.*

103 *La Patrie Suisse* (Geneva), 10 December 1959, 50.

104 "Loisirs et Récréation."

105 Tillotson, *The Public at Play*, 15.

106 Jean-Paul Gilbert, "Origine et justification du Policier-éducateur," *Police Jeunesse* (Montreal: Graph-o Pier, 1970): 19–34.

107 MPJG, III.

108 "Loisirs et Récréation."

109 The Montreal Council of Social Agencies was a coordinating organization for English-speaking, non-Catholic social agencies that had its origins in the McGill University Department of Social Studies/Work.

110 McGill University Archives, MO 2076, C30, file 520, "Juvenile Delinquency Prevention Bureau Study."

111 Ibid., 2.

112 Ibid., 3.

113 "Friend of Youth," *La Presse*, 1 April 1958, 6. Parc Ovila-Pelletier is in the east end of Montreal near the Olympic Stadium.

114 "Les Clubs Juvéniles vont disparaître," *La Presse*, 3 May 1965.

115 Marcus H. Miles, "Firearms Training for Juveniles," *Police Chief News* 19, no. 12 (December 1952): 14.

116 Sisson, "Police-Sponsored Rifle Club," 42.

Chapter Five

1 Library and Archives Canada, RG 33, 131–1, Royal Commission on the Criminal Law Relating to Criminal Sexual Psychopaths, Remarks by Chief Constable John Chisholm, 9–10 February 1956, page 3.

2 Elizabeth Chant Robertson, MD, "The Greatest Child Killer of Them All – Accidents," *Chatelaine*, April 1953, 110.

3 See, for example: Conley and McLaren, eds., *Car Troubles*; Flink, *The Automobile Age*; Norton, *Fighting Traffic*.

4 Parusel and McLaren, "Cars before Kids, 129–47, at 131.

5 For a discussion of citizenship and competency see Schumann, ed., *Raising Citizens in the 'Century of the Child,'* Introduction.

6 The phrase belongs to Swedish reformer Ellen Key, *The Century of the Child* (New York: G.P. Putnam's Sons, 1909).

7 Davies, "Reckless Walking Must Be Discouraged," 123–38. According to Davies, in 1904 there were 535 automobiles registered. This number grew to 490,906 by 1930.

8 Ibid.; Cournoyer, "Les accidents impliquant des enfants et l'attitude envers l'enfance à Montréal (1900–1945)," 47.

9 McShane, *Down the Asphalt Path*; see chapter 9, "Red Light, Green Light," especially 174–6.

10 Norton, *Fighting Traffic*, 19; see McShane on New York City's anti-automobile incidents: *Down the Asphalt Path*, 177–9.

11 Norton, *Fighting Traffic*, 2.

12 Ibid., 23.

13 Lorenzkowski, "The Children's War," in High, ed., *Occupied Saint John's*, 113–50, at 48.

14 *Hamilton Spectator*, 6 May 1924, cited in Davies, "Reckless Walking."

15 Cournoyer, "Les accidents impliquant des enfants," 54.

16 Norton, *Fighting Traffic*, 24; Zelizer, *Pricing the Priceless Child*, 23.

17 Cournoyer, "Les accidents impliquant des enfants," 54–5.

18 Norton, *Fighting Traffic*, 242.

19 Ibid., 27.

20 Cournoyer, "Les accidents impliquant des enfants," 135.

21 On New York City and the American safety movement see Zelizer, *Pricing the Priceless Child*, 32–40. On Montreal, see Fahrni, "La Lutte Contre L'Accident" in Fahrni, Niget, and Petitclerc, eds., *Pour une histoire du risque*, 181–202.

22 Stearns, *American Fear*; Stearns, *Anxious Parents*.

23 McShane, *Down the Asphalt Path*, 175.

24 Zelizer, *Pricing the Priceless Child*, 40.

25 Ibid., 41–3.

26 Gaboury, *La lutte contre l'accident*, 13–14.

27 Ibid., 14.

28 Zelizer, *Pricing the Priceless Child*, 42.

29 Ibid., 51; Norton, *Fighting Traffic*, 242; some of these slogans are from baby boomers' childhood memories.

30 *Hamilton Times*, 6 July 1918, as cited in Davies, "Reckless Walking."

31 Zelizer, *Pricing the Priceless Child*, 38.

32 Cournoyer, "Les accidents impliquant des enfants," 138–9.

33 Norton, "Four Paradigms," 326.

34 This formed part of what Zelizer terms the sacralization of children in the twentieth century. *Pricing the Priceless Child*, 54.

35 Norton, "Four Paradigms," 326.

36 Ford advertisement, *Maclean's*, 15 October 1920.

37 Norton, *Fighting Traffic*, 226.

38 Cournoyer, "Les accidents impliquant des enfants," 138.

39 *Toronto Daily Star*, 10 March 1910, as cited in Davies, "Reckless Walking."

40 Parusel and McLaren, "Cars before Kids," 131, 133.

41 Ibid.

42 Dummitt, *The Manly Modern*, 128.

43 Ibid., 128–31.

44 Flink, *The Automobile Age*, chapter 9; on automobility and the dominance of the car, see Parusel and McLaren, "Cars before Kids," and Conley and McLaren, eds., "Introduction," *Car Troubles*.

45 Owram, *Born at the Right Time*, 70.

46 Metro Toronto Archives, *Annual Report of the Chief Constable of the City of Toronto for the Year 1931*, 21 (hereafter MTA, ARCC), *1940* and *1952*.

47 On driving as a modern masculinist project, see Dummitt, *The Manly Modern*, 126. On youth and drag racing in Vancouver see Genovese, "T-Bucket Terror to Respectable Rebels," in Conley and McLaren, eds., *Car Troubles*, 21–36. Genovese notes that while the American film *Rebel without a Cause* portrayed the drag race as a youthful frontier of alienation, the history of racing in Vancouver and its depiction in the NFB's *Fun for All: Car Crazy* show it became a path to respectability around skill and sportsmanship (33). On the jaywalker see McShane, *Down the Asphalt Path*, 188.

48 Jain, "Dangerous Instrumentality," 61–94, at 74–5. On the revolution of the American family lifestyle in this period see Flink, *The Automobile Age*, 158.

49 City of Vancouver Archives (hereafter CVA), Vancouver Traffic and Safety Council Fonds, Health General Studies – Pedestrian Traffic Accident Study, box 146-0-5, folder 20, letters from David A. Clarke, Director of

Research, Traffic Accident Study, no dates. Clarke was acting on behalf of Dr John Read. Read et al., "The Epidemiology and Prevention of Traffic Accidents Involving Child Pedestrians," 689. Children were defined as under fifteen years of age.

50 MTA, ARCC, 1955, 70; in 1951, there were sixteen child pedestrian fatalities (46). A child was considered as being fourteen years of age and younger.

51 Archives Municipales de la Ville de Montréal, Département de Police, *Annual Reports*, 1950, 1951, 1952, 1953. Statistics on pages 22–5. Numbers are for children between zero and fourteen years of age.

52 Zelizer, *Pricing the Priceless Child*, 35.

53 The Annual Reports of the Chief Constable in Toronto mentioned that, in the late 1940s and 1950s, it was the young and "old" (those over fifty-five years of age) who were particularly vulnerable as pedestrians.

54 Elizabeth Chant Robertson, MD, "Accidents: Your Child's Worst Enemy," *Chatelaine*, September 1949, 88.

55 Chant Robertson, "The Greatest Child Killer of Them All – Accidents," 110.

56 Acres, "Twentieth-Century Disease," 221–2.

57 Wilson, "Accident Prevention in Infants and Preschool Children," 287.

58 Fowler, "Accidents in Childhood," 241.

59 Read et al., "The Epidemiology and Prevention of Traffic Accidents Involving Child Pedestrians," 694.

60 Ibid., 698.

61 Ibid., 699.

62 Ibid.

63 Chant Robertson, "Accidents: Your Child's Worst Enemy," 88.

64 Guild, "Nursing Service: The Promotion of Safety," 457.

65 Norton, *Fighting Traffic*, chapter 2; Albert, "Order Out of Chaos," chapter 3.

66 McShane, *Down the Asphalt Path*, 184.

67 Norton, *Fighting Traffic*, 47.

68 Marquis, *Policing Canada's Century*, 169.

69 Ibid., 170.

70 MTA, ARCC, 1931.

71 MTA, ARCC, 1938, 34; 1937.

72 Ibid., 1937.

73 Ibid., 1935.

74 Ibid., 1937.

75 "Saving the Kids," *Canadian Police Gazette* 10, no. 7 (October 1935).

76 Marquis, *Policing Canada's Century*, 171. The *Canadian Police Gazette* proudly reported Canadian officers taking the three-week course in Evanston, Illinois, in 1952. "Traffic Course," *Canadian Police Gazette* 27, no. 7 (September 1952): 11.

77 Marquis, *Policing Canada's Century*, 209–10.

78 Albert, "Order Out of Chaos," 115–23.

79 Max Braithwaite, "Don't Cuss the Traffic Cop," *Maclean's*, 1 September 1951, 14–15. Journalist Sidney Katz wrote in "Why Do We Hate the Police?" that the exorbitant fines levied for traffic violations turned the public against the police. *Maclean's*, 30 August 1958, 9–11, 38

80 MTA, ARCC, 1939, 32 and 51.

81 MTA ARCC, 1947, 51.

82 Archives Municipales de la Ville de Montréal, Département de Police, *Annual Reports*, 1950, 21.

83 Ibid., 1937, 36.

84 "But Officer, I Didn't Know," *Canadian Police Gazette* 25, no. 3 (June 1950): 4.

85 "Every Third Victim a Child," *Canadian Police Gazette* 25, no. 1 (April 1950): 26.

86 Zelizer, *Pricing the Priceless Child*, 217.

87 *Montreal Daily Star*, 26 July 1930, 11.

88 Parr, *Sensing Changes*, 14.

89 Tumarkin, "Productive Death," 885–900 at 889. Tumarkin builds on the work of Pellegrini, "What Do Children Learn at School?" 97.

90 In 1935, *Reader's Digest* described in prurient detail the "daily mangling of human beings in crashing automobiles" in an article, aptly entitled, " – And Sudden Death." It formed part of a popular textual genre that purported to deliver the real facts of accidental death. These dramatic sudden-death stories proliferated in newspapers in the mid-1930s during what Peter D. Norton suggests was a "popular safety rebellion." This literature was directed at adults. Norton, *Fighting Traffic*, 245–6.

91 Jalland, *Death in the Victorian Family*, 380; Ariès, *The Hour of Our Death*, 576.

92 These addressed such issues as popularity, respect for oneself and adult authority, dating, etc.

93 Smith, *Mental Hygiene Classroom Films, 1945–1970*, 78.

94 *Hell's Highway: The True Story of Highway Safety Films*, directed by Bret Wood (New York: Livin' Man Productions, 2003); Smith, *Mental Hygiene Classroom Films, 1945–1970*, 79.

95 Smith, *Mental Hygiene Classroom Films, 1945–1970*, 80. In 1961's
    Mechanized Death, the producers of Signal 30 began to include
    accompanying audio from accident scenes, replete with the sounds of
    the dying victims.

96 This conclusion comes from filmmakers.

97 Stearns, *American Fear*, 95–9.

98 Ibid., 112.

99 This sanitizing of children's culture and the management of emotional
    responses to fright by relegating fear to entertainment venues are
    evidence of "new directions in American personality goals around
    mid-century." Stearns and Haggerty, "The Role of Fear," 91. Happiness
    in childhood then came to trump other qualities and emotions as
    it became a measure of good parenting and a reflection of both the
    individual and the collective.

100 W.P. Hinkens, *First Day of School*, photograph, Los Angeles Police
    Department, from *Traffic Review*'s annual photography contest for
    1949; Hinkens won in the category "Traffic Policing." See "Police Photo
    Contest Winners," *Police Chief News* 16, no. 12 (December 1949): 6–7; also
    the *Canadian Police Gazette* 25, no. 1 (April 1950): 11.

101 Elizabeth Chant Robertson, "Your Child's Worst Enemy," 73, and her
    "Accidents Needn't Happen," *Chatelaine*, June 1960, 133.

102 Low, NFB *Kids*, 70 and 73.

103 *Look Alert, Stay Unhurt*, directed by Gordon Burwash (National Film
    Board, 1955); see also Low, NFB *Kids*, 83.

104 The National Film Board's website indicates it won first place in the
    category of Traffic and Transportation by the National Committee
    on Films for Safety (Chicago), http://www2.nfb.ca/boutique/
    XXNFBibeCCtpItmDspRte.jsp?formatid=11045&lr_ecode=collection
    &minisite=10005&respid=50409.

105 See Sangster, "The Beaver as Ideology: Constructing Images of Inuit and
    Native Life in Postwar Canada," 191–209 at 192.

106 On indigeneity and performance see Corbey, "Ethnographic Showcases,
    1870–1930," 338–69; Maddox, "Politics, Performance, and Indian Identity,"
    7–37; Morgan, "A Wigwam to Westminster," 319–41. On rodeos see Kelm,
    A Wilder West; for theorizing the performance of "otherness" see Davis,
    "Spectacles of South Asia at the American Circus, 1890–1940," 121–38.

107 http://www.elmer.ca/elmers-story.

108 MTA, ARCC, 1954, 66.

109 MTA, ARCC, 1955, 72; "Road Safety: An Elephant Brings Safety to Our Schools," CBC Television, 27 March 1955, Digital Archives.

110 On reflections of a school patroller, see "Curb Crusaders," *Westward Alberta*, September 2002, 43–54.

111 "The School Patrol," *Canadian Police Gazette* 26, no. 7 (October 1951): 1.

112 "Youthful Policemen," *Canadian Police Gazette* 13, no. 2 (May 1938).

113 Parusel and McLaren, "Cars before Kids," 136. Two students were from Dawson Elementary School and were killed at Burrard and Comox Streets in downtown Vancouver. *Vancouver Courier*, 5 September 2008, online at Canada.com.

114 "Traffic Patrols for Three City Schools," *Vancouver Sun*, 15 September 1936, 2; CVA, Collection PDS 25: City Records of Police Public Documents, box 152-B-3, Annual Report of the Chief Constable of the City of Vancouver, BC, for the Year 1943, 11; CVA, Collection PDS 25: City Records of Police Public Documents, box 152-B-3, Annual Report of the Chief Constable of the City of Vancouver, BC, for the Year, 1953, 5.

115 "Are School Patrols Safe?," *Edmonton Sun*, 27 January 1961.

116 "Police Proud of Calgary School," *Canadian Police Gazette* 26, no. 11 (January 1952): 6.

117 CVA, Collection PDS 25, Annual Report of the Chief Constable of the City of Vancouver, BC, 1961, 30; "School Boy Patrol," *Canadian Police Gazette* 27, no. 5 (July 1952): 9; "School Patrol Boy Kenny Cobbs," *Canadian Police Gazette* 30, no. 7 (September 1955): front cover.

118 "Curb Crusaders," 54.

119 Calgary City Archives, Transportation Fonds, folder 6303, Jack O'Neill, Patrol Sergeant, Calgary City Police, "School Patrol and Safety Bulletin," no. 6 (February 1969): 1.

120 "Calgary's School Patrol," *Canadian Police Gazette* 13, no. 10 (January 1939): 6.

121 CVA, Collection PDS 25, Annual Report of the Chief Constable of the City of Vancouver, BC, 1950, 21; O'Neill, Bulletin no. 11, 1.

122 "Police Proud of Calgary School," 6.

123 "School Patrol and Safety Bulletin" #1, 19 September 1969, 1.

124 "Curb Crusaders," 43.

125 CVA, Collection PDS, Annual Report 1960, 31. As early as 1953, praise for, and pride in, the Vancouver School Boy Patrol for building an accident-free record came from the local police. "School Boy Patrols," *Canadian Police Gazette* 27 no. 12 (February 1953): 36.

126 City of Calgary, Archives, Transportation Department Fonds, series III, box 3, folder 6303, "Calgary School Patrol file," Letter from C/Inspector J.C. Stagg, Commanding Traffic Division, Calgary City Police Department, n.d., 1.

127 "Every Third Victim a Child."

128 "Traffic Course," *Canadian Police Gazette* 27, no. 7 (September 1952): 11. In fall 1952, officers from Oshawa, ON, Calgary, Edmonton, and Halifax attended a three-week course on traffic at Northwestern.

129 "Police Proud of Calgary School," 6.

130 Ibid.

131 "Praise for School Patrols," *Canadian Police Gazette* 29, no. 1 (March 1954): 67.

132 "Police Proud of Calgary School," 6.

133 "Curb Crusaders," 43.

134 "Traffic Patrols for Three City Schools," 2.

135 CVA, Police and Traffic Committee Meeting, box 27-C-3, folder 5, "Re: Safety Patrols," 23 August 1935.

136 MTA, ARCC, 1946, 33.

137 City of Calgary, Archives, Transportation Department Fonds, series III, box 3, folder 6303, Calgary School Patrol file, "Safety Patrol Committee Report (and Minutes)," 4 July 1967, 2.

138 Read et al., " Epidemiology and Prevention of Traffic Accidents," 700.

139 In this case, normalization refers to the actuarial persistence of accidents. That is, local police forces, like the Montreal Police Department, recorded traffic fatalities for annual reports, making them not unexceptional but, rather, creating yearly norms. Accidents, paradoxically, "may seem to be random and arbitrary, yet at the same time be expected or preordained." See Cooter and Luckin, eds., "Introduction," in *Accidents in History*, 3–4.

Epilogue

1 Pelletier joined the force as a young man in the early 1920s and worked his way up to inspector just prior to his death. Archives Municipales de la Ville de Montréal, Département de Police, Personnel File, Ovila Pelletier.

2 Archives Municipales de la Ville de Montréal, Département de Police, Personnel File, Ovila Pelletier, letter from Captain P. Brodeur to the Directeur du Service de la Police, 10 October 1932.

3 "To Teach and Not to Punish," *Montreal Gazette*, 3 April 1958, 8.

4 Ibid.

5 "Friend of Youth: Insp. O. Pelletier Dies at Age of 55," *Montreal Star and Herald*, 1 April 1958, 1;" "Ovila Pelletier," *Montreal Star and Herald*, 2 April 1958, 10; "L'insp. Ovila Pelletier, l'ami des jeunes, meurt subitement à l'hôpital," *La Presse*, 1 April 1958, 6. "Park Name Honors Boys' Club Founder," *Montreal Star*, 16 June 1960. Archives Municipales de la Ville de Montréal, Bureau du Greffier, Dossiers de presse, Bobine 251 [hereafter AMM Bob. #]; Parcs et Terrains de Jeux, Dossier Parc Ovila-Pelletier; and Administration Municipale, Comité Executif, Série 1: Procès-Verbeaux, Bobine 24, 2 April 1959–27 May 1960, "Le procès-verbal de la séance tenue le 16 février 1960," resolution 118400-14.

6 "Les Clubs Juvénile vont disparaître!" *La Presse*, 3 May 1965. AMM Bob. 251.

7 In 1961 the mayor convened a committee to look into the problem of goofballs, involving the Montreal Catholic School Commission (La Commission des Écoles Catholiques de Montréal), which surveyed its secondary schools to illuminate the extent of the problem. While very few students were caught using goofballs, it was clear that youth spaces – restaurants, buffets, snack bars, and dance clubs – were implicated in making the drugs available to teenagers. See Commission Scolaire de Montréal, Fonds d'archives du services des études, box 21, file "Drogues," Memo from the CECM to Mayor, "Commerce illicite des barbituriques," 24 March 1961.

8 See Garland, *The Culture of Control*.

9 See Beger, "Expansion of Police Power in Public Schools and the Vanishing Rights of Students," 119–30; Na and Gottfredson, "Police Officers in Schools," 1–32; Brown, "Understanding and Assessing School Police Officers," 591–604; Hirschfield, "Preparing for Prison?, 79–101; Hopkins et al., "Police-Schools Liaison and Young People's Image of the Police," 203–20; Jackson, "Police-School Resource Officers' and Students' Perception of the Police and Offending," 631–50. News coverage is extensive: see, for example, "With Police in Schools, More Children in Court," *New York Times*, 12 April 2013; "Criminalizing Children at School," *New York Times*, 18 April 2013; Desmond Cole, "7 Things to Know about How Armed Cops Came to Be in Toronto High Schools," *Buzzfeed*, https://www.buzzfeed.com/desmondcole/7-reasons-to-get-police-out-of-torontos-schools?utm_term=.yqnagk0D4#.wloOjMmrD.

10 Brown, "Understanding and Assessing School Police Officers," 592.

11 "Police Juvenile Clubs," *On the Spot* (National Film Board of Canada, 1954).

12 Myers, "Didactic Sudden Death," 451–75.

13 Mack, "Police Juvenile Liaison Schemes," 362.

14 Jackson, *Policing Youth*, chapter 2.

15 See Bennett, "Décisions des policiers-éducateurs"; "Baisse de la delinquance juvenile dans les classes ou passent les "Policiers éducateurs" de Montréal," *La Presse*, 10 July 1968.

16 Jean-Paul Gilbert, "Origine et justification du policier-éducateur," *Police Jeunesse* (Montreal: Graph-o Pier, 1970): 19–34 at 21.

17 "We Asked Canada's Police Chiefs," *Canadian Star Weekly*, 4–11 February 1967, 3–4; AMM Bob. 251; Gilbert, "Origine et justification du policier-éducateur," 19–34; Hanigan, *La jeunesse en difficulté*, 287.

18 "Le directeur Gilbert souligne que la police ne peut affronter seule la délinquance juvénile," *Le Devoir*, 25 November 1965; AMM Bob. 251.

19 The Juvenile Aid Squad was merged with several other squads (missing persons, sexual offences, and policewomen) in 1968 to form the Juvenile Aid Section, and the Craig Street office was closed. "Nouvelle section à la police de Montréal: L'aide à la jeunesse," *Dimanche/Dernière Heure*, 24 March 1968; AMM Bob. 251.

20 Gilbert, "Origine et justification du policier-éducateur," 22.

21 "Delinquency Fight Pays Off," *Montreal Star*, 14 December 1966. René Mongeau replaced Trépanier in 1967.

22 "La police retourne à l'école," *La Patrie* (Quebec), 19 March 1967; "L'expérience-pilote de l'unité préventive," *La Presse*, 6 December 1967; AMM Bob. 251.

23 "Delinquency Fight Pays Off." By the end of 1966 the Montreal Police Department boasted a 17 per cent decline in juvenile delinquency.

24 "Baisse de la delinquance juvenile dans les classes ou passent les 'policiers éducateurs' de Montréal"; AMM Bob. 251.

25 Ibid.

26 "Il n'est pas facile d'être adolescent, avec le peu de maturité des parents aujourd'hui," *Le Devoir*, 2 November 1967; AMM Bob. 251.

27 Bennett, "Décisions des policiers-éducateurs," 11–12.

28 "Une philosophie 'nouvelle' de police déjà publiée en 1946," *La Patrie* (Quebec), 31 March 1968. The police-educator program formed a "preventive unit" or *unité preventive*.

29 It's worth noting that although Montreal school boards were still organized confessionally (Catholic and Protestant), from 1964 the Quebec school system was secularized with a new government ministry in charge of education.

30 Claude Labelle, "Service de la Police de Montréal Section Aide à la jeunesse," *Police Jeunesse* (Montreal: Graph-o Pier, 1970), 106; "Conseillés par des policiers: Des Adolescents apprennent à devenir des hommes," *La Semaine*, 17–23 June 1968; AMM Bob. 251.

31 "Initiative de Montréal qui devrait être imitée à travers la province," *La Revue Municipale* (January 1969); AMM Bob. 251.

32 "Montréal est devenu un veritable Chicago," *Photo-Journal*, 22–9 March 1967.

33 "Des policiers de Montréal donnent des cours de criminologie aux jeunes," *La Presse*, 18 March 1967; AMM Bob. 251.

34 "En collaboration avec la CECM et la police de Montréal: Cours sur la délinquance juvénile dans nos écoles," *Les Nouvelles de l'Est*, 17 November 1966; AMM Bob. 251

35 "Des adolescents apprennent à devenir des hommes," *La Semaine*, 17–23 June 1968. See also "Une escouade anonyme surveille les jeunes filles qui 'poucent'," *Photo-Journal*, 5–12 June 1968; AMM Bob. 251

36 "Delinquency Fight Pays Off"; "Des adolescents apprennent à devenir des homes," AMM Bob. 251.

37 "City Policewomen Look After the Children's World," *Montreal Gazette*, 30 January 1968; AMM Bob. 251

38 "Un policier explique son travail aux jeunes Chinois dans leur langue," *La Presse*, 4 December 1968; AMM Bob. 251

39 "Initiative de Montreal qui devrait être imitée à travers la province;" AMM Bob. 251.

40 "La télévision educative au service de la police," *La Patrie* (Quebec), 1 December 1968.

41 Claude Labelle, "Service de la Police de Montréal Section Aide à la jeunesse," 103.

42 Commission Scolaire de Montréal, Fonds d'archives du services des études, box 21, file "Drogues," Letter from Viateur Ravary to Monsieur Jean-Paul Tardif, Directeur general adjoint, CECM, 20 December 1968.

43 Labelle, "Service de la Police de Montréal Section Aide à la jeunesse," 103–4. Martel, *Not This Time*, 55.

44 "Montréal et Paris s'entendent sur l'échange de policiers-éducateurs," *La Presse*, 21 December 1968; "Plusieurs pays s'intéressent au travail de l'Aide à la Jeunesse," *La Patrie* (Quebec), 2 March 1969; AMM Bob. 251.

45 "Des Policiers de Montréal vont enseigner en France!," *La Patrie* (Quebec), 2 February 1969; "Plusieurs pays s'intéressent au travail de l'Aide à la Jeunesse"; AMM Bob. 251.

46 "City Police Youth Program Praised," *Montreal Star*, 16 July 1970; AMM Bob. 251.

47 "Des policiers qui se font 'grands frères,'" *La Patrie* (Quebec), 21 January 1968; AMM Bob. 251.

48 "Les jeunes et le policier-éducateur," *La Patrie* (Quebec), 2 March 1969; AMM Bob. 251.

49 Sergeant Labelle believed that the problem with parents was that they influenced their children to distrust the police officer, like a "bête noire." "Baisse de la délinquance juvenile dans les classes ou passent les policiers éducateurs de Montréal," *La Presse*, 10 July 1968, AMM Bob. 251.

50 "Les jeunes et le policier-éducateur," *La Patrie* (Quebec), 2 March 1969; AMM Bob. 251.

51 Martel, *Not This Time*, 56.

52 Mark Lalonde, "The Canadian Experience: School Policing Perspective," *School Safety* (Fall 1995): 20–1.

53 Ibid., 20.

54 Kahn, *Police and Children*, 10.

55 "Toronto Police Board to Consider Suspending School Officer Program," *Toronto Star*, 23 May 2017, https://www.thestar.com/news/crime/2017/05/23/toronto-police-board-to-consider-suspending-school-officer-program.html.

56 Beger, "Expansion of Police Power in Public Schools," 119.

57 Ibid., 121.

58 Na and Gottfredson, "Police Officers in Schools," 2.

59 Beger, "Expansion of Police Power in Public Schools," 122.

60 Na and Gottfredson, "Police Officers in Schools," 2.

61 Beger, "Expansion of Police Power in Public Schools," 122.

62 In the first decade of the twenty-first century, 96 per cent of US schools required guests to sign in; 80 per cent had a closed-campus policy that forbids students to leave at lunchtime. Beger, "Expansion of Police Power in Public Schools," 120.

63 Na and Gottfredson, "Police Officers in Schools," 4.

64 Ibid.

65 Beger, "Expansion of Police Power in Public Schools," 119.

66 Ibid., 120.

Bibliography

Primary Sources

ARCHIVAL COLLECTIONS

Archives Municipales de la Ville de Montréal, Montreal, Quebec
    Bureau du Greffier
    Département de Police
    Fonds du Conseil de Ville de Montréal
Archives Nationales du Québec à Québec
    Fonds Procureur Général
Bibliothèque et Archives Nationales du Québec à Montréal, Montreal,
    Quebec
    Local Council of Women Fonds
    Fonds de la Cour des Jeunes Délinquants de la Cité de Montréal/Montreal
        Juvenile Delinquents' Court
Calgary City Archives, Calgary, Alberta
    Transportation Fonds
City of Toronto Archives, Toronto, Ontario
City of Vancouver Archives, Vancouver, British Columbia
    Vancouver Traffic and Safety Council Fonds
Commission Scolaire de Montréal
Library and Archives of Canada, Ottawa, Ontario
    Canadian Committee on Social Development
    Local Council of Women Fonds
    Royal Commission on the Criminal Law Relating to Criminal Sexual
        Psychopaths

McGill University Archives, Montreal, Quebec
Metro Toronto Archives, Toronto, Ontario
New York City Public Library, New York, New York
    Citizens' Committee on Children of New York City
    Mayor's Committee on Juvenile Delinquency
    New York City Police Department

NEWSPAPERS

Canadian Police Gazette
Canadian Star Weekly
CBC *News Online*
Charlottetown Guardian
Dimanche/Dernière Heure
Edmonton Sun
Financial Post
Fort Morgan Times
Globe and Mail
Hamilton Spectator
La Patrie
La Patrie Suisse
La Presse
Le Devoir
Le Petit Journal
Les Nouvelles de l'Est
Los Angeles Times
Montreal Gazette
Montreal Matin
Montreal Star
Montreal Star and Herald
Municipal Gazette of Canada
New York Times
Northern Beacon
Ottawa Citizen
Times (Fort Frances, ON)
Toronto Daily Star
Toronto Star
Vancouver Courier
Vancouver Sun

Westward Alberta
Winnipeg Free Press

JOURNALS AND MAGAZINES
Bulletin des Recherches Historiques
Canadian Journal of Public Health
Canadian Medical Association Journal
Canadian Nurse
Canadian Police Bulletin
Canadian Police Gazette
Chatelaine
Evangelical Churchman
La Revue des Constables/Police Constables Review
La Revue Municipale
La Semaine
Maclean's Magazine
Montreal Police Juvenile Guide
Municipal Review of Canada
North American Review
Oeuvre des Tracts
Photo-Journal
Police Chief News
Police Chief's Newsletter
Police Jeunesse
Reader's Digest
Revue des Agents de Police/Constables' Review
Royal Canadian Mounted Police Quarterly
Saturday Night Magazine

PUBLISHED PRIMARY SOURCES
Additon, Henrietta. "The Crime Prevention Bureau of New York." In
    Preventing Crime: A Symposium, edited by Sheldon Glueck and Eleanor T.
    Glueck, 215–36, New York: McGraw-Hill, 1936.
Archambault, R.P., S.J. *Le couvre-feu*. Montreal: L'Oeuvre des Tracts no. 274,
    April 1942.
Davis, Philip. *Street-Land: Its Little People and Big Problems*. Boston, 1915.
Gaboury, Arthur. *La lutte contre l'accident.* Montreal: La Ligue de Securité de
    la Province de Québec, 1934.

Glueck, Sheldon and Eleanor Glueck, eds. *Preventing Crime: A Symposium*. New York: McGraw-Hill, 1936.

Kahn, Alfred. *Police and Children: A Study of the Juvenile Aid Bureau of the New York City Police Department*. Citizens' Committee on Children of New York City, 1 June 1951.

Kelso, J.J. *Revival of the Curfew Law. A Paper Presented for the Twenty-Third National Conference of Charities and Corrections, Held at Grand Rapids, Michigan, June 4–10, 1896*. Toronto: Warwick Bros & Rutter, 1896.

Key, Ellen. *The Century of the Child*. New York City: G.P. Putnam's Sons, 1909.

Labelle, Claude. "Service de la Police de Montréal Section Aide à la Jeunesse." *Police Jeunesse*. Montreal: Graph-o Pier, 1970.

The Report of the Curfew Committee of the Law Enforcement Students of the Twenty-Third Class of the Delinquency Control Institute of the University of Southern California. 1970.

Service de Police de la Ville de Montréal [Communauté Urbain de Montréal], Centre du Documentation. "Youth Aid Section, History."

FILMS

Guerre à la délinquance: des policières montréalaises. National Film Board of Canada, 1952.

Hell's Highway: The True Story of Highway Safety Films. Directed by Bret Wood. New York: Livin' Man Productions, 2003.

Look Alert, Stay Unhurt. Directed by Gordon Burwash. National Film Board, 1955.

On the Spot. "Police Juvenile Clubs." National Film Board of Canada, 1954.

The Policeman. Produced by Gudrun Parker. National Film Board of Canada, 1946.

A Sergeant Sees It Through. Montreal: Omega Productions, 1954.

Secondary Sources

PUBLICATIONS

Acres, S.E. "Twentieth-Century Disease." *Canadian Journal of Public Health* 55, no. 5 (May 1964): 221–2.

Adams, Mary Louise. *The Trouble with Normal: Postwar Youth and the Making of Heterosexuality*. Toronto: University of Toronto Press, 1997.

Agee, Christopher Lowen. "Crisis and Redemption: The History of American Police Reform since World War II." *Journal of Urban History* 43, no. 3 (May 2017): 1–10.

Appier, Janis. "'We're Blocking Youth's Path to Crime:' The Los Angeles
Coordinating Councils during the Great Depression." *Journal of Urban
History* 31, no. 2 (2005): 190–218.

Ariès, Philippe. *The Hour of Our Death*. New York: Alfred A. Knopf, 1981.

Austin, Joe, and Michael Nevin Willard, eds. *Generations of Youth: Youth
Cultures and History in Twentieth-Century America*. New York: New York
University Press, 1998.

Backhouse, Constance. *Petticoats and Prejudice: Women and the Law in
Nineteenth-Century Canada*. Toronto: Women's Press, 1991.

Baldwin, Peter C. *In the Watches of the Night: Life in the Nocturnal City,
1820–1930*. Chicago: University of Chicago Press, 2012.

– "Nocturnal Habits and Dark Wisdom: The American Response to
Children in the Streets at Night, 1880–1930." *Journal of Social History* 35,
no. 3 (2002): 593–611.

Bard, Christine, Frédéric Chauvaud, Michelle Perrot, and Jacques-Guy Petit,
eds. *Femmes et justice pénale, XIX–XX siècles*. Rennes: Presses Universitaires
de Rennes, 2002.

Beger, Randall R. "Expansion of Police Power in Public Schools and the
Vanishing Rights of Students." *Social Justice* 29, nos. 1–2 (2002): 119–30.

Bourdieu, Pierre "Sport and Social Class." *Social Science Information* 17, no. 6
(1978): 819–40.

Brewer, Holly. *By Birth or Consent: Children, Law, and the Anglo-American
Revolution in Authority*. Chapel Hill: University of North Carolina
Press, 2005.

Brodeur, Jean-Paul. *La délinquance de l'ordre: recherches sur les commissions
d'enquête*. La Salle: University of Montreal Press, 1984.

Brown, Ben. "Understanding and Assessing School Police Officers: A
Conceptual and Methodological Comment." *Journal of Criminal Justice* 34
(2006): 591–604.

Brown, R. Blake. "'Every Boy Ought to Learn to Shoot and to Obey Orders':
Guns, Boys, and the Law in English Canada from the Late Nineteenth
Century to the Great War." *Canadian Historical Review* 93, no. 2 (2012):
196–226.

Burchell, Graham, Colin Gordon, and Peter Miller, eds. *The Foucault Effect:
Studies in Governmentality*. Chicago: University of Chicago Press, 1991.

Bush, William S. *Who Gets a Childhood? Race and Juvenile Justice in Twentieth-
Century Texas*. Athens: University of Georgia Press, 2010.

Caldwell, Mark. *New York Night: The Mystique and Its History*. New York:
Scribner, 2005.

Carrigan, D. Owen. *Juvenile Delinquency in Canada: A History*. Toronto:
    McClelland and Stewart, 1991.

Chambliss, William, ed. *Juvenile Crimes and Justice*. Los Angeles: Sage, 2011.

Chenier, Elise. *Strangers in Our Midst: Sexual Deviancy in Postwar Ontario*.
    Toronto: University of Toronto Press, 2008.

Chudacoff, Howard. *How Old Are You?: Age Consciousness in American Culture*.
    Princeton, NJ: Princeton University Press, 1989.

Cohen, Stanley. *Visions of Social Control: Crime, Punishments, and Classification*.
    Cambridge: Polity Press, 1985.

Cole, Desmond. "7 Things to Know about How Armed Cops Came to Be in
    Toronto High Schools." *Buzzfeed*, 14 June 2017. https://www.buzzfeed.com/
    desmondcole/7-reasons-to-get-police-out-of-torontos-schools?utm_term=.
    yqnagk0D4#.wloOjMmrD.

Collins, Damian C.A., and Robin A. Kearns. "Under Curfew and Under
    Siege? Legal Geographies of Young People." *Geoforum* 32, no. 2 (2001):
    389–403.

Comacchio, Cynthia. "Dancing to Perdition: Adolescence and Leisure
    in Interwar English Canada." *Journal of Canadian Studies* (Autumn
    1997): 5–35.

– *The Dominion of Youth: Adolescence and the Making of Modern Canada,
    1920–1950*. Waterloo, ON: University of Waterloo Press, 2005.

– *"Nations Are Built of Babies": Saving Ontario Mothers and Children,
    1900–1940*. Montreal and Kingston: McGill-Queen's University Press, 1990.

Conley, Jim, and Alison Tigar McLaren, eds. *Car Troubles: Critical Studies of
    Automobility and Auto-mobility*. Farnham, UK: Ashgate, 2009.

Cooter, Roger, and Bill Luckin, eds. *Accidents in History: Injuries, Fatalities, and
    Social Relations*. Amsterdam: Rodopi, 1997.

Corbey, Raymond. "Ethnographic Showcases, 1870–1930." *Cultural
    Anthropology* 8, no. 3 (August 1993): 338–69.

Cox, Pamela. *Gender, Justice, and Welfare: Bad Girls in Britain, 1900–1950*.
    Basingstoke: Palgrave, 2003.

Davies, Stephen. "'Reckless Walking Must Be Discouraged': The Automobile
    Revolution and the Shaping of Modern Canada to 1930." *Urban History
    Review* 18, no. 2 (October 1989): 123–38.

Davis, Janet. "Spectacles of South Asia at the American Circus, 1890–1940."
    Visual Anthropology 6 (1993): 121–38.

Decker, Scott, ed. *Policing Gangs and Youth Violence*. Belmont, CA: Thomson,
    Wadsworth, 2003.

Deleuze, Gilles. "Postscript on the Societies of Control." *October* 59, no. 1 (1992): 3–7.

Donzelot, Jacques. *The Policing of Families*. Translated by Robert Hurley. New York: Pantheon, 1979.

Dummitt, Christopher. *The Manly Modern: Masculinity in Postwar Canada*. Vancouver: University of British Columbia Press, 2007.

Ekirch, A. Roger. *At Day's Close: Night in Times Past*. New York: Norton, 2005.

Escobar, Edward J. *Race, Police, and the Making of a Political Identity: Mexican Americans and the Los Angeles Police Department, 1900–1945*. Berkeley: University of California Press, 1999.

Fahrni, Magda. "The Romance of Reunion: Montreal War Veterans Return to Family Life, 1944–1949." *Journal of the Canadian Historical Association* 9, no. 1 (1998): 187–208.

Fahrni, Magda, David Niget, and Martin Petitclerc, eds. *Pour une histoire du risque: Québec, France, Belgique*. Rennes: Presses universitaires de Renne, 2012.

Fass, Paula S. *The Damned and the Beautiful: American Youth in the 1920s*. New York: Oxford University Press, 1977.

Felker-Kantor, Max. "'Kid Thugs Are Spreading Terror through the Streets': Youth, Crime, and the Expansion of the Juvenile Justice System in Los Angeles." *Journal of Urban History* 42, no. 1 (January 2016): 1–25.

Field, Corinne T., and Nicholas L. Syrett, eds. *Age in America: The Colonial Era to the Present*. New York: New York University Press, 2015

Fishman, Sarah. *The Battle for Children: World War II, Youth Crime, and Juvenile Justice in Twentieth Century France*. Cambridge, MA: Harvard University Press, 2002.

Flamm, Michael W. *Law and Order: Street Crime, Civil Unrest, and the Crisis of Liberalism in the 1960s*. New York: Columbia Univeristy Press, 2005.

Flink, James J. *The Automobile Age*. Cambridge, MA: MIT Press, 1988.

Fogelson, Robert. *Big-City Police: An Urban Institute Study*. Cambridge, MA: Harvard University Press, 1977.

Fowler, Rodney S. "Accidents in Childhood: A Survey of 150 Cases on Private Paediatric Practice." *Canadian Medical Association Journal* (15 August 1958): 241.

Freedman, Estelle B. "'Uncontrolled Desires': The Response to the Sexual Psychopath, 1920–1960." *Journal of American History* 74, no. 1 (1987): 83–106.

Garland, David. *The Culture of Control: Crime and Social Order*. Chicago: University of Chicago Press, 2001.

George, Marie-Amelie. "The Harmless Psychopath: Legal Debates Promoting the Decriminalization of Sodomy in the United States." *Journal of the History of Sexuality* 24, no. 2 (2015): 225–61.

Gilbert, James. *A Cycle of Outrage: America's Reaction to the Juvenile Delinquent in the 1950s*. New York: Oxford University Press, 1984.

Gilfoyle, Timothy. *City of Eros: New York City, Prostitution, and the Commercialization of Sex, 1820–1920*. New York: Norton, 1992.

– "Street Rats and Guttersnipes: Child Pickpockets and Street Culture in New York City, 1850–1900." *Journal of Social History* 37, no. 4 (2004): 853–82.

Gleason, Mona. *Normalizing the Ideal: Psychology, Schooling, and the Family in Postwar Canada*. Toronto: University of Toronto Press, 1999.

Goluboff, Risa. *Vagrant Nation: Police Power, Constitutional Change, and the Making of the 1960s*. New York: Oxford University Press, 2016.

Grant, Julia. *The Boy Problem: Educating Boys in Urban America, 1870–1970*. Baltimore: Johns Hopkins University Press, 2014.

Grossberg, Michael. *Governing the Hearth: Law and Family in Nineteenth-Century America*. Chapel Hill: University of North Carolina Press, 1985.

Guild, Dorothy J. "Nursing Service: The Promotion of Safety." *Canadian Nurse*, June 1955, 456–9.

Hahn, Harlan, and Judson L. Jeffries. *Urban America and Its Police: From the Postcolonial Era through the Turbulent 1960s*. Boulder: University of Colorado Press, 2003.

Hanigan, Patricia. *La Jeunesse en difficulté: Comprendre pour mieux intervenir*. Quebec: Presses de l'Université du Québec, 1990.

Harring, Sidney R. *Policing a Class Society: The Experience of American Cities, 1865–1915*. New Brunswick, NJ: Rutgers University Press, 1983.

Hemmens, Craig, and Katherine Bennett. "Juvenile Curfews and the Court: Judicial Response to a Not-So-New Crime Control Strategy." *Crime and Delinquency* 45, no. 1 (1999): 99–121.

Hess, Kären, Christine H. Orthmann, and John P. Wright. *Juvenile Justice*. 6th ed. Belmont, CA: Wadsworth, 2013.

High, Steven, ed. *Occupied Saint John's: A Social History of a City at War*. Montreal and Kingston: McGill-Queen's University Press, 2010.

Hinton, Elizabeth. *From the War on Poverty to the War on Crime: The Making of Mass Incarceration in America*. Cambridge, MA: Harvard University Press, 2016.

Hirschfield, P.J. "Preparing for Prison? The Criminalization of School Discipline in the USA." *Theoretical Criminology* 12, no. 1 (2008): 79–101.

Hogeveen, Bryan. "'The Evils with Which We Are Called to Grapple':
     Elite Reformers, Eugenicists, Environmental Psychologists, and the
     Construction of Toronto's Working-Class Boy Problem, 1860–1930."
     Labour/LeTravail 55 (2005): 37–68.

Holloway, Sarah L., and Gill Valentine, eds. *Children's Geographies: Playing,
     Living, and Learning.* London: Routledge, 2000.

Hopkins, Nick, Miles Hewstone, and Alexandra Hantzi. "Police-Schools
     Liaison and Young People's Image of the Police: An Intervention
     Evaluation." *British Journal of Psychology* 83 (1992): 203–20.

Houston, Susan. "'The Waifs and Strays' of a Late Victorian City." In
     Childhood and Family in Canadian History, edited by Joy Parr, 129–42.
     Toronto: McClelland and Stewart, 1982.

Iacovetta, Franca, and Wendy Mitchenson, eds. *On the Case: Explorations in
     Social History.* Toronto: University of Toronto Press, 2006.

Jackson, A. "Police–School Resource Officers' and Students' Perception of the
     Police and Offending." *Policing: An International Journal of Police Strategies
     and Management* 25 (2002): 631–50.

Jackson, Louise A., with Angela Bartie. *Policing Youth: Britain, 1945–70.*
     Manchester: Manchester University Press, 2014.

Jain, Sarah S. Lochlann "'Dangerous Instrumentality': The Bystander as
     Subject in Automobility." *Cultural Anthropology* 19, no. 1 (February 2004):
     61–94.

Jalland, Pat. *Death in the Victorian Family.* Oxford: Oxford University Press,
     1996.

Jenkins, Philip. *Moral Panic: Changing Concepts of the Child Molester in Modern
     America.* New Haven, CT: Yale University Press, 1998.

Johnson, Craig M. "It's Ten O'Clock: Do You Know Where Your Children
     Are? QUTB v. Strauss and the Constitutionality of Juvenile Curfews."
     St. John's Law Review 69 (1995): 327–63.

Jones, Andrew, and Leonard Rutman. *In the Children's Aid: J.J. Kelso and Child
     Welfare in Ontario.* Toronto: University of Toronto Press, 1981.

Joyal, Renée, ed. *Entre surveillance et compassion: l'évolution de la protection
     de l'enfance au Québec.* Sainte Foy, QC: Presses de l'Université du
     Québec, 2000.

– *Les enfants, la société et l'état au Québec, 1608–1989.* Montreal: Hurtubise
     HMH, 1999.

Kelm, Mary Ellen. *A Wilder West: Rodeo in Western Canada.* Vancouver:
     University of British Columbia Press, 2011.

Keshen, Jeffrey A. *Saints, Sinners, and Soldiers: Canada's Second World War*. Vancouver: University of British Columbia Press, 2004.

– ed. *Age of Contention: Readings in Canadian Social History, 1900–1945*. Toronto: Harcourt, Brace Canada, 1997.

L., H., and R.R.O. "Note: Curfew Ordinances and the Nocturnal Control of Juvenile Crime." *University of Pennsylvania Law Review* 107, no. 1 (1958): 66–101.

Lapointe, Mathieu. *Nettoyer Montréal: les campagnes de moralité publique, 1940–1954*. Quebec: Septentrion, 2014.

Lewis, Norah. "'Isn't This a Terrible War? The Attitudes of Children to Two World Wars." *Historical Studies in Education* 7, no. 2 (1995): 193–215.

Lindenmeyer, Kriste. *A Right to Childhood: The U.S. Children's Bureau*. Urbana: University of Illinois Press, 1997.

Loewen, James W. *Sundown Towns: A Hidden Dimension of Segregation in America*. New York: New Press, 2005.

Lossing, Elisabeth. "The Crime Prevention Work of the Berkeley Police Department." In *Preventing Crime: A Symposium*, edited by Sheldon Glueck and Eleanor Glueck, 237–63. New York: McGraw-Hill, 1936.

Low, Brian J. NFB *Kids: Portrayals of Children by the National Film Board of Canada, 1939–1989*. Waterloo, ON: Wilfrid Laurier University :Press, 2002.

Mack, J.A. "Police Juvenile Liaison Schemes." *British Journal of Criminology* 3, no. 4 (April 1963): 361–75.

MacLeod, David I. *Building Character in the American Boy: The Boy Scouts, YMCA, and Their Forerunners, 1870–1920*. Madison: University of Wisconsin Press, 1983.

Maddox, Lucy. "Politics, Performance, and Indian Identity." *American Studies International* 40, no. 2 (June 2002): 7–37.

Marquis, Greg. "The Police as a Social Service in Early Twentieth-Century Toronto." *Histoire Sociale/Social History* 25, no. 50 (November 1992): 335–58.

– *Policing Canada's Century: A History of the Canadian Association of Chiefs of Police*. Toronto: University of Toronto Press, 1993.

– *The Vigilant Eye: Policing Canada from 1867 to 9/11*. Halifax: Fernwood, 2016.

Marr, Lucille. "Church Teen Clubs, Feminized Organizations? Tuxis Boys, Trail Rangers, and Canadian Girls in Training, 1919–1939." *Historical Studies in Education* 3, no. 2 (1991): 249–67.

Martel, Marcel. *Not This Time: Canadians, Public Policy, and the Marijuana Question, 1961–1975*. Toronto: University of Toronto Press, 2006.

Maynard, Steven. "'Horrible Temptations': Sex, Men, and Working-Class Male Youth in Urban Ontario, 1890–1935." *Canadian Historical Review* 78, no. 2 (June 1997): 191–235.

McShane, Clay. *Down the Asphalt Path: The Automobile and the American City.* New York: Columbia University Press, 1994.

Mennel, Robert M. *Thorns and Thistles: Juvenile Delinquents in the United States, 1825–1940.* Hanover, NH: University Press of New England, 1973.

Mills, Sarah. "Youth on Streets and Bob-a-Job Week: Urban Geographies of Masculinity, Risk, and Home in Postwar Britain." *Environment and Planning* 46 (2014): 112–28.

Mintz, Steven. *Huck's Raft: A History of American Childhood.* Cambridge, MA: Harvard University Press, 2004.

Mitrani, Sam. *The Working Class in American History: The Rise of the Chicago Police Department: Class and Conflict, 1850–1894.* Champaign: University of Illinois Press, 2013.

Monkkonen, Eric H. *Police in Urban America, 1860–1920.* New York: Cambridge University Press, 1981.

Morgan, Celia. "A Wigman to Westminster: Performing Mohawk Identity in Imperial Britain, 1890s–1900s." *Gender and History* 25, no. 2 (August 2003): 319–41.

Moss, Mark. *Manliness and Militarism: Educating Young Boys in Ontario for War.* New York: Oxford University Press, 2001.

Myers, Tamara. *Caught: Montreal's Modern Girls and the Law, 1869–1945.* Toronto: University of Toronto Press, 2006.

– "Didactic Sudden Death: Children, Police, and Teaching Citizenship in the Age of Automobility." *Journal of the History of Childhood and Youth* 8, no. 3 (Fall 2015): 451–75.

– "Embodying Delinquency: Boys' Bodies, Sexuality, and Juvenile Justice History in Early Twentieth-Century Quebec." *Journal of the History of Sexuality* 14, no. 4 (October 2005): 383–414.

– "Women Policing Women: A Patrol Woman in Montreal in the 1910s." *Journal of the Canadian Historical Association* 4 (1993): 229–45.

Myers, Tamara, and Mary Anne Poutanen. "Cadets, Curfews, and Compulsory Schooling: Mobilizing Anglophone Children in WWII Montreal." *Histoire Sociale/Social History* 76 (November 2005): 367–98.

Na, Chongmin, and Denise C. Gottfredson. "Police Officers in Schools: Effects on School Crime and the Processing of Offending Behaviors." *Justice Quarterly* (2011): 1–32.

Norton, Peter D. *Fighting Traffic: The Dawn of the Motor Age in the American City*. Cambridge, MA: MIT Press, 2008.

– "Four Paradigms: Traffic Safety in the Twentieth-Century United States." *Technology and Culture* 56, no. 2 (April 2015): 319–34.

Odem, Mary. *Delinquent Daughters: Protecting and Policing Female Adolescent Sexuality in the United States, 1885–1920*. Chapel Hill: University of North Carolina Press, 1995.

Ossian, Lisa L. *The Forgotten Generation: American Children and World War II*. Columbia: University of Missouri Press, 2011.

Owram, Doug. *Born at the Right Time: A History of the Baby-Boom Generation*. Toronto: University of Toronto Press, 1997.

Oxford English Dictionary. Oxford: Oxford University Press, 2004.

Parr, Joy. *Sensing Changes: Technology, the Environment, and the Everyday*. Vancouver: University of British Columbia Press, 2009.

– ed. *Childhood and the Family in Canadian History*. Toronto: McClelland and Stewart, 1982.

Parusel, Sylvia, and Arlene Tigar McLaren. "Cars before Kids: Automobility and the Illusion of School Traffic Safety." *Canadian Review of Sociology* 47, no. 2 (2010): 129–47.

Pellegrini, Ann. "What Do Children Learn at School? Necropedagogy and the Future of the Dead Child." *Social Text* 26, no. 4 (2008): 97–105.

Platt, Anthony M. *The Child Savers: The Invention of Delinquency*. New Brunswick, NJ: Rutgers University Press, 2009.

Potter, Claire Bond. *War on Crime: Bandits, G-Men and the Politics of Mass Culture*. New Brunswick, NJ: Rutgers University Press, 1998.

Poutanen, Mary Anne. *Beyond Brutal Passions: Prostitution in Early Nineteenth-Century Montreal*. Montreal and Kingston: McGill-Queen's University Press, 2015.

Powers, Ron. "The Apocalypse of Adolescence." *Atlantic*, March 2002. https://www.theatlantic.com/magazine/archive/2002/03/the-apocalypse-of-adolescence/302449/.

Putney, Clifford. *Muscular Christianity: Manhood and Sports in Protestant America, 1880–1920*. Cambridge, MA: Harvard University Press, 2001.

Read, John H., Eleanor J. Bradley, Joan D. Morison, David Lewall, and David A. Clarke. "The Epidemiology and Prevention of Traffic Accidents Involving Child Pedestrians." *Canadian Medical Association Journal* (5 October 1963): 689.

Robertson, Stephen. "What's Law Got to Do with It? Legal Records and Sexual Histories." *Journal of the History of Sexuality* 14, nos. 1–2 (January/April 2005): 161–85.

– "Shifting the Scene of the Crime: Sodomy and the American History of Sexual Violence." *Journal of the History of Sexuality* 19, 2 (May 2010), 223–43.

Romesburg, Don. "Wouldn't a Boy Do? Placing Early-Twentieth-Century Male Youth Sex Work in the Histories of Sexuality." *Journal of the History of Sexuality* 18, no. 3 (2009): 367–92.

Rooke, P.T., and M.R. Schnell. *Discarding the Asylum: From Child Rescue to the Welfare State in English Canada, 1800–1950*. Lanham, MD: University Press of America, 1983.

Ruefle, William, and Kenneth Mike Reynolds. "Curfews and Delinquency in Major American Cities." *Crime and Delinquency* 41, no. 3 (1995): 347–63.

Ryerson, Ellen. *Best Laid Plans: America's Juvenile Court Experiment*. New York: Hill and Wang, 1978.

Sangster, Joan. "The Beaver as Ideology: Constructing Images of Inuit and Native Life in Postwar Canada." *Anthropoligica* 49, no. 2 (2007): 191–209.

– *Girl Trouble: Female Delinquency in English Canada*. Peterborough, ON: Broadview Press, 2002.

Schlossman, Steven. *Love and the American Delinquent: The Theory and Practice of 'Progressive' Juvenile Justice, 1825–1920*. Chicago: University of Chicago Press, 1977.

– *Transforming Juvenile Justice: Reform Ideals and Institutional Realities, 1825–1920*. DeKalb: Northern Illinois University Press, 2005.

Schlossman, Steven L., and Michael Sedlak. "The Chicago Area Project Revisited." *Crime and Delinquency* 26 (1983): 398–462.

Schmidt, Bonnie Reilly. *Silenced: The Untold Story of the Fight for Equality in the RCMP*. Halfmoon Bay, BC: Caitlin Press, 2015.

Schneider, Eric C. *In the Web of Class: Delinquents and Reformers in Boston, 1810s–1930s*. New York: New York University Press, 1992.

– *Vampires, Dragons, and Egyptian Kings: Youth Gangs in Postwar New York*. Princeton, NJ: Princeton University Press, 1999.

Schneider, Eric C., Christopher Agee, and Themis Chronopolous. "Dirty Work: Police and Community Relations and the Limits of Liberalism in Postwar Philadelphia." *Journal of Urban History* 43, no. 3 (2017): 1–19.

Schor, Joachim. *Nights in the Big City: Paris, Berlin, London, 1840–1930.* Translated by Pierre Gottfried Imhof and Dafydd Rees Roberts. London: Reaktion Books, 1998.

Schumann, Dirk, ed. *Raising Citizens in the 'Century of the Child': The United States and German Central Europe in Comparative Perspective.* Oxford: Berghahn Books, 2010.

Smith, Ken. *Mental Hygiene Classroom Films, 1945–1970.* New York: Blast Books, 1999.

Stansell, Christine. *City of Women: Sex and Class in New York, 1789–1860.* New York: Knopf, 1987.

Stearns, Peter N. *American Fear: The Causes and Consequences of High Anxiety.* New York: Routledge, 2006.

– *Anxious Parents: A History of Modern Child-Rearing in America.* New York: New York University Press, 2004

Stearns, Peter N., and Timothy Haggerty. "The Role of Fear: Transitions in American Emotional Standards for Children, 1850–1950." *American Historical Review* 96, no. 1 (1991): 63–94.

Straw, Will. "Montreal and *The Captive City.*" *Quebec Studies* 33, no. 48 (Fall-Winter, 2009–10): 13–24.

Sutherland, Neil. *Children in English-Canadian Society: Framing the Twentieth-Century Consensus.* Toronto: University of Toronto Press, 1976.

Sutphen, Richard D. and Janet Ford. "The Effectiveness and Enforcement of a Teen Curfew Law." *Journal of Sociology* 28, no. 1 (March 2001): 55–78

Tanenhaus, David S. *Juvenile Justice in the Making.* New York: Oxford University Press, 2004.

Thrasher, Frederic M. "The Lower West Side Crime Prevention Program, New York City." In *Preventing Crime,* edited by Sheldon Glueck and Eleanor Glueck, 46–67.

Tillotson, Shirley. *The Public at Play: Gender and the Politics of Recreation in Post-War Ontario.* Toronto: University of Toronto, 2000.

Townsend, Mrs John D. "Curfew for City Children." *North American Review* (December 1896): 725–30.

Tumarkin, Maria. "Productive Death: The Necropedagogy of a Young Soviet Hero." *South Atlantic Quarterly* 110, no. 4 (Fall 2011): 885–900.

Turmel, Jean. *Police de Montréal, historique du service: premières structures et évolution de la police de Montréal: 1796–1971.* Montreal: Service de la Police de la Communauté Urbaine de Montréal, 1974.

Tuttle, Jr., William M. *Daddy's Gone to War: The Second World War in the Lives of America's Children.* New York: Oxford University Press, 1993.

Umbach, Fritz. *The Last Neighborhood Cops: The Rise and Fall of Community Policing in New York Public Housing*. New Brunswick, NJ: Rutgers University Press, 2011.

Valentine, Gil. "Angels and Devils: Moral Landscapes of Childhood." *Environment and Planning Society and Space* 14 (1996): 581–99.

Valverde, Mariana. *The Age of Light, Soap, and Water: Moral Reform in English Canada, 1885–1925*. Toronto: University of Toronto Press, 2008.

Vissing, Yvonne. "Curfews." In *Juvenile Crime and Justice*, edited by William J. Chambliss, 59–72. London: Sage, 2011.

Walker, Samuel. *The Police in America: An Introduction*. New York: McGraw Hill, 1999.

Ward, Geoff K. *The Black Child-Savers: Racial Democracy and Juvenile Justice*. Chicago: University of Chicago Press, 2012.

Weintraub, William. *City Unique: Montreal Days and Nights in the 1940s and '50s*. Montreal: Robin Brass Studio, 1996.

Wilson, Mary. "Accident Prevention in Infants and Preschool Children." *Canadian Nurse*, April 1954, 287.

Wolcott, David B. *Cops and Kids: Policing Juvenile Delinquency in Urban America, 1890–1940*. Columbus: Ohio State University Press: 2005.

Zelizer, Viviana. *Pricing the Priceless Child*. New York: Basic Books, 1985.

UNPUBLISHED THESES AND PAPERS

Albert, Daniel Marc. "Order Out of Chaos: Automobile Safety, Technology and Society, 1925 to 1965." PhD diss., University of Michigan, 1998.

Bennett, Constance. "Décisions des policiers-éducateurs." Master's thesis, Université de Montréal, 1969.

Cournoyer, Catherine. "Les accidents impliquant des enfants et l'attitude envers l'enfance à Montréal (1900–1945)." Master's thesis, Université de Montréal, 1999.

Hill, Janice M. "Building a Nation of Nation Builders: Youth Movements, Imperialism, and English Canadian Nationalism, 1900–1920." PhD diss., York University, 2004.

Kuplowsky, Adam. "A Captivating 'Open City': The Production of Montreal as a 'Wide-Open Town' and 'Ville Ouverte' in the 1940s and '50s." Master's thesis, McGill University, 2014.

Trepanier, James. "Building Boys, Building Canada: The Boy Scouts Movement in Canada, 1908–1970." PhD diss., York University, 2015.

Index

abortion, as sting operation, 67
Additon, Henrietta, 36–7, 119
Adolescence: Its Psychology and Its Relations to Physiology, Anthropology, Sociology, Sex, Crime and Religion (Hall), 11, 87, 110
adolescents: adults versus, 46, 53; changing meaning of, 10–11; concern for, 95, 103, 110, 171; criminalization of, 3, 108, 172, 174; girl, 7, 12, 51; panic over, 94, 108; policing of, 3–4, 46, 78, 98, 129; programming for, 30, 113, 170 (*see also* clubs: boys' and girls'); provocation of, 3, 100–1; rehabilitation of, 24, 54–5, 171; sexuality, 44, 51–5
adults, 9, 26, 76, 93, 163; concern about, 13, 23, 32, 67, 80; corruption of youth, 39, 47, 50–6, 67, 81; criminality, 5, 19, 43, 97, 169–70; hegemony of, 44, 86, 102, 108, 176; policing of, 84, 146, 172; predatory, 8, 44–9, 53, 75–6, 84; saving youth from, 83–8; youth opposition to, 22, 91

African Americans, 12, 121; curfews, 83, 99–100; discrimination against, 20; imprisonment of, 14, 22; policewoman, first, 33; programming for, 17, 121, 123, 159; targeting of youth, 33–4, 99–100, 115–16
American Social Hygiene Association, 36
Appier, Janis, 14, 30
Archambault, Father, 94–6
arrests, 54, 67, 77, 91, 140; adult, 39, 47–56, 63; African American youth, 14; children's, 25, 67, 74, 98, 154; curfews, 98–100; gender imbalance in, 70–2; growth in, 24–5, 27; mass, 19; reduction in, 15, 35, 38, 61; school and, 154, 178; youth, 45, 58, 74, 93, 124
article 33. *See* Juvenile Delinquents Act
Asian Canadians, 159, 175
asylums, 26
Attorney General, office of the, 74–5
authority, police, 4, 7, 23, 70, 163–4; changing image of, 18–19, 62–5,

107, 154, 166–71; embedding of, 40, 43–4, 47, 124–9; opposition to, 22, 24, 86, 91–2, 176; parents versus, 92–7; youth hangouts, 30, 37, 39, 103, 150

automotive revolution. *See* traffic safety

baby boom, 42, 134, 141–3, 164, 171; automobility, 141–5
Baldwin, Peter C., 84, 89
Barnes, Charles, 63–4
beat officers, 98, 122; attitudes of, 21; evolution of, 62–3, 66–7, 76; stereotypes of, 23–4, 56
Beger, Randall R., 177
Berkeley, CA, 15; crime prevention, 31–4, 40, 43
Bieler, Zoe, 65–6
Big Sisters, 36
black communities. *See* African Americans
Boston, 5, 23
Bourdieu, Pierre, 108
Boy Scouts, 9, 110–12, 114–17, 125, 132
boywork, 109–11, 113–15, 128
bribery, police, 6, 24
broken homes. *See* single parenting
Brown, R. Blake, 105
Bush, William, 14

Caldwell, Mark, 84
Calgary, 63; school safety patrols, 158–61, 163
Canada: automobility, 134, 137, 139–47, 158; Boy Scouts (*see* Boy Scouts); colonialism, 20; crime prevention programs, 8, 20,

62–3, 178; crime rates, 8, 57–8, 93, 101; curfews (*see* curfews); delinquency (*see* delinquency); films (*see* National Film Board of Canada); juvenile justice system, 5, 45, 177; national narratives, 34, 87, 153–63; penal reform, 13–14, 22, 99, 110; police–youth relations, 11, 24–6, 175
Canadian Automobile Association (CAA), 158–9
Canadian Penal Association, 31
Canadian Police Gazette (CPG), 25, 63, 115, 132, 148, 161–2
Canadian Women's Voluntary Services, 26
car culture. *See* traffic safety
Catholicism, 43, 112; curfews, support for, 94–5; tensions with, 128–9, 210n93; youth organizing in, 46, 69, 71, 172–5
Caught: Montreal's Modern Girls and the Law, 1869–1945, 5
charities, private, 20, 32, 94
Chatelaine, 143–4, 152
Chicago, 21, 53, 82, 158; Area Project (CAP), 40, 112–13; curfews, 99–100; police–youth relations, 22–5, 63, 77
childhood, 144; curfews, 80–9, 95–6, 100–3; deficits in, 14, 28–9; definition of, 4, 10–12, 106; diseases, 136, 138, 141–4, 164; domesticated, 136, 140–1, 144–5, 155, 165, 170; environment, importance of (*see* environment); moulding of, 8, 12–13, 17, 90, 111; perceptions of, 21, 150–5; police presence in,

30–3, 40–1, 63, 169, 179; risks, 12, 23, 134–45, 163–5, 170; safeguarding, 3, 19–20, 74–5, 134–40

child labour, 5, 138

children: "accident," 142–4; control of, 7, 25–35, 57–8, 107–8, 135; "corruption" of, 22, 44, 46–50, 54–60, 76; curfews (*see* childhood: curfews); future crime avoidance, 9, 29–40, 73–5, 86, 119, 172; police involvement with, 8–12, 43–52, 117–22, 135–40, 145–64 (*see also* policewomen); rescuing, 18–23, 61, 147; safety campaigns, 134–50; sports involvement (*see* sports). *See also* childhood

Children's Aid Societies, 82, 85, 90, 92, 95

Children's Protection Act, Ontario, 82, 85, 88, 92

child-saving: rhetoric of, 4–5, 143; middle-class, 20, 80–2, 87, 96; police campaigns, 33, 40, 54, 160

Chisholm, John, 134

churches, 118–19, 148; inadequacy of, 27; youth programming, 71, 94, 111

citizenship, 158, 165, 176; notions of good, 16, 35, 61–3, 93–7, 114; training, 34, 87, 102–3, 127–36, 172; worthiness of, 20–2, 105–10, 149

civic leadership, 18, 61, 64–5, 80; award, 131, 167; boy problem, 110; crime prevention work, 14, 28, 30, 40, 106

class: barriers, 14, 84, 125, 141, 159; delinquency and, 5, 13, 22, 24, 57; middle (*see* middle class); regulation by, 4, 16, 107–9;

working (*see* working class)

Cleveland, 99, 116; Common Sense Policy, 31–2

Cloutier, Marguerite, 66–7

clubs: boys' and girls', 94; crime prevention, 30, 39–41, 121, 125; denominational, 126, 167; membership to, 73, 105–9, 114, 126–30, 133; police-run, 34, 62, 70–7, 104–21, 170–1. *See also* Police Juvenile Clubs (PJC, Montreal); YMCA/YWCA

Cohen, Stanley, 12

Cold War, 152, 165

colonialism, Canada, 20

Columbine High School, 177

Communism, 7, 47

coordinating councils, 14, 30, 32

Cournoyer, Catherine, 137, 140

courts, juvenile. *See* juvenile courts

Couzens, James R., 25–6

Cowan, Oliver A. 12

crime: adult, 5, 19, 47–51, 134 (*see also* adults); "breeding grounds," 28, 35, 37, 186n52; deterrence of, 23, 69, 120–2, 177; drug, 175; etiology of, 19, 29–30, 54, 73, 169; growing levels of, 23, 31–2, 57, 61–2, 164; juvenile, 27, 57–9, 69–73, 92, 103; organized, 18, 34, 43, 169; petty, 23, 35, 86, 121, 172; rates, 14, 57–9, 85, 125, 174; sensationalization of, 7–8, 81; sexual, 44, 47, 56, 72, 76; war on, 14, 27, 30, 65, 99; waves, 7, 13, 30, 58, 170. *See also* crime prevention: curfews

crime prevention: anti-delinquency programs, 21, 27–35, 40–1, 73, 113;

Berkeley, 31–4, 40, 43; Chicago, 77, 112 (*see also* Chicago: Area Project [CAP]); crime-fighting praxis, 16–19; curfews (*see* curfews); Detroit, 21, 25, 77, 99; juvenile justice system, 5–8, 19–20, 40, 74; Montreal, 14–17, 42–6, 59, 70, 123–31 (*see also* Juvenile Morality Squad [JMS, Montreal]); New York City, 28–9, 34–40, 43, 116–22, 177; police role in, 21, 40–1, 77, 173, 177 (*see also* youth-conscious policing); programming, 8–14, 19, 70, 113, 132; reconfiguration of, 21, 62–70, 110, 166–70; rhetoric of, 19–20, 54, 61–2, 73, 124; strategies, 28–30, 43–4, 46, 79–80, 106–10; study of, 32–6, 40, 69, 99, 169; Toronto, 26, 41, 113, 115, 177; Vancouver, 34, 63.

crime prevention advocacy, 8, 19–20, 29, 114

Criminal Code of Canada, 4, 48–9

criminality, 59, 113; causes of, 28–32, 86, 124, 132; latent, 8, 18–19, 53, 169; single male neighbours, 50

criminal justice system, 33; adult, 5, 21, 45; exposure to, 29–30, 178; harshness of, 9, 21, 30, 39–40; juvenile, 20, 24–6, 39–45, 74–5, 169. *See also* juvenile courts

criminology, 8; child welfare, 29; courses, 32, 171, 173; crime prevention, 19, 31

curfews, 3, 102; acceptance of, 12, 79–89, 92–8; critiques of, 79–80, 89, 93, 100–4; justification for, 3–4, 16, 94–5, 103; opposition to, 92,

97, 101–2; origins of, 81–2; protest, quelling of, 99–101, 103; "revival," 82, 90–8, 102–3; sunset crimes, 71–2, 80, 98; targeted, 58–9, 80–3, 89, 102

death, 100–1; abortion-related, 67; automobiles, 134–5, 136–40, 142–7; children and youth, 51, 135, 137–8, 140–4; didactic sudden, 149–52, 154, 170; parental, 90; safety patrols reducing, 158, 163–4; sentences, 28

delinquency, 5; as boy problem, 7–8, 22–3, 106, 109–17, 128; causes of, 13, 32–3, 73; class-based, 13, 22–4, 27–8, 57, 107; development of, 8, 13, 15, 35; education campaigns, 21, 35, 54, 105, 168; "elimination" of, 22–3, 46, 132, 177; growth of, 27, 44, 90–3, 106, 114–17; incipient, 29, 33–5, 77, 106, 119, 166–7; panics, 13, 73, 94–5, 98–9, 117; persistence of, 7, 18, 24, 119–22; police ambivalence to, 10, 24, 41, 76–7; postwar, 44, 57, 61, 98–103, 167; predelinquency, 9–17, 44, 71, 80, 123–4, 170; prevention of, 43–4, 70–6, 105–6, 112–14, 171–7; prosperity, 91, 141–2; regulation of, 6, 11, 23, 85, 102; safety patrols and, 39, 161; sports to combat, 129–32; wartime, 25, 44, 57–61, 81, 125

Delinquency Prevention Bureau (DPB, Montreal), 43, 59–61, 77, 127, 129–30; women in, 65, 67–9

Delinquency Prevention Week conference (Montreal), 61

Depression, Great, 25–8, 42, 44, 115, 123

detention centres, 14, 45, 97–8

Detroit, 21, 99, 157; police reform in, 25–6, 77

discrimination: gender, 89; racialized groups, 10, 83, 100, 177

diseases, childhood. *See* childhood: diseases

"Dr Watson's Corner," 49, 51

drugs: delinquency and, 167–68; use of, 171, 175–6, 219n7

Dufresne, Fernand, 46–7, 75

Dummit, Christopher, 141

Durivage, Louis–Philippe, 46, 69

Edmonton, 92, 158–9

educators, 16; crime prevention, 30, 98; police as, 21, 35, 148, 168–9, 172–7

Ekirch, A. Robert, 82

elites, 6, 139

England, 51, 63, 110; curfew laws, 82; Liverpool, 171; London, 4, 84. *See also* United Kingdom

environment, children's, 109, 178; adult (in)action, 27–9, 87, 153; delinquency, 37, 43–4, 70, 144, 169; influence on crime, 8–9, 11, 18–21, 111; play, importance of, 111, 115, 119; urban crime, 13, 29–30, 132

Everleigh, Ronald G., 34

Federal Bureau of Investigation (FBI), 8, 19, 27, 30

femininity: notions of, 34, 128; police work, 66–8

films, National Film Board of Canada. *See* National Film Board of Canada

films, safety. *See* traffic safety: didactic sudden death messaging

First World War, 36, 62; lawlessness, 7

Flamm, Michael, 13

Fontaine, Rosario, 49–50

Foucault, Michel, 107, 183n29

gambling, 42–3, 48, 72

gangs, youth, 12–13, 66, 118, 133, 174; Archie's story, 72–3, 127; curfews and, 90, 92, 99–100; drugs and, 167–8; police breakup of, 34–5, 70–1, 86, 176; recreation clubs and, 106–8, 111–15, 121–5, 170

gangsterism, 18, 27–9, 105, 109, 169

Garland, David, 6

gay men, policing of, 51–2, 56, 91

gender: curfews, 84, 86–7, 89; police recruitment, 7, 33, 63–6; policewomen's work, 7, 31, 62–70; recreational clubs, 112–13, 159; regulation, 4–5, 106–7, 174

Gendron, Stéphane, 100–1

Genovese, Vincent, 3

Gilbert, James, 57

Gilbert, Jean-Paul, 16–17, 171

Gilfoyle, Timothy, 22

girls: clubs, 30, 39, 106–11, 116–17; crime prevention, 33–5, 61, 98–100, 176; "khaki-mad," 13, 103; problem, 7, 12, 58–9, 72, 174; prostitution, 22, 33, 56; protection of, 28, 36, 47–51, 86–9; recreation programs, 74, 120–8; regulation of, 44, 53, 89, 91, 174; safety patrols, 154–5, 159–60, 167; street life, 83, 94

Gleason, Mona, 51, 143–4

Globe and Mail, 83–4, 87–9

Glueck, Sheldon and Eleanor, 29
G-Men. *See* Junior G-Men
Grant, Julia, 111, 113
Greis, Walter, 27–8
guns, youth use of, 105, 131–2

Haggerty, Timothy, 151–2
Hall, G. Stanley, 11, 87, 110
Harshaw, Robert, 115
health: delinquency and, 87, 103,
   137–8; ill, 22, 37; moral, 47, 95;
   promotion, 33, 38, 64, 110, 128;
   traffic accidents, 144, 152
Healy, William, 29
Hinton, Elizabeth, 14
Hirschfield, P.J., 178
Hogeland, Alexander, 81, 83, 85, 87
Hollywood, 34; violence, 8, 105, 151;
   youth portrayals in, 59
homeless shelters, 26
homophobia, 44, 47, 54
homosexual relations, 44, 47, 51–5, 91
homosexuality, 52, 55, 174
Hoover, J. Edgar, 8, 19, 27, 30
Huckleberry Finn, 109
Huntingdon, QC, 100–1

idleness, youth, 7–8, 19, 73, 124;
   programming for, 34, 107, 170
immigrants: citizenship, 20;
   neighbourhood delinquency, 29,
   83; as problematic, 5, 85; programs
   for, 40, 109, 112, 173
immigration, 4, 42, 115
incest, 48–9
"inclusive" social control, 12
indecency, charge of, 45, 48–9, 51
Indigenous peoples, 155–6;
   incarceration of children, 20,

109; recreational clubs, 107;
   youth curfews, 82, 89, 101. *See also*
   residential schools
industrialization, 164; curfews, 82–3,
   89, 94; features of, 5, 22, 106, 109,
   138; schools in, 26, 88
inspections, police, 23, 39, 67, 129,
   146–7
institutions: bourgeois values,
   22, 94; failure of, 12, 30, 86, 88;
   innovation, 19–27, 81, 167–8, 175,
   179; juvenile rehabilitation, 5–6,
   53, 61, 113–14
International Association of Chiefs
   of Police (IACP), 18, 99, 117, 146
interwar period: crime prevention,
   19, 27, 77, 139–40, 169; policing
   in, 4, 8, 29–30, 146–7; recreation
   programs, 106, 111–12; youth
   culture, 46

JAB-2 cards, 38
Jackson, Louise A., 13, 171
Japanese communities, 34
Jim Crow era, juvenile justice, 20
jobs, youth, 28, 82
Jones, Beverley, 82, 86
judges, 47, 65, 95, 99; sympathetic, 21,
   49, 55–6, 97; youth regulation, 5,
   46, 58, 74–5, 130
Junior G-Men, 34
junior police (New York City), 12,
   34–5, 40, 117
Juvenile Aid Bureau (JAB, New York
   City), 19, 37–9, 63, 117, 121–2. *See
   also* JAB–2 cards
juvenile courts: appearance in,
   12, 61, 127, 130; avoidance of,
   8–9, 28, 38–40, 74–5; curfews,

92, 94–5, 97–8; diversion to, 5, 20, 47–59; movement, 12–13, 20–1, 23, 26; police versus, 29, 43–6, 77; proliferation of, 5–6, 45, 179; scrutiny of, 30; urban, 20; usurpation of authority, 29, 43, 74–5

Juvenile Delinquents Act, 45–9, 74, 76, 98, 128; article 33, 48–53, 56, 76, 192n36

Juvenile Morality Squad (JMS, Montreal), 5, 14–15; "corruption" of youth, 43, 46, 49–50, 56; growth of, 42–7, 57; juvenile justice policy, 75; prevention work, 60–4, 71, 76; professionalization, 42–3; raids, 56, 98; youth-conscious policing, 70–4, 127, 130; youth response to, 75–6

Katz, Sidney, 10
Kelso, J.J., 81–9
Kidman, John, 31

Labelle, Claude, 172–6
labour organizers, 47
Langlois, Albert, 65, 75–6
La Presse, 97, 131
Laramée, Arthur, 47, 75
"latchkey" children, 46, 90, 92
Latinos, targeting of, 33–4, 91
Legrand, Émile, 52
liberal democracies: citizenship, 105, 108, 116, 127–8, 176; penal reform in, 6, 8, 13–14, 19–20; Second World War, 28; threats to, 23, 39–40
Ligues du Sacré-Coeur, 46–7, 94
Lochlann Jain, Sarah S., 142

Los Angeles, 33–4, 91, 100, 169; crime prevention, 21, 77
Lossing, Elizabeth, 32–3, 40
low-income communities. See working class

Maclean's, 63, 65–6, 93
Mail and Empire, 41
Marquis, Greg, 8, 13, 26, 146
marriage, encouragement of, 55
masculinity, 67, 142; crisis of, 13; hegemonic, 16–17, 62, 105, 108–12. See also muscular Christianity
masturbation, youth, 48, 54–5
media, 7–8, 41, 47–8, 76, 175–6; crime coverage, 13, 37, 84, 93, 99–101; curfew coverage, 103; on delinquency, 44, 57–9, 70–4, 166–7; gender, portrayals of, 64–9; sports club coverage, 107, 114, 123–4, 127–33; traffic safety coverage, 134, 138–9, 151, 159. See also Hollywood
mental health issues, 35, 96, 150, 154; sexuality and, 47–55, 67
Metropolitan Toronto Police Youth Bureau, 26
Mexican American youth. See Latinos, targeting of
middle class, 136, 142; reformers, 4–5, 19–20, 139; values, 22, 105, 111, 143; youth, 27, 109–11
Miles, Marcus H., 132
Mills, Sarah, 108
minority communities, 90, 121; curfews, 81–3, 89, 99–102, 107; police-related resentment, 10, 41, 178; police relations, 10, 17, 20, 91, 177

Montreal: le chemin des amoreux
   (lover's lane), 56; crime in, 16–17,
   42–3, 56–9, 70–3, 167–8; curfews,
   58–60, 70–2, 80–2, 89–98, 103;
   Juvenile Delinquents Act (*see*
   Juvenile Delinquents Act); Local
   Council of Women, 64, 94;
   miracle, anti-delinquency, 48,
   70–7; Police Athletic League, 17;
   police-educators, 168–77; Police-
   Jeunesse, 17; Police Juvenile
   Clubs for Boys (*see* Police
   Juvenile Clubs [PJC, Montreal]);
   policewomen, 62–7, 153, 174;
   recreational clubs, 106–9, 125–30,
   145, 170; *Revue des Agents de Police/
   Constables Review*, 49, 59–60, 66,
   69; Royals (baseball team), 74,
   126, 129; traffic safety, 136–40, 148,
   161–3; youth culture in, 22, 46,
   55–6, 84, 168; youth squads, 42–51,
   56, 59–62, 68–80, 124
Montreal Boys' Association, 28, 94
Montreal Council of Social Agencies
   (MCSA), 129
Montreal Gazette, 66, 82
Montreal Juvenile Delinquents
   Court (MJDC), 44–6, 74, 78, 91,
   94, 98
Montreal Police Department, 42–3,
   64, 71, 98, 126, 166–7; Bureau de
   la Prévention des Accidents, 148;
   Youth Aid Section, 43, 56–8, 75–7,
   171–2, 174
morality, 115; correction of, 22, 52–4;
   liberal, 108–16, 150; lowering of, 13,
   47, 52, 83–6; role modelling of, 16,
   19–21, 87, 167; transformation of,
   27–8, 95–6, 106, 123–5
moral panics, 13, 27, 42, 73, 140;
   delinquency, 30, 46–7, 81, 93–4,
   167; sexual relations, 47–9, 51, 70,
   134, 174
Mulrooney, Edward Pierce, 36, 119
municipal committees. *See*
   coordinating councils
muscular Christianity, 62, 105,
   110–12, 142. *See also* masculinity:
   hegemonic

National Film Board of Canada,
   129–30; films, 68, 75–6, 79, 152–7;
   television series, 130
National Safety Councils (United
   States), 138, 147, 151
Naud, Paul-Émile, 48, 50, 69, 75
Nelson, BC, 115
newsboys, 22, 82, 85
New York City, 16, 19, 100; Advisory
   Committee on Crime Prevention,
   36–7; Crime Prevention Bureau,
   36–8, 117–19 (*see also* Juvenile
   Aid Bureau); Police Department
   (NYPD), 23, 29–31, 35–40, 43, 116;
   policewomen, 63; recreational
   clubs, 106, 109, 111, 123, 177 (*see also*
   Police Athletic League [PAL, New
   York]); traffic safety, 138–9, 145;
   youth culture, 22, 53, 84
Nicholson, J.G., 75, 95–7
night-time: destructiveness of, 81,
   84–7, 94; immoral behaviour,
   55–6, 72, 83–6; patrols, 78, 80–3,
   91–2, 98–103; sleep deprivation,
   87–9, 95–6; social costs, 72, 79,
   94–7, 102–3. *See also* curfews

nineteenth century: childhood, protection of, 19–22, 27, 109–12; curfews, 79–91, 95, 102; delinquency, 21, 26, 56; juvenile justice systems, 23–4, 45, 179; social regulation, 4–10, 50, 139, 150–1

Nolan, James B. 19

Nordstrom, Hilmer, 105–6, 112

Norton, Peter D., 137, 140, 145

order, public: civic-mindedness and, 34, 64, 172; curfews and, 79–83, 89, 100; juvenile delinquency versus, 59, 61, 116, 119; maintenance of, 11–14, 147, 168; police and, 6, 18–23, 26–7, 45, 145

orphanages, 20, 22, 26, 74, 81

Ottawa, 92, 159

parens patriae, doctrine of, 4

parenting: absence of, 57, 90, 93; curfews, 80, 85–9, 92–5, 101–3; delinquencies, 32, 49, 67, 122, 139; duty of, 55–8, 61, 96–9, 171; failure of, 15, 47, 144, 149, 161; impact of, 12–13, 27, 44, 141; police presence in, 9, 76, 136, 164, 175–6; single (*see* single parenting); state intervention into, 20–1, 151, 169–72

Parr, Joy, 149

patriotism, 90, 109, 111–12

patronage, police 6

pedophilia, 51; conflation with homosexuality, 52

Peel, Robert, 4

Pelletier, Ovila, 67–77, 172; accolades, 15, 61, 92, 129–31, 167; case decision

making, 50, 51–6, 74; recreational clubs, 123–8; youth squad, 13, 43–8, 57–9, 113, 166

penal reform, 4–6, 13–14, 25; progressive, 6, 16, 18–19, 179; standards, 31–32

Philadelphia, 36, 99, 145

police, 40, 106, 140; ambivalence of, 23–4, 41, 76–7, 81, 176; attitudes toward, 33, 65, 76, 161, 179; avoidance of, 10, 25–6, 97, 172; curfews by, 3–4, 80–1, 88–93, 96–100; -educators, 168–77; evolution of, 18–22, 35, 38–41, 116, 135; friendliness, 8–9, 31, 39–41, 61–3, 172; growth of, 42, 57, 166, 169–70; legitimacy of, 15, 25–6, 126, 165, 168; modern forces, 4, 8, 32–3, 77, 112–15; paternalism, 21, 23, 61–4, 70, 154–5; pragmatism, 23–4, 31–2; public image, 43, 129–35, 140, 148, 166–7; reform (*see* penal reform); rehabilitation systems, 5–7, 20–1, 45, 80–1, 121; repression, 4, 19, 105, 169, 178–9; resentment of, 10, 21, 24, 104, 172; scandals, 6, 10, 67, 91; scrutiny of, 74, 130, 176–8; school authorities versus, 176–9; social service work, 9, 26, 36, 122, 170–1; tension between roles, 4, 10, 21, 118, 177; traffic safety, 135, 145–51, 157–8, 161–5; urban forces, 20–7, 44–6, 87, 134, 147; youth turn, 4–7, 18, 36–7, 61–4, 166 (*see also* youth squads); youth workers (*see* youth workers)

Police Athletic League (PAL, New York), 109, 117–23, 128, 132, 138

police athletic leagues, 16–17, 106, 170
Police Boys' Rifle Club, 105–6, 112
Police Juvenile Clubs
    (PJC, Montreal), 73, 101, 123–33,
    171–2; outreach, 109; PAL
    modelling, 123; recruitment, 70–1,
    166–7
policewomen, 6–7, 25–6, 43; crime
    prevention, 33, 36, 153, 174; first, 33;
    hiring of, 21, 62–70
postwar era, 13, 51, 170–1; curfews, 79–
    80, 98–9, 103; recreational clubs,
    108, 123, 125; traffic safety, 134–5,
    141–5, 152–5, 159, 163–4; youth
    squads, 42–5, 57, 61–6, 69, 167
poverty, 67, 121; effects of, 10, 50–1,
    56, 67, 100; juvenile justice and,
    20, 39, 53, 63, 119; neighbourhood
    crime, 12, 29–30, 109, 111; youth, 5,
    22, 44, 90, 125
press. See media
prison, 86–7, 127; sentences, 14, 22, 28,
    54; reform, 19, 63, 73, 124, 177–8
probation: officers, 5, 21, 24, 45, 74–5;
    system, 33, 36, 53–6, 130
prostitution, 42–3, 49, 66, 83; boys',
    47–8, 53; girls', 53, 86; juvenile, 5,
    22, 33, 91
protection, paradox of, 3, 8, 44, 177
public anxiety, 18, 53, 152, 179;
    curfews, 79; delinquency, 13, 28,
    46, 58–61; school safety, 177
public relations campaigns, police,
    10, 17–19, 41–3, 161, 168

Quebec Human Rights
    Commission, 17, 101

race, 38, 41, 100; barriers, 14, 107–8,
    128; child welfare, 20, 121, 102;
    delinquency, 10, 12–13, 22;
    regulation by, 4–5, 10–12, 16, 89;
    riots, 91, 99–100, 103
racialized discrimination, 29, 33, 38,
    90, 177; in sports clubs, 107–8,
    112–15, 121, 128
rape, 48–9, 53, 91
rebellious youth, 12, 27, 46, 142
recreation, youth clubs, 74, 127–8;
    delinquency prevention, 30, 61,
    110–13, 132, 163; need for, 11, 27,
    70, 114; police-initiated, 17, 38–41,
    106–9, 116–22, 170–1. See also sports
reform schools, 4, 20–2, 26, 45,
    98; state guardianship and,
    85–6, 88, 179; workers, 5. See also
    institutions
rehabilitation, 102, 125, 179;
    exclusionary, 20, 26, 38; failure of,
    7, 80–1; programs, 5, 24, 45, 73, 121
residential schools, 20, 22
Riedel, A.E., 34
Robertson, Elizabeth Chant, 143–5
Robinson, Georgia Ann, 33

safety films. See traffic safety: didactic
    sudden-death messaging
safety leagues, Canadian, 139
same-sex relations. See homosexual
    relations
Sampson, Mrs E.T., 28
Sangster, Joan, 155–6
Saskatoon, 105, 107. See also Police
    Boys' Rifle Club
Saturday Night (magazine), 48, 70

Schneider, Eric C., 5

school, 22, 61, 111–16; attendance monitoring, 20, 38–9; patrols, 12, 65–6, 134–8, 148–53, 157–65; police involvement in, 11, 59, 78, 167–79; reform (see reform schools); youth squads, 9, 16, 30, 41

School Resource Officer (SRO) programs, 168–72, 177–8

Second World War, 28; curfews, 79–80, 90, 92–3, 99, 103; "khaki-madness," 13; recreation clubs during, 106, 113, 117, 128; safety patrols, 131, 135–7, 141–2, 150–2, 159; youth squads, 12, 31, 42, 57, 63

Sergeant Sees It Through, A (film), 105–6

sexual assaults, 49, 51, 54–5, 69, 174

sexuality, regulation of, 51–6

sex work, youth. See prostitution

Shaw, Clifford R., 29, 112

Short, Jean, 64

single parenting, 10; delinquency, 27–8, 37, 57, 94

social science, 20, 34; crime prevention, 30, 40, 109, 169

Social Welfare Court. See Juvenile Delinquents' Court

social workers, 36–7; crime prevention, 29, 30, 32, 45; duties, 14, 31, 64–5; versus police, 24, 44, 130

socialized justice model, 20–1

Sparrows Point, MD, 132

sports, 4, 34, 116, 170, 175; clubs, 71, 106–8, 114, 124, 130; girls' participation in, 106, 111–13,

121–3, 128–9; police use of, 10–12, 105–9, 112–14, 116–33; solution, 106, 117, 124–5, 127, 129–30. See also muscular Christianity; Police Juvenile Clubs (PJCS, Montreal)

state, the, 108; authority of, 85, 151, 158, 168, 170; child welfare policies, 80–2, 87–8, 128; police work and, 6, 151, 158, 168, 170; protection of, 5, 100, 102–3; social contract, 18–20, 179

Stearns, Peter N., 151–2

"stranger danger," 50–1, 76

surveillance, youth, 23, 41, 53, 170, 178; hangouts, 59, 61, 70, 72–4, 124; homosexual relations, 55–6 (see also homophobia); Montreal crime prevention, 10, 44, 70, 95; police-led clubs, 107, 136

teenager, term coining, 11

theft, youth, 22, 45–8, 61–3, 98, 174

Thrasher, Frederic M., 29

Tillotson, Shirley, 128

Toronto, 18, 53, 63, 83; crime prevention, 26, 41, 113, 115, 177; curfews, 86, 89, 92, 103; traffic safety, 134–7, 146–8, 154, 157–8, 161–3

tough-on-crime approach, 19, 27–8

traffic safety, 145, 164, 168; automotive revolution, 134–5, 137, 141–2; campaigns, 135, 138–40, 143, 147–9, 158–62; car culture, 134–6, 140–1, 164; deaths from automobiles, 134, 136–40, 142–7; didactic sudden-death messaging, 149–57; Elmer the Elephant, 157–8; police

involvement, 135, 145–51, 157–8,
    161–5; school patrols, 135, 139,
    158–63
Trahan, Marcel, 74, 172
Trepanier, James, 112
truancy, youth, 31, 38, 84, 98, 174

Umbach, Fritz, 14
unemployment, 22, 44, 46, 119
United Kingdom, 6, 63, 170. *See also*
    England
United States, 7, 111, 129–30; child
    welfare policies, 20, 30, 80, 89,
    100; penal reform, 5–6, 12–14,
    177–8; popular culture, 8, 13, 91,
    151, 158. *See also* Federal Bureau of
    Investigation (FBI); Hoover,
    J. Edgar

vagrancy, crime of, 3, 22–3, 45, 61, 83
Valentine, Gill, 102
Vancouver, 34, 69, 92, 142–4, 158–61
vandalism, youth, 7, 81, 99–100, 105
veterans, 64–5, 115
vice: spread of, 35, 46–7, 84–6, 95, 175;
    squads, 42–3
Victoria, BC, 114, 158
violence, 53, 109, 113, 128, 151;
    escalating, 18, 27, 81, 90–1; police,
    24–5, 100; youth, 13, 69, 99, 101–2,
    177
Vollmer, August, 31–3
vulnerability, youth, 17–19, 35–7, 50–1,
    79–80, 179

Ward, Geoff K., 14, 20
Washington, DC, 12

Waterloo, ON, 81, 88
welfare, child, 29, 73, 78, 128–9;
    police role in, 21, 25, 27, 37, 45;
    policies, 20, 22, 81, 83–4, 179; racial
    ideologies, 20; reformers, 4–7,
    31–3, 80, 102, 111; services, 26, 35, 61,
    92–3, 172
Wells, Alice Stebbins, 33
White, Julien, 69, 126
white supremacy, 20, 38, 90, 133, 156
Winnipeg, 81, 101, 157–8
Wolcott, David B., 6, 21, 23, 77
Woman's Christian Temperance
    Union (WCTU), 85, 88
women, 90, 94, 166; crime
    prevention, 31–4, 88, 109;
    independence, 7, 22; police
    bureaus, 26, 62–70, 73–4, 77;
    protection of, 36, 50, 84; youth
    squads, 26–7, 32–4, 49, 114. *See also*
    policewomen
working class, 7; communities, 26,
    40, 43, 83–5; crime prevention,
    14, 22, 70, 105–7; middle class
    versus, 20, 69, 109–11, 136–9; police
    involvement with, 10, 62, 91,
    118; visibility, 5, 53, 57, 173; youth
    vulnerability, 28, 34, 66, 95, 153
Wylie, C.A., 28

YMCA/YWCA (Young Men's/Women's
    Christian Associations), 9, 71,
    110–15, 126, 132
young offender, category of, 4–5,
    59–61
Youth Aid Section. *See* Montreal
    Police Department

youth-conscious policing, 12, 39–44, 79, 114–15, 169–70; movement toward, 17, 46, 56–62, 124, 179

youth squads, 167; beliefs of, 8–9, 44–5, 166, 174; crime prevention programs, 19, 30, 109, 116, 168–72; expertise, claims of, 7–16, 18, 26–7, 40–1; Montreal (*see* Juvenile Morality Squad [JMS, Montreal]); New York City (*see* Juvenile Aid Bureau [JAB, New York City]); officer qualifications, 32, 34

youth workers, 7, 9, 69; crime prevention, 28–30, 168; police as, 31, 43, 46, 49; tensions with police, 21

Zelizer, Viviana, 138, 140, 143

zoot suiters, 91